Tolley's
Stakeholder Pensions:
A Practical Guide
Volume 1

by
Sasha Butterworth
and
Tom Collinge
Hammond Suddards

Tolley

A member of the Reed Elsevier plc group

Whilst every care has been taken to ensure the accuracy of the contents of this work, no responsibility for loss occasioned to any person acting or refraining from action as a result of any statement in it can be accepted by any of the authors, editors or the publishers.

Published by
Tolley
2 Addiscombe Road
Croydon Surrey CR9 5AF England
020 8686 9141

Printed in Great Britain by
Hobbs the Printers,
Southampton

Preface

Stakeholder pensions have been discussed at great length in the press and specialist publications. However, there is no book that pulls together all this detail and the various strands of thought to give a clear overview to those who must either sell the product or provide a stakeholder scheme for their employees.

This is a complex area that has involved several Government departments, including the Department of Social Security, the Inland Revenue, the Treasury and the regulatory bodies of the Financial Services Authority (FSA) and the Occupational Pensions Regulatory Authority (OPRA). Understandably, there has been a great deal of consultation and some of the final detail of tax regulations and the authorisation process and documentation for contract based stakeholder schemes has yet to be revealed. A list of the legislation and guidance still awaited is at Appendix 3.

Despite these gaps, it was felt that due to the pressure of a tight timescale, with stakeholder pension schemes able to be approved from October 2000, practitioners would welcome a practical handbook early on in their decision making process. With this in mind, Volume 1 of the book concentrates on the information available at June 2000. Volume 2 will cover the tax regulations to be issued by the Inland Revenue and the FSA's framework for contract based stakeholder pensions and other relevant material.

Stakeholder pensions offer an opportunity for employers to provide access to a low cost pension scheme as an attractive benefit for employees. Providers, who are to be given workplace access by employers if their scheme is designated, will have further opportunities for cross-selling direct to the workforce. Those outside the workplace benefit from the opportunity to contribute to a pension, in some cases for the first time.

The prospect of an ever-increasing ageing population, living longer in retirement, makes the move towards a greater level of private pension provision imperative for the government. Much time, effort and political will has been invested in stakeholder pensions. Whether the public can be persuaded to invest their savings is the big question.

Sasha Butterworth
Tom Collinge
June 2000

Contents

Contents

Table of Statutes

Table of Statutory Instruments

List of Abbreviations

AVC	Additional Voluntary Contribution
DB	Defined Benefit
DC	Defined Contribution
DSS	Department of Social Security
EEA	European Economic Area
EU	European Union
FSA	Financial Services Authority
FSAVC	Free Standing Additional Voluntary Contribution
GPP	Group Personal Pension
IDR	Internal Dispute Resolution
IFA	Independent Financial Adviser
IRA	Individual Retirement Account
ISA	Individual Savings Account
IVA	Individual Voluntary Arrangement
LEL	Lower Earnings Limit
LET	Low Earnings Threshold
MIG	Minimum Income Guarantee
MNT	Member Nominated Trustee
NIC	National Insurance Contribution
OPAS	Pensions Advisory Service
OPRA	Occupational Pensions Regulatory Authority
PAYE	Pay as You Earn
PAYG	Pay as You Go
PEP	Personal Equity Plan
PPI	Pooled Pension Investment
PSA	Pension Savings Account
S2P	State Second Pension
SDA	Severe Disablement Allowance
SERPS	State Earnings Related Pension Scheme
SIP	Statement of Investment Principles
SRI	Socially Responsible Investment
UEL	Upper Earnings Limit

1 – Introduction To Stakeholder Pensions

This chapter covers the following.

- ○ What is a stakeholder pension?
- ○ The current framework for pension provision.
- ○ The government's objectives in its Green Paper 'A New Contract For Welfare: Partnership in Pensions'.
- ○ The key features of the stakeholder consultation papers.
- ○ The key dates for stakeholder pensions.

Summary   [1.1]

Stakeholder pensions are to be introduced from 6 April 2001. They are aimed primarily at those earning between £10,000 and £20,000 a year, both employees and the self-employed. Other groups that are being targeted are those outside the workplace, such as carers and those in ill health. Contributions up to £3,600 can be made without reference to earnings, so that those without earnings can pay into a stakeholder pension and benefit from the tax advantages.

Stakeholder schemes will be classed as Defined Contribution (DC) schemes. This means that the pension paid out is dependent on the contributions made and the investment returns produced on the pension fund. They can be taken out as personal pensions or an employer's occupational scheme can opt into the stakeholder DC tax regime if it meets the requisite criteria.

The current framework of pension provision includes the basic state pension and the State Earnings Related Pension Scheme (SERPS), occupational schemes, personal pensions, group personal pensions (GPPs) and other private provision. The Green Paper 'A New Contract for Welfare: Partnership in Pensions' was issued by the government in December 1998. This outlines the concept of stakeholder pensions and how they will fit within this framework. Stakeholder pensions form part of the new Insurance Contract for Pensions, together with the Minimum Income Guarantee (MIG) and the replacement for SERPS, the State Second Pension (S2P).

The Welfare Reform and Pensions Bill containing the draft stakeholder legislation was published in February 1999. The draft legislation for the tax regime for stakeholder pensions was published in the Finance Bill in February 2000. Six consultation papers on aspects of stakeholder pensions were issued between June and September 1999. The key issues to be considered were:

○   minimum standards;
○   employer access;
○   clearing arrangements;
○   regulation, advice and information;
○   governance; and
○   tax.

The Bill came into force on 11 November 1999 as the *Welfare Reform and Pensions Act 1999*. This, together with the Finance Bill 2000, Schedule 1, will be the primary legislation governing stakeholder pensions. The detail is provided by secondary legislation, in the *Stakeholder Pension Schemes Regulations 2000* and other associated regulations.

The Current UK Pension Framework   [1.2]

Here in the UK our pension provision is based on a three tier approach.

○   The first tier consists of the basic State pension.
○   The second tier is a mix of State and private provision. The State provision is via the State Earnings Related Pension Scheme (SERPS), which is due to be replaced by the new State Second Pension (S2P), in 2002. The private provision comprises occupational pension schemes and personal pensions.
○   The third tier covers insurance schemes and other voluntary private provision.

First Tier: State Provision   [1.3]

The first tier, the basic State pension, is funded via compulsory National Insurance Contributions (NICs) for all employees and self-employed people, except for the lowest paid.

Second Tier: State and Private Provision [1.4]

State Provision – SERPS and S2P

Employees, but not the self-employed, also have to contribute towards a second pension, SERPS. This is due to be replaced by S2P in 2002. (S2P is explained in more detail at paragraph 1.15). Employees can 'contract out' of SERPS and make their own provision in a private scheme. This is then reflected through the payment of reduced rate NICs.

Private Provision – Occupational Pension Schemes [1.5]

Occupational pension schemes of a recognisable modern form have been in existence since 1921. Private employers have been encouraged to provide them for their employees through tax concessions. They form an important part of the infrastructure of pension provision, though there is no obligation for employers to make private pension provision for its employees. However, occupational schemes are seen as a valuable part of the overall remuneration package that helps retain good employees. Occupational schemes are either Defined Benefit (DB) schemes, where the employer guarantees the employee a pension based on a percentage of his final salary, or DC schemes, or combine the two approaches in a hybrid arrangement. They are not available to the self-employed.

The assets of UK pension schemes are estimated at over £1,000 billion. The *Pensions Act 1995* and the associated regulations regulate and govern the operation of occupational schemes. These were introduced in the wake of Robert Maxwell's death in 1991, when £600 million of pension fund money was found to have disappeared.

Private Provision – Personal and Group Pension Schemes [1.6]

Personal pensions first became available on 1 July 1988 and were introduced via the *Social Security Act 1986*. Personal pensions are available to anyone who is working, either employed or self-employed, who does not have access to an occupational pension scheme. Personal pensions operate on a DC basis.

There are two different types of personal pensions:

○ an appropriate personal pension which is a 'contracted-out' personal pension (not available to the self-employed, because they are excluded from SERPS); and

○ an ordinary personal pension (open to the employed and self-employed alike).

People with an appropriate personal pension pay the full rate of NICs, and a refund is paid into their pension as they have contracted-out of SERPS. Those with an ordinary personal pension pay the full rate of NICs, with no rebate. Personal pensions can also be grouped together as a group personal pension (GPP) for the employees of one employer or for a group of self-employed people.

Personal pensions have been the subject of a mis-selling scandal. People in occupational schemes were incorrectly advised to switch to a personal pension plan. By so doing many lost out on employer contributions, as the majority of employers only contribute to their own occupational schemes.

The Green Paper 'A New Contract for Welfare: Partnership in Pensions' [1.7]

Faced by the challenges of an increasing ageing population, living longer due to advances in health care and diet, the government introduced its Green Paper on reforming the pension system in December 1998. Consumer confidence in pensions was at a low ebb following the Maxwell affair and the personal pensions mis-selling scandal. A new strategy to encourage people to save for their retirement was needed.

The Government's stated aims in the Green Paper were to:

'reform...the whole pension system, to rebuild trust and ensure that everyone can look forward to a secure retirement.'

The Prime Minister went on to say:

'We are building a new contract for pensions between the State and the private sector, and the individual. We believe that those who can save for their retirement have the responsibility to do so, and that the State must provide effective security for those who cannot.'

The Lack of Private Pension Provision [1.8]

In its Green Paper, the government stated that 'the current pension system does not provide adequate security for people who cannot afford to save and does not have the trust of people who can afford to do more to help themselves'. There are many reasons why people do not save or have private pension provision. It is not simply because they do not have the money.

It is estimated that up to 4 million people, earning between £10,000 – £20,000 a year, are not contributing anything to their pensions above the compulsory minimum via NICs. Pensions are difficult to understand due to a lack of information about how much one has saved and how much one needs to save to provide for an adequate income in retirement. People therefore delay rather than act, which tends to be the most dangerous strategy.

Non-savers [1.9]

Those who cannot save or who find it very difficult to save within the current pension system include the following.

❍ People earning less than the Lower Earnings Limit (LEL) a year (£3,484 in 2000/2001) who do not pay NICs and are not entitled to either the basic State pension or SERPS, and depend on the minimum income guarantee (MIG) to give them security in retirement. The introduction of the National Minimum Wage is intended to ensure that those who work long hours at low rates will be paid enough to build up entitlement to a basic State pension. However, this still leaves a large group of part-timers, mainly women, who are on low earnings for long periods, only working a few hours a week, which makes it difficult to contribute to a pension.

❍ Lower earners, earning between the LEL and £10,000 a year, who find that the charges and administrative costs of personal pensions are too high and tend to rely on state provision, unless they belong to an occupational pension scheme.

❍ Carers and disabled people who are unable to contribute to a pension as they have no earnings.

❍ Contract workers, the self-employed and employees who do not have access to occupational schemes.

❍ Those between jobs who can find it difficult to maintain continuity in their pension provision.

Potential Savers – Why They Do Not Save [1.10]

The current system also fails to convince those who could save, to do so. In the Green Paper the reasons stated were:

O   changes in the regulation of occupational pension schemes;
O   changes in the labour market not reflected in current pension products;
O   personal pension inflexibility and charging structures; and
O   a lack of trust in the pension system post-Maxwell and the mis-selling of personal pensions.

Market Forces [1.11]

Occupational pension schemes are seen as an attractive part of an employment package but there have been changes to the regulation of occupational schemes and a decline in the number of people in occupational schemes. This is partly due to fewer people being employed by large companies and in the public sector (the traditional providers of occupational schemes). There has also been a switch in current fashion from establishing DB schemes to establishing DC schemes with the employee, rather than the employer, bearing the investment risk. While DC schemes are more suitable for those who change jobs frequently, many employers have taken the opportunity when switching to a DC scheme to reduce their own contributions.

The labour market of the twenty-first century requires mobility and flexibility from its workforce, both factors that militate against building up pension rights. The current pension system does not reflect this. Fewer people expect a 'job for life' and new employment patterns include a mixture of work practices: self-employment, full time work, contract work and part-time work. This reflects changes people encounter in their lifestyle, due to major events, such as redundancy, retraining, family care responsibilities or maybe winding down prior to retirement. The current system does not allow for periods when people's income fluctuates between higher and lower levels. More jobs are also being provided by small and medium enterprises, which are less likely to offer an occupational scheme.

The State pension provision is paternalistic: it is based on the premise that the man would provide and that his wife would have access to a pension via the contributions he made during his working life. This no longer reflects the profile of the working population today, with more and more women building up their own pension rights. Marriage is no longer seen as being 'for life' and women can no longer depend directly on their husbands to provide for them in retirement. The move will be increasingly towards individualisation of pension rights, reflecting the new working and social patterns of today's population.

The Shortcomings of Personal Pensions [1.12]

Personal pensions are targeted at those people who do not have access to an occupational pension scheme and who change jobs frequently. However, many personal pension schemes have high up-front charges, which means that in the first few years of making contributions most, if not all, of the contributions are taken up with recouping the selling and distribution costs, whilst administration charges eat up a further slice of a member's contributions. The charging structures of personal pensions are not transparent, making it difficult to compare products.

The mis-selling scandal, mentioned at paragraph 1.6 above, has also dented people's confidence. Widespread coverage in the press has led to misgivings about the pensions industry. People are unwilling to entrust their retirement provision to those whose behaviour has been found wanting, especially when low and middle earners find it difficult to put money aside to pay towards a pension.

A New Insurance Contract for Pensions [1.13]

The government in its Green Paper 'A New Contract For Welfare: Partnership in Pensions' proposed a new Insurance Contract for Pensions. This comprises three interrelated types of pension provision.

○ A minimum income guarantee (MIG) for pensioners to be increased each year, 'as resources allow'. The aim over the longer term is for this to rise in line with earnings.
○ Better pension provision for low and middle earners, carers and disabled people through the introduction of enhanced rates under S2P which is to replace SERPS in 2002.
○ The introduction of flexible stakeholder pension schemes with low charging structures for middle and higher income earners.

The government's stated aim is to ensure that the current split between

State and private provision of 60/40 is reversed by 2050 to only 40% of pension provision being provided by the State and 60% provided by the private sector. As people are living longer due to improvements in healthcare and diet, the State will face an increasing burden if it does not manage to pass a greater part of that burden over to the individual. Although the State's spending on pensions will increase as people live longer, the government hopes that this will be offset by greater private provision.

Minimum Income Guarantee [1.14]

The MIG for pensioners was introduced in April 1999 through Income Support. The 2000/01 rates provide at least £78 a week for single pensioners and £121 for couples. The MIG is for pensioners who have not built up any entitlement to the basic State pension or SERPS. This is because they have not had paid employment or only very low paid employment under the LEL. They will receive benefits provided they only have savings of below £3,000. Those with savings of between £3,000 - £8,000 will be entitled to reduced benefits on a sliding scale. People with savings over £8,000 will not qualify. Those with a modest second pension will also not be eligible, which means that voluntary savers amongst the lowest earners are penalised. However, these capital limits are due to increase from April 2001 with the lower savings limit of £3000 doubling to £6000 and the upper limit increasing to £12,000.

S2P [1.15]

Those earning under £9,500 (or the prevailing Lower Earnings Threshold) will all be treated as though they had earned £9,500 when calculating their S2P. From 2007, S2P is intended to become a flat-rate rather than an earnings related scheme for contributors with a lower lifetime earnings history, to be defined at a later date.

The government's aim is to encourage moderate earners, on between £10,000 – £20,000, to have their own pension. For 2001/02, the existing rebates for contracted-out DC schemes and appropriate personal pensions will apply to occupational stakeholder schemes and personal stakeholder pensions respectively. It is intended that NIC rebates for those who have 'opted-out' of the new S2P into stakeholder and other personal pension schemes will be enhanced. This will allow moderate earners to derive greater benefits from the contributions made and encourage them to move to private pension provision.

The long-term disabled or sick, who have previously worked but no longer do so, and may already have some second pension rights, will be given credits under S2P, if they can show they have worked at some time in the past and may do so again in the future. They will be treated as though they earned £9,500 a year. Disabled people who have never worked are covered by the benefit system.

Some carers manage to combine their caring responsibilities with full time or part time employment, though most find it difficult to build up enough contributions for entitlement to a second pension. Carers include those who care for children below school age, for the disabled and for those with chronic illnesses. Provided their annual earnings are below the LEL, they will be treated under S2P as though they earned £9,500 in that year and given credits.

Stakeholder Pensions [1.16]

Stakeholder pensions will allow those on lower incomes to increase their pension provision. The government aims to put in place a pensions education campaign and ensure in future, that every adult receives an annual pension statement. This will mean that people are much more aware of their projected pension and should encourage them to take steps to increase their contributions, if financially possible.

Stakeholder pensions will also have simple charging structures, with a maximum annual charge of 1% on the value of the fund throughout the life of the stakeholder pension plan. This will avoid 'front-end loading' of charges and ensure that contributions made in the early years are applied to the plan rather than being swallowed up by large charges when the plan is first started. They will also be flexible enough to reflect today's changing lifestyles and work patterns, allowing people to change from one stakeholder plan to another without exit charges.

Consultation Papers [1.17]

The draft Welfare Reform and Pensions Bill was issued in February 1999, outlining a framework for stakeholder pension schemes. The detailed provisions were the subject of 6 consultation papers issued by the Department of Social Security (DSS) (nos. 1–5) and the Inland Revenue (no. 6) between June and October 1999. Details of the tax regime for stakeholder pensions appeared in the Finance Bill, issued in

February 2000. The draft regulations for stakeholder pensions and the proposed tax regime were issued in March 2000. A detailed summary of the consultation briefs and of decisions announced in press releases from Alistair Darling, Secretary for Social Security appears below.

Consultation Brief no. 1 – Minimum Standards   [1.18]

Summary

The introduction of minimum standards is to encourage saving as the current investment vehicles have a wide range of charging conditions which makes it difficult for consumers to compare what is on offer. However, minimum standards will not offer a guarantee of performance or suitability.

Charges   [1.19]

A single percentage charge will be levied on the value of the fund to cover all the normal operating costs. This total annual charge will be limited to 1% maximum. Comments were invited as to whether this charge would only cover the costs of basic advice and explanation, with additional services being paid for separately. The taking up of any additional advice and services will be discretionary.

Minimum Contributions   [1.20]

A minimum contribution of £10 for regular or one-off contributions with no minimum frequency of contributions was suggested. The pension's industry felt that this was a very low level of contribution for the administrative burden involved in large numbers of small payments. Contributions are to be collected via direct debits or from employer payrolls.

Investment   [1.21]

There is to be a clearly defined default investment choice, for those stakeholder entrants who have failed to make an explicit choice of investment fund.

The Treasury and the DSS also issued a joint consultation document entitled 'Flexibility in pension investment: helping to deliver stakeholder pensions'. The suggestion was to have a pooled pension investment (PPI) allowing stakeholder schemes to offer investment choice to members. It would also be possible for PPI schemes to limit investment choices and include a default option.

Information [1.22]

The information to be provided for stakeholder schemes is in line with other DC schemes.

- How the scheme operates.
- The benefits that are offered.
- The tax rules governing the scheme.
- The contribution limits.
- Regular information on the value of a member's fund.
- Information on the contributions paid in by the member, and where appropriate those paid by the employer.
- The charges levied by the scheme.

Transfers – In and Out [1.23]

No additional charges should be made for transfers into or out of stakeholder schemes. Schemes must accept transfers of pension rights from other schemes, where consistent with any requirements for the tax approval of the stakeholder scheme.

Tax Approval [1.24]

Schemes must be tax approved by the Inland Revenue.

Registration [1.25]

Stakeholder pension schemes must register with OPRA, before they begin to operate. The trustees (or the stakeholder manager in a contract based scheme) must state that the scheme complies with the minimum standards and other regulatory requirements for stakeholder schemes.

Sanctions [1.26]

Trustees (or stakeholder managers) of schemes which fail to meet the minimum standards can be fined. The last resort will be for the scheme to be removed from the register of stakeholder schemes managed by OPRA.

Decisions – 10 January 2000 [1.27]

The decisions announced on minimum standards were:

O A maximum 1% annual charge on the value of the member's fund, to include marketing, administrative and generic advice costs and basic information and explanatory material;

O Any individual financial advice about which stakeholder pension to choose is to be subject to a separate fee, though providers can include this within the 1% charge if they wish to do so;

O Minimum contribution level of £20 with no requirement to make regular or frequent contributions;

O No additional charges for transfers into stakeholder pensions, or if members choose to transfer to another pension scheme.

Consultation Brief no. 2 – Employer Access [1.28]

Summary

O All employees earning above the National Insurance lower earnings limit are to have access to stakeholder pension schemes;

O Employees must be eligible to join an occupational scheme within six months (later extended to one year) of starting work;

O Changes to contributions via the payroll whenever the employee wishes to make them;

O Employers have one year (later reduced to six months) from the introduction of stakeholder pension schemes to make arrangements before the requirements come into force.

Employer Access Requirement [1.29]

This is a key point in the government's proposals since access via employment gives employees an easy route to join and contribute to stakeholder pension schemes. It also gives scheme providers access to potential members via a single point of entry without high marketing overheads.

In the Green Paper, the components of employer access were to nominate a scheme, provide information on a point of contact for the scheme and to offer a payroll deduction facility. Concerns which were voiced during the consultation process of the Green Paper were:

○ that employers could be perceived as advising that the scheme they had chosen was the right choice to make, which could in turn lead to the employers being liable if the scheme did not perform well;
○ the costs of consulting staff on the scheme choice and payroll deductions would be an additional administrative burden on staff;
○ employers offering GPPs wanted exemption from the need to also provide a stakeholder scheme; and
○ employers felt that any information provided by them had to be supported by a government campaign.

Designation of a scheme   [1.30]

Employers must designate one or more stakeholder schemes, to include at least one which is open to all employees, unless they benefit from an exemption listed at paragraph 1.56. All stakeholder schemes must be registered with OPRA. It is the employer's responsibility to check the register to ensure that the designated scheme is registered.

Consultation of the Workforce   [1.31]

The employer should consult the workforce, though it decides which scheme is ultimately chosen. If the employees are not satisfied with the choice of scheme they can choose their own scheme, though the employer will not initially be obliged to make payroll deductions to such schemes.

An employer is not obliged to recommend a scheme — merely to designate one and make it clear to employees that he is not recommending this scheme above any other. The employer must also provide contact information for employees in the form of the name, address and telephone number of the contact at the designated scheme.

Role of Providers [1.32]

Providers could assist employers by offering incentives such as bespoke payroll software or assistance with staff training. Other ways of assisting employers would be via the use of stakeholder decision trees to help employees decide if stakeholder pensions are the best option for them. Information on the designated stakeholder scheme could be provided via wage packets, on induction or through routine workplace meetings.

Employers can engage independent advisers to advise on which stakeholder scheme they should choose, if they wish to do so, though there is no obligation to do this. Alternatively they can just designate a provider, following consultations with their workforce.

Employee Contributions [1.33]

Payroll Deduction Facility

The employer has an obligation to provide a payroll deduction facility to the designated scheme and comply with the following requirements.

○ The employer must deduct and record the amount requested from the employee's pay and forward it to the designated scheme.
○ Contributions must be passed to the designated scheme within 19 days of the end of the month in which the contribution was made. This can be checked on the employee's annual statement.
○ OPRA is to police compliance with the access requirements and ensure the timeliness of payments.
○ The employer is only required to provide payroll deduction facilities to the designated scheme, though later on clearing house arrangements may be possible.
○ Payments can be changed, stopped or re-started once every six months.
○ Employees can also make top up payments within the prescribed limits, either as a one off payment or as a fixed amount of their salary.

Direct Debit [1.34]

Employees have more control over payments via direct debit as:

○ they can continue payments if they change employers and during periods of absence from work; and
○ there is no limit to the number of changes to payment levels during the year.

Employer Contributions [1.35]

There is no obligation on an employer to contribute to a stakeholder pension scheme, even if the employer makes contributions to other pension arrangements for his employees.

Decisions − 10 January 2000 [1.36]

The decisions announced on employer access were as follows.

○ The access requirement will come into force on 8 October 2001, six months after the introduction of stakeholder pension schemes.
○ Employers with fewer than five employees or employees who earn less than the LEL are not required to provide access to a stakeholder scheme.
○ Employers who become liable to comply with the employer access requirements, if for example they take on a fifth employee, have three months to designate a stakeholder scheme.
○ Employers who contribute three percent of employees' salaries to group personal pensions (GPPs) and offer payroll deduction for the contributions are to be exempted from the stakeholder access requirements provided there are no exit charges if people wish to leave the GPP.
○ If employees are eligible to join the employer's occupational scheme within a year of starting work, employers are exempt from providing access to a stakeholder scheme − this exemption is not affected if the scheme restricts access to those aged 18 and over with more than five years to go before retirement.
○ Employers who do not benefit from an exemption should provide access to a stakeholder scheme within three months of an employee starting work.
○ Employees can vary the contributions every six months.

○ Employers can offer either flat-rate or salary percentage deductions or both.

Consultation Brief no. 3 – Clearing Arrangements [1.37]

Summary

Three options were proposed for dealing with the payroll deductions for stakeholder pensions:

○ the payroll deduction system could be operated without clearing arrangements; or
○ the current clearing arrangements could be used to make payroll deductions; or
○ separate clearing house facilities could be established for stakeholder pensions, though primary legislation would be needed.

No Clearing Arrangements   [1.38]

Initially there is only a requirement for employers to pass contributions to a single nominated scheme, so there is no benefit in having a clearing house.

Use Current Clearing Arrangements   [1.39]

Using current commercial facilities is simpler and more effective than establishing a dedicated clearing house for stakeholder pension contributions. This option does not need any further legislation.

Establish Dedicated Facilities   [1.40]

Over time the need for a clearing house could increase as employers find that they have to transfer stakeholder deductions to different schemes where:
○ individuals move jobs and find that the new employer operates a different scheme but stay with the old one, despite being offered a transfer at no additional costs;

○ employers may wish to give access to more than one scheme or to any stakeholder scheme;
○ employers wish to make a single payment for all employees.

However, it is difficult to judge the likely take up for stakeholder pensions and the exact numbers required for a dedicated clearing house to be financially viable, unless it were compulsory for all employers.

Decisions – 10 January 2000 [1.41]

The decisions announced on clearing arrangements were:

○ employers will initially only be required to pass contributions to their designated scheme; and
○ current commercial clearing arrangements are to be used rather than a dedicated clearing house for stakeholder pensions.

Consultation Brief no. 4 – Regulation, Advice and Information [1.42]

Summary

Key features.

○ The scheme should specify the advice and other services that the standard stakeholder charge of 1% of the annual fund covers and any charge for extra advice should be specified.
○ The information provided to prospective members of a stakeholder scheme should include:
  ● information on the scheme's key features, including a suggested fourteen day cooling off period;
  ● generic advice on its suitability for people in a particular group;
  ● projections of potential benefits; and
  ● encourage consumers who are uncertain about the suitability of a stakeholder scheme for them to seek specific advice.
○ The promoter who advises the employer on the suitability of a particular stakeholder scheme is subject to Financial Services Authority (FSA) regulation, but the employer who designates a

scheme and provides contact information is able to give factual information and generic advice, without being subject to FSA regulation. Only if the employer endorses a particular scheme will FSA authorisation be needed.

O   OPRA will monitor the registration of all schemes and regulate trust based schemes.

O   The FSA will regulate the promotion and marketing of all stakeholder schemes.

Advice [1.43]

The government provides basic pension information on the DSS website and the FSA offers consumer guides to pensions. FSA rules do not require that anyone marketing pensions and other investments should give advice or that anyone buying a pension should take advice. However, when someone seeks or takes advice, then the FSA rules come into play. Decision trees to help consumers work out whether stakeholder is right for them, combined with the provision of information via workplace meetings, telephone help-lines and the Internet will be the likely ways to deliver advice.

Decisions – 10 January 2000 [1.44]

The decisions announced on regulation, advice and information were:

O   OPRA will be responsible for registering schemes and regulating their compliance with registration requirements and for certain aspects of the conduct of trust-based stakeholder schemes; and

O   the FSA will regulate the promotion and marketing of all schemes, including occupational schemes that are established as stakeholder schemes.

Consultation Brief no. 5 – Governance [1.45]

Summary

There were two suggestions for the governance arrangements for stakeholder pension schemes: trust based schemes and authorised stakeholder management (now known as contract based schemes).

The trust based schemes will be subject to the *Pensions Act 1995* and to specific provisions for stakeholder schemes with supervision by OPRA. Stakeholder managers running contract based schemes, will be authorised by the FSA. However, contract based schemes will also have to register with OPRA and comply with its registration requirements. The investment options for pension funds under the contract based schemes are set out below at paragraph 1.48.

Trust Based Schemes [1.46]

Key features.

○ There is no requirement for Member Nominated Trustees or the appointment of professional trustees.
○ There is no prohibition on paying trustees.
○ Trustees are responsible under the terms of the trust deed for ensuring that the scheme does not breach conditions for registration as a stakeholder scheme.
○ Insurance costs and costs of trustees to be met from 1% annual charge.

Contract Based Schemes [1.47]

Key features.

○ This would be an alternative to trust based schemes and run by a stakeholder manager from a firm authorised by the FSA, responsible for ensuring compliance with minimum standards and a number of the same duties as trustees.
○ Members' rights in the scheme would be set out in a contract.
○ The stakeholder manager is to report to members on the scheme performance, compared with certain defined benchmarks.
○ An optional advisory committee can be established to represent stakeholder members' interests.
○ The stakeholder manager would have to comply with the same minimum standards and registration requirements with OPRA.
○ The manager must have a statement of investment principles, including the scheme's policy on socially responsible investment.
○ A default investment option and other investment options must be provided.

○ Annual reports and personal reports with a forecast of future pension entitlements must be produced at least once a year.
○ Delays in paying over contributions must be reported to OPRA.

Investment of Funds by Stakeholder Managers [1.48]

There are two suggested options.

Either:

○ Stakeholder funds are to be invested in one or more Pooled Pension Investments (PPIs) which are a 'wrapper' for unit and investment trusts allowing them to provide a tax free option. These are due to be introduced at the same time as stakeholder. Normally there will be one PPI per scheme member, with a default investment option. Stakeholder managers must make scheme members aware of the choice to switch between the eligible PPIs at least once every three years.

Or:

○ Stakeholder schemes' assets are held by a stakeholder depository independent of the scheme manager, which is authorised by the FSA according to specific rules:
  ● The assets must be prudently spread according to the FSA rules, with no more than 5% of the scheme assets in any single security;
  ● The assets must be unitised and priced daily at net asset value; and
  ● Limited stock lending and borrowing will be allowed to ensure efficient portfolio management.

Decisions – 10 January 2000 [1.49]

The decisions announced on governance were:

○ trust based schemes will be overseen by OPRA and subject to similar regulatory requirements as occupational schemes;
○ at least one third of trustees should be independent of the service provider from the time the scheme is established;
○ there is no additional requirement for member nominated trustees or for the appointment of professional trustees;

- trustees can contract with service providers for as long as they see fit;
- there is no requirement to appoint an actuary;
- trust based schemes can restrict membership eligibility e.g. to a trade union or affinity group; and
- there should be clear rules requiring schemes to be wound-up if they cease to qualify as stakeholder schemes.

Consultation Brief no. 6 – Tax [1.50]

Summary

The key features of the proposed tax framework for stakeholder pensions were as follows.

- An integrated tax regime for all DC pension schemes, with concurrent membership as long as the overall personal pension age and earnings related limits are not exceeded.
- Contributions into Defined Contribution (DC) schemes can be up to the higher of £3,600 per year, or the existing earnings and age related personal pension limits. The link with earnings is removed where contributions are no more than £3,600 in a year.
- Contributions in excess of £3,600 may continue for up to five years after relevant earnings have ceased. Thereafter, contributions cannot exceed £3,600.
- All contributions into DC schemes will be paid net of basic rate tax. Pension providers will recover tax at the basic rate from the Inland Revenue with contributors recovering, if appropriate, tax at higher rates through their self assessment tax return.
- The £3,600 contribution limit applies to the total of all contributions from employers, individuals and the tax relief recovered on the individual's contributions from the Inland Revenue. It excludes any contracted out National Insurance contribution rebate.
- Employers' money purchase pension schemes may opt into this new DC regime.
- Carry forward and carry back tax relief for those wishing to use up unused limits on pension contributions over a period of six years to be abolished.

Advantages of the New Tax Regime [1.51]

Key features:

O More flexible scheme for individuals;

O The opportunity of pension provision for more people with the abolition of an earnings link for contributions up to £3,600;

O Simpler advice and lower costs of advice;

O By removing the cap on contributions individuals can remain with the stakeholder scheme as income increases which is attractive for providers;

O An integrated tax regime for all DC schemes gives lower costs for providers;

O No need to provide evidence of earnings;

O Contributions are paid net of basic rate tax by all, replacing the current system of net and gross contributions;

O The complex carry forward and carry back rules will be replaced with a simpler system.

Administrative Points [1.52]

These are the main areas to consider.

O Trustees of money purchase schemes are to be given an irrevocable option to transfer to the new DC regime.

O From April 2001, tax approval will only be given to those DC schemes that have a standard application and adopt model rules to be issued by the Inland Revenue.

O Concurrent membership of DB and occupational DC schemes that have not opted into the new DC regime, is not permitted.

O Now that the link with earnings has been abolished there will be a residency test so that in order to open a DC pension, the member will have to be resident, or ordinarily resident, in the UK or performing Crown duties treated as being performed in the UK or in receipt of earnings taxable in the UK.

O There is no lower age limit for stakeholder schemes, though the upper limit is 75.

O Schemes within the new DC regime will include personal pensions which are registered as stakeholder schemes and all other personal pension plans including appropriate GPPs and DC occupational pension schemes where the employer has opted into the new DC regime.

Decisions – 22 February 2000 [1.53]

The decisions announced on tax were:

○ an integrated tax regime for all DC schemes to take effect from 6 April 2001;

○ contributions of up to £3,600 each tax year with no link to earnings;

○ contributors are to be resident in the UK, unless serving or the spouse of someone serving abroad or undertaking Crown duties;

○ carry forward reliefs are to be abolished, with carry back only available on election;

○ 10% of the pension contribution can be used for life assurance;

○ tax relief for waiver of pension contributions insurance will be simplified and broadened to give tax relief on the pension contributions paid out on ill health and unemployment, rather than on the insurance premium itself;

○ shares from an approved employee exempt scheme can be put into the pension and attract tax relief, if within the contribution limits;

○ there is no concurrency allowed for members of a DB or DC scheme that has not opted into the new DC regime;

○ telephone and electronic applications to join stakeholder schemes will be allowed;

○ from April 2001, information about earnings for one year will cover higher level contributions above £3,600 for the next 5 years;

○ phased vesting for annuities from a single pension arrangement is to be introduced.

Key Features of Stakeholder Pensions [1.54]

For Consumers

The key points for consumers are as follows.

○ Aimed primarily at those earning £10,000 – £20,000 a year.

○ For both employees and the self-employed.

○ Also for those without access to occupational schemes or unable to contribute to a pension as they are not earning.

- The link with earnings removed – for all who satisfy the UK residency test and are to save at least £3,600 a year unless in a DB scheme or an occupational DC scheme that has not opted into the new DC regime.
- Low annual charges of a maximum of 1%.
- Life assurance can be included.
- Ability to change, stop and re-start contributions whenever they wish via direct debit and able to alter employee payroll deductions every six months and, also pay in lump sums.
- Transferable without exit charges.
- Low minimum contribution of £20.
- Three months maximum waiting period before joining an occupational stakeholder scheme; and
- Can have concurrent membership of a personal stakeholder pension and a DC occupational stakeholder scheme.

For Employers   [1.55]

The key points for employers are as follows.

- Employers should consult their workforce about stakeholder schemes, but they designate the stakeholder scheme.
- The designated scheme should be accessible to all employees earning above the lower earnings limit (LEL) within three months of joining the company provided they satisfy the UK residency test.
- Employers must provide access to the designated scheme by giving employees contact details, such as a telephone number, address and a contact name at the stakeholder provider.
- Employers must check that the scheme is registered with the Occupational Pensions Regulatory Authority (OPRA).
- Employers have to provide payroll deduction facilities at a flat rate or percentage of salary, if requested to do so by employees.
- Employers must allow employees to alter their deductions every six months and pass the contributions deducted over to the designated stakeholder scheme within specified time limits.
- There is no obligation for employers to contribute to the designated stakeholder scheme, even if they contribute to other pension arrangements.
- By designating a scheme employers are not to be perceived as endorsing it and will not be liable in the event of poor performance.

○ If employers have a DC occupational scheme that complies with the stakeholder requirements, they have a one-off opportunity to 'opt-in' to the new stakeholder tax regime.

Exemptions for Employers [1.56]

Employers are exempt from designating a stakeholder scheme if:

○ they have 1–4 employees or only have employees earning less than the LEL;
○ they offer an occupational scheme which staff are eligible to join after a year of employment, even if membership of the occupational scheme is restricted to those over aged 18 or over and new employees with more than 5 years left before retirement;
○ they offer employees membership of a GPP within 3 months of starting work to which they contribute at least 3% of an employee's salary, which has no cessation charges or exit charges when an employee wishes to leave the scheme and move to a new employer;
○ none of their employees satisfies the UK residency test.

For Providers [1.57]

The key points for providers are as follows.

○ Maximum 1% annual charge on the value of each member's fund.
○ Basic information, explanatory material, marketing and administration to be provided within 1% charge.
○ Advice can be charged for separately.
○ Must accept minimum £20 contribution, with no specification on minimum frequency of contributions allowed.
○ Must allow contributor to change, stop or re-start contributions as and when required.
○ Can refuse contributions made in cash or by credit card.
○ A default investment option must be specified for those not wishing to exercise a choice.
○ No additional charges for transfers into stakeholder pensions or transfers to another pension scheme.
○ The stakeholder scheme they offer must comply with all the above requirements and register with OPRA.

Key Dates for Stakeholder Pensions [1.58]

The stakeholder calendar will run as follows:

1 October 2000	Registration of stakeholder schemes with OPRA and the Inland Revenue begins.
6 April 2001	Stakeholder pension schemes can begin to accept contributions.
October 2001	Unless employers benefit from one of the exemptions listed at paragraph 1.56, by this date they must have designated a stakeholder scheme that allows access for all relevant employees.

2 – Legal Framework For Stakeholder Pensions

This chapter covers the following:

○ The *Welfare Reform and Pensions Act 1999*.
○ The Finance Bill 2000.
○ The Child Support, Pensions and Social Security Bill.

Summary [2.1]

The legal framework for stakeholder pension schemes is found in the *Welfare Reform and Pensions Act 1999, Part I, ss 1 – 8* and *Schedule 1,* and in the Finance Bill 2000, Schedule 1. There are also provisions that apply to stakeholder schemes in further sections of the *Welfare Reform and Pensions Act 1999, ss 9–16* dealing with general changes to the regulatory framework for personal and occupational pensions and *ss 19–51* which deal with pension sharing on divorce. The detailed provisions for stakeholder schemes are in the *Stakeholder Pension Scheme Regulations 2000* (discussed in Chapters 3, 4 and 5) and other regulations.

Stakeholder pension schemes are defined contribution (DC) schemes and many of the provisions will be known to those who are already familiar with DC occupational trust based schemes. The tax regime for stakeholder pensions resembles the personal pension regime and is outlined in the Finance Bill 2000, Schedule 1. This means that the government is not introducing a totally new structure, but rather combining elements of existing structures, with some specific variations for the authorised stakeholder management structure.

The mechanics for calculating the State Second Pension (S2P) and how it will dovetail with stakeholder pension schemes is examined. The provisions are outlined in the Child Support, Social Security and Pension Bill.

The Welfare Reform and Pensions Act 1999, Part I [2.2]

Section 1–Definition and Requirements for Stakeholder Pensions

This section defines a stakeholder pension in a way which allows much of the existing legislative framework applying to occupational and personal pensions to apply to stakeholder pensions. It also lists a number of additional requirements which schemes will have to meet in order to be classed as stakeholder pensions.

Section 1(1) – Definitions [2.3]

The *Pension Schemes Act 1993, section 1*, defines two relevant types of pension scheme:

O   occupational pension schemes; and
O   personal pension schemes.

Membership of an occupational pension scheme is via employment for an employer or group of employers, allowing the employee to build up rights in a scheme. A personal pension is open to all those who have net relevant earnings from which to make contributions. This subsection states that these two types of schemes can be registered as stakeholder pension schemes, providing they meet a number of specific conditions detailed below. In addition, this section provides a power to prescribe other additional conditions in the future, giving flexibility in the light of experience of operating stakeholder schemes.

Section 1(2) – Governance [2.4]

Stakeholder pension schemes are to be set up under a trust based, or a contract based, arrangement as specified in the *Stakeholder Pension Schemes Regulations 2000*. Occupational pension schemes have trustees who administer the trust for the benefit of the scheme's members under the terms of the trust deed and rules, general trust law and according to the relevant legislation.

Contract based schemes also have to provide similar protection and security for scheme members' interests. These details are specified in the *Stakeholder Pension Schemes Regulations 2000* and are discussed in Chapter 5.

Section 1(3) – Contents of Governing Instruments [2.5]

The instruments that set up a stakeholder scheme will be the trust deed and rules for a trust based scheme, and other specified instruments that are necessary for contract based schemes. The requirements for the scope of the trust deed are to:

O ensure trustees are able to appoint and dismiss those who advise them, such as actuaries, investment managers, auditors and administrators;
O specify what proportion of the trustees are to be member nominated (not a current requirement) and if independent trustees should be appointed; and
O specify if the scheme should provide additional benefits such as life assurance and permanent health insurance.

The requirements for the documentation for contract based schemes are intended to offer similar protection to members and beneficiaries.

Section 1(4) – DC Benefits   [2.6]

Stakeholder schemes must offer DC benefits to members. This excludes defined benefit (DB) schemes from stakeholder pension schemes, though there is also a regulation-making power to prescribe exceptions. This power provides flexibility for the future by allowing the framework to be amended to accommodate schemes which may wish to offer benefits on a suitable alternative basis.

Section 1(5) – Charges and Expenses   [2.7]

The power to make regulations to detail how much may be deducted from scheme members' pension funds in respect of charges and expenses is covered in this subsection. The *Stakeholder Pension Schemes Regulations 2000* set out how any charge is to be calculated, specify limits on the charging levels and when a charge can be imposed. This is examined in Chapter 4. Requirements for charges will be reviewed in the light of experience of operating stakeholder schemes, giving consideration to future flexibility.

Section 1(6) – Stakeholder Pension Schemes Compliance   [2.8]

Schemes must comply with the obligations under the *Pension Schemes Act*

1993, s 113 and the *Occupational Pension Schemes (Disclosure of Information) Regulations 1996* (SI 1996 No 1655). Trustees are obliged to disclose:

○ certain documents and information to scheme members, prospective members, beneficiaries and appropriate trade unions;
○ basic scheme information to all the above, although other documentation need only be provided on request; and
○ details of the scheme's governing documentation, and an annual statement on the accounts, funding of the scheme and details of the benefits payable.

The *Stakeholder Pension Schemes Regulations 2000* detail the minimum standards in respect of the annual information that must be provided concerning:

○ the value of a pension;
○ the contributions that have been paid in; and
○ the charges deducted by the scheme.

Section 1(7) – Flexible Contributions [2.9]

Contributions from members can either be on a regular basis or whenever possible. Many existing personal pensions do not provide this level of flexibility for their members, which has contributed to the fact that a large percentage of personal pension contributions lapse within three years. There is also a regulation-making power to prescribe minimum contribution levels (currently £20) and other restrictions which schemes would be allowed to impose. Setting minimum contribution levels is intended to balance flexibility for members against the costs to schemes and providers of handling numerous small and intermittent contributions.

Section 1(8) – Transfers-in [2.10]

The definition of stakeholder pension schemes in the *Welfare Reform and Pensions Act 1999, s 1*, brings them within the 'pension scheme' definitions in the *Pension Schemes Act 1993, Part I*.

○ Stakeholder scheme members will share with occupational and personal pensions scheme members the automatic right to transfer-out their rights to another scheme (subject to certain limitations specified in the *Pensions Schemes Act 1993* and the *Pensions Act 1995*).

○ There is an additional requirement on stakeholder schemes to accept transfers-in of members' rights from other schemes, though not if a transfer-in comes from an 'unapproved' scheme as this would prejudice its tax-approved status and be contrary to Inland Revenue rules. There is currently no obligation on occupational and personal pension plans to accept transfers-in, though this can be provided for within their rules.

Section 1(9) – Approval by Inland Revenue [2.11]

Stakeholder schemes will need to apply for Inland Revenue approval for exemption to qualify for tax benefits. Contributions by members (and employers) will qualify for income tax relief at the basic rate. Investment returns and capital gains on the scheme's funds will be tax exempt. Schemes must have Inland Revenue exemption or approval to meet the conditions for registration as stakeholder schemes.

Section 2 – Registration of Stakeholder Pension Schemes [2.12]

To be classed as stakeholder schemes, pension schemes have to comply with all the requirements in the *Welfare Reform and Pensions Act 1999, Part I*. The *Welfare Reform and Pensions Act 1999, s 2* details the procedure for the registration of stakeholder pension schemes and the Occupational Pensions Regulatory Authority's (OPRA) role in this. OPRA's role is discussed in Chapter 4.

Section 2(1) – OPRA's Register of Stakeholder Schemes [2.13]

OPRA will maintain a register of stakeholder pension schemes. This will give members of the public easy access to the names of providers of stakeholder schemes. The register will assist employers who will be able to check that their designated scheme is on the register in order to comply with the employer access requirements of the *Welfare Reform and Pensions Act 1999, s 3*.

Section 2(2) – Declaration on Registration [2.14]

Scheme trustees and stakeholder managers are to support applications for registration with a declaration that the scheme meets all the conditions contained in the *Welfare Reform and Pensions Act 1999, s 1*. OPRA is required to register schemes on the basis of this application, subject to *s 2(3)*. It has a discretionary power to impose a fee for registering schemes.

Section 2(3) – Registering and Removing Schemes [2.15]

OPRA has a power to refuse to register schemes if they do not comply with the conditions in the *Welfare Reform and Pensions Act 1999, s 1*. It also has a power to remove schemes from the register, if it has evidence that the scheme no longer complies with the conditions in s *1*.

Section 2(4) – OPRA's Sanctions [2.16]

OPRA has a power to sanction trustees and stakeholder managers who have not ensured that a scheme they wish to register as a stakeholder scheme complies with the requirements in *s 1* and, once registered, continues to do so. Two sanctions from the *Pensions Act 1995* are to be applied by OPRA where trustees are in breach of this obligation:

O   The *Pensions Act 1995, s 3* allows OPRA to prohibit a person from being a trustee of a particular scheme;
O   The *Pensions Act 1995, s 10* provides for civil penalties for trustees and stakeholder managers following breaches of the *1995 Act*.

Section 2(5) – Criminal Sanctions for Trustees [2.17]

Trustees can be subject to criminal sanctions for knowingly or recklessly providing misleading information when applying to register a scheme as a stakeholder pension scheme. A Justice of the Peace can issue a warrant for OPRA to search an employer's premises under the *Pensions Act 1995, s 100*, where OPRA has reasonable grounds for believing that misleading information was provided. This is consistent with a number of requirements in the *Pensions Act 1995*, which are underpinned by criminal sanctions for more serious breaches in relation to occupational pension schemes.

Section 2(6) – Criminal Sanctions for Corporate Bodies and Others [2.18]

The *Pensions Act 1995, s 115* provides that offences committed by corporate bodies or Scottish partnerships can apply to individuals, such as a manager, director or partner where, for example, the offence has been committed with the consent of that individual. The *Welfare Reform and Pensions Act 1999, s 2(6)* applies the *Pensions Act 1995, s 115* to offences under *s 2(5)* (listed above at 2.17).

Section 2(7) – Inspection of Register [2.19]

This subsection contains a power for the register of stakeholder pension schemes (or copies or extracts from it) to be made available for inspection or supplied to prescribed persons, subject to certain conditions. This will allow the general public and employers access to inspect the register.

Section 3 – Duty of Employers to Facilitate Access to Stakeholder Pension Schemes [2.20]

This section defines the employers' obligation to provide access to stakeholder pension schemes. Employer access is discussed in Chapter 3.

Section 3(1) – Who Must Comply [2.21]

Unless regulations state otherwise, any employer who employs relevant employees, defined in *s 3(9)* must comply with the requirements set out in this section.

Section 3(2) – Employers to Choose Stakeholder Scheme [2.22]

Employers are to choose at least one registered stakeholder scheme which offers membership to all employees. Trade unions or other membership based organisations may establish trust based member-only schemes which fail to meet the universal membership criterion. Employers then have to choose an additional scheme open to all. Employers must consult with employees and any organisation representing them, such as a trade union, about the choice of scheme. They also have an ongoing responsibility to ensure at all times that the designated stakeholder scheme remains on the OPRA register.

Section 3(3) – Scheme Contact Details [2.23]

The employer must inform employees of the name and address of the designated scheme. This subsection also contains a power to specify other information which the employer must provide. This allows flexibility to modify the information requirements for stakeholder schemes in the future.

Section 3(4) – Workplace Access for Providers [2.24]

The employer must allow the providers of the stakeholder scheme 'reasonable access' to the relevant employees to provide information about the scheme. 'Reasonable access' could be via workplace meetings in larger firms or information provided via payslips in smaller firms.

Section 3(5) – Deduction of Employee Contributions [2.25]

Employees who are members of a stakeholder scheme can request that the employer deducts contributions from their wages and pays them to the trustees of the chosen scheme. The employer is then obliged to do so. However, in order to balance the cost to the employer with flexibility for the member, there is a regulation-making power to prescribe restrictions on this requirement. There is an additional power to make regulations for deductions to be paid to an alternative approved person, for example, to an authorised stakeholder manager.

Section 3(6) – Withdrawal of Employer's Designation [2.26]

If the employer's designated stakeholder scheme under the terms of *s 3(2)* ceases to be registered under *s 2*, the employer must withdraw his designation.

Section 3(7) – Civil Penalties for Non-Compliance with Access Requirements [2.27]

This applies the civil penalties of the *Pensions Act 1995, s 10* to an employer's breaches of the access requirements. The civil penalties include monetary fines of up to £5,000 for an individual who is an employer and up to £50,000 for a company.

Section 3(8) – Limiting Employer Liability for Scheme Designation [2.28]

When an employer designates a scheme to comply with employer access requirements, he has to check that it is registered with OPRA, has universal membership and that scheme contact details are available. He is under no duty to make any enquiries or act on any information about the scheme other than for the above requirements.

In particular, he is:

> 'not... under any duty... to investigate or monitor, or make any judgement as to, the past, present or future performance of the scheme.'

This *s 3(8)(b)* is of great importance to employers concerned about the issue of liability for a scheme's performance following designation of a scheme, which in some employees' eyes could be seen as a recommendation of the merits of the scheme. This subsection exempts them from that liability.

Section 3(9) – Definitions [2.29]

There are three definitions in this subsection: employer, relevant employees and qualifying schemes.

❍ 'Employer' means any employer whether or not resident or incorporated in any part of the UK.
❍ 'Qualifying scheme' means the employer's designated scheme(s) or, if the regulations permit, any stakeholder scheme.
❍ 'Relevant employees' are all those employed by the employer in the UK, and for an employer resident or incorporated in the UK all his employees employed from outside the UK. It does not include:
  ● those already in the employer's occupational pension scheme;
  ● those who are eligible to join it within one year of entering employment;
  ● those below the lower earnings limit as defined in the *Pension Schemes Act 1993, s 181* (a statutory limit which is increased each year); or
  ● where the employer only has 4 or fewer employees.

Regulations will allow for these exemptions to be altered at a later date.

Section 4 – Obtaining Information to Comply with Section 3 [2.30]

OPRA has to ensure that the employer is complying, or has complied with the requirements under the *Welfare Reform and Pensions Act 1999, s 3* to provide employer access. If OPRA gives notice in writing to a person who seems likely to hold information on compliance with access requirements, then that person must produce any relevant document within the time scale and at the place specified. 'Document' includes information recorded in any form (and if not in legible form, then a document must be produced in legible form e.g. a print-out of information from a computer).

The *Pensions Act 1995, s 100* deals with OPRA's powers to:

○ ask relevant persons to supply documentation;
○ question people on the premises;
○ apply for a warrant if it believes that documents on premises have not been supplied; and
○ search and retain documents for six months or longer if proceedings have commenced within that period.

These provisions will apply to the relevant persons who deal with compliance with access requirements for stakeholder schemes. The *Pensions Act 1995, ss 101 – 103,* which impose penalties, such as fines for non-cooperation with OPRA, will also apply.

Section 5 – OPRA's Powers to Enter Premises and Question People [2.31]

To check that an employer is complying with the *Welfare Reform and Pensions Act 1999, s3* employer access requirements, OPRA's powers of inspection are to be applied to stakeholder schemes. An OPRA inspector has the power to enter premises for inspection at any reasonable time, question people, examine documents and ask for them to be produced. These powers are already available to OPRA for the inspection of premises under the *Pensions Act 1995* to check compliance with occupational pension schemes.

Any premises where the inspector has reasonable grounds to believe that employees have been working can be inspected, if the inspector believes that documents relevant to the administration of the employer's business are kept there, or administration is carried on there. This does not apply if the premises are a private dwelling house not used by or with the permission of the occupier for a trade or business.

Section 6 – Provisions of the Employment Rights Act 1996 [2.32]

The *Employment Rights Act 1996, ss 46* and *102,* protects 'relevant occupational scheme' trustees from unfair dismissal. *Section 58* gives trustees time off for trustee training and duties. These provisions are extended to include employees or a director of a company who are trustees of a designated stakeholder scheme, which is a 'relevant occupational scheme' for the purposes of the *Employment Rights Act 1996.*

Section 7 – Reduced Rates of NICs for Stakeholder Schemes [2.33]

Under the *Pension Schemes Act 1993, s 42B(2),* the Secretary of State can make an order specifying reduced rate National Insurance contributions (NICs) for members of contracted-out DC occupational schemes. The reduced rate of NICs reflects the cost to employers of providing members with benefits of an equivalent value to SERPS. Occupational DC schemes that have opted into the stakeholder regime, and personal pension schemes that are registered under *s 2* as a stakeholder pension scheme, will have the appropriate rebate rates for occupational pension schemes and personal pensions applied to them for 2001/02. A full review of the rebate rates is due to take place in summer 2000, in advance of the introduction of S2P. It is expected that members of stakeholder schemes will receive enhanced rebate rates.

Section 8 – Interpretation and Application of Part I [2.34]

The Secretary of State can make provisions via regulations for a stakeholder scheme that is to all intents and purposes an occupational scheme, to be treated as if it were a personal pension scheme, so the full range of occupational scheme regulations do not apply. This reflects the single taxation regime for occupational and personal stakeholder pensions introduced by the new DC regime.

Schedule 1 [2.35]

This schedule gives a detailed breakdown of how the *Pension Schemes Act 1993* and the *Pensions Act 1995* apply to stakeholder pension schemes. In some cases existing provisions are extended to include stakeholder schemes and in others new provisions that will apply to stakeholder schemes are listed.

Trust based stakeholder schemes and those set up under contract are to be under the same regulatory regime as occupational pension schemes as defined by the *Pension Schemes Act 1993*. This brings stakeholder schemes within the supervisory scope of the Occupational Pension Schemes Regulatory Authority (OPRA). Trustees of stakeholder pension schemes will be supervised in the same way as trustees of occupational pension schemes to ensure a consistent approach. The sales and marketing of these schemes will fall within the ambit of the Financial Services Authority (FSA).

The *Pension Schemes Act 1993* is extended to allow the Pensions Compensation Board (PCB) to impose a levy on all stakeholder pension schemes to contribute to the PCB's ability to cover this new class of pensions.

Provisions of the *Pensions Act 1995* that will apply to stakeholder schemes are as follows.

- O   OPRA's powers.
- O   Trustees' general powers.
- O   Functions of trustees.
- O   Duty of scheme trustees to provide scheme documents.
- O   Appointment of professional advisers and 'whistle blowing'.
- O   Keeping of accounts.
- O   Internal dispute resolution procedures.
- O   Trustees' power to modify scheme.
- O   Compensation payments.
- O   Assignment and forfeiture for occupational schemes.
- O   OPRA's review of own determinations to disqualify a trustee.
- O   OPRA's permitted disclosure.
- O   Provision of information to the PCB by trustees, professional advisers or employers.
- O   Any requirement of the *Welfare Reform and Pensions Act 1999, Part I* will override scheme rules where there is a conflict, and terms shall be interpreted in accordance with the *Pensions Act 1995, Part I.*

The definition of an employer in the *Pensions Act 1995* is widened to include the role of an employer who is complying with the access requirements to a stakeholder scheme. The definition of occupational schemes is broadened to include stakeholder pension schemes which are not occupational schemes, such as personal pensions and GPPs, though the definition of 'member' is excluded, as it is not appropriate to stakeholder schemes that are not occupational schemes.

The Welfare Reform and Pensions Act 1999, Part II
Pensions – General   [2.36]

Section 9 – Monitoring Employers' Payments to Personal Pension Schemes

The *Pensions Act 1995* introduced time limits for the payment of employee and employer contributions to occupational schemes and penalties for failing to comply. The contributions have to be transferred to the trustees within 19 days of the end of the month in which they are deducted from employees' pay. This section introduces corresponding provisions for personal pensions, which will also apply to stakeholder schemes registered under the *Welfare Reform and Pensions Act 1999, s 2* under a new *s 111A* in the *Pension Schemes Act 1993*.

Employers have to keep a record of the rates and due dates of contributions payable under direct payment arrangements to the designated stakeholder scheme, or to another scheme if the regulations allow. The employer has to send a copy of the record to the trustees or managers of the scheme and send the employee a statement setting out the amounts and dates of the payments made under the direct payment arrangements. The Pensions Ombudsman's determination in 1999, involving a member of the Merrill Lynch pension scheme, indicates that employers can still be guilty of maladministration if payments that are due to be passed to the pension provider are delayed even if they are made within the 19 day period of grace. Further details on employers' payments are discussed in Chapter 3.

Section 10 – Late Payments by Employers to Occupational Pension Schemes   [2.37]

If the employer and/or any trustee or manager of the scheme has failed to comply with his obligations, OPRA can impose fines not exceeding the statutory maximum or remove a trustee of a scheme. If there is evidence of fraudulent evasion of payments, a term of imprisonment not exceeding seven years, or a fine, or both, may be imposed on conviction. However, if an employer has already paid a penalty under the *Welfare Reform and Pensions Act 1999* for failing to conform to the employer access requirements, he will not be required to pay another penalty under this section.

Section 11 – Effect of Bankruptcy on Pension Rights: Approved Arrangements [2.38]

Pension rights in approved arrangements have statutory protection with effect from 29 May 2000, which ensures that pension rights are not counted as an asset in bankruptcy. Approved pension arrangements are those recognised by the Inland Revenue, under the *Income and Corporation Taxes Act 1988, Part XIV,* which has been amended to include stakeholder schemes. The effect of bankruptcy on stakeholder pensions is discussed in Chapter 7.

The Welfare Reform and Pensions Act 1999, Part IV – Pension Sharing on Divorce [2.39]

Pension sharing on divorce is to apply to any type of pension arrangement, which includes stakeholder schemes, apart from excepted public service pension schemes, under the *Welfare Reform and Pensions Act 1999, s 27.* The provisions for pension sharing on divorce are due to be implemented for divorce or nullity proceedings begun on or after 1 December 2000.

Pension sharing is a step forward from the current provisions, which allow pension earmarking. Earmarking has been an unsatisfactory solution on divorce as there is no clean break. If the former spouse whose pension has been earmarked dies before taking that pension, then the remaining former spouse is left with no pension provision.

Two of the pension sharing provisions in the *Welfare Reform and Pensions Act 1999, ss 31* and *38,* override scheme rules. These deal with pension debits, the reduction in a member's benefits which occur where a pension sharing order has been made and a provision giving pension credit rights statutory priority on winding up. These provisions will also apply to stakeholder schemes and scheme rules will need to include provisions for these requirements. Pension sharing on divorce is discussed in Chapter 7.

The Finance Bill 2000, Schedule 1 [2.40]

The main tax provisions that apply to stakeholder schemes are detailed in the Finance Bill 2000, Schedule 1. Stakeholder pensions are to be DC schemes and will fall under the new simplified tax regime that is being introduced for DC pensions, examined in detail in Chapter 6. Under this, stakeholder schemes, including occupational DC schemes that decide to opt into the stakeholder regime, are to be treated under tax legislation as a type of personal pension.

Those occupational DC schemes that choose not to opt-in and all DB schemes will continue under the tax regime for occupational schemes. Stakeholder pensions will also be subject to the specific rules for stakeholder pensions in the *Welfare Reform and Pensions Act 1999, Part I.*

Tax Charges and 'Opting-in' to the New DC Regime [2.41]

The Inland Revenue will not impose a tax charge on a DC occupational scheme that elects to be treated as a DC pension scheme. Detailed rules on how a DC scheme can 'opt-in' to the new regime are provided in the Finance Bill 2000, Schedule 23ZA.

'Opting-in' to the DC tax regime includes the following steps.

O The trustees of an occupational DC scheme can elect on or after 1 October 2000 to transfer into the DC tax regime with an effective date from 6 April 2001 (more detail on the information needed to support the election is found in Volume 2).

O The Inland Revenue can refuse an application where the scheme is over-funded (more detail on the criteria for over-funding is found in Volume 2).

O It is assumed that existing pension scheme rules cover the transfer of an occupational DC scheme into the new simplified DC tax regime.

Earnings Threshold [2.42]

The earnings threshold below which DC contributions may be paid without any reference to earnings or the need to produce any confirmation of these earnings is currently £3,600 a year, which can be changed at a later date by a Treasury Order. The removal of any link with earnings means that for the first time, someone without earnings can contribute to a pension and benefit from the tax relief on contributions and on the investment growth. Contracting-out rebates are disregarded in calculating the allowable contributions.

Eligibility Criteria   [2.43]

A member is eligible to make contributions to a stakeholder scheme, if he:

○   is resident and ordinarily resident in the UK; or
○   was resident and ordinarily resident during the relevant year or at some time during the five years of assessment preceding the relevant year; or
○   was resident and ordinarily resident when he made the personal pension arrangements; or
○   is performing Crown duties, in the armed forces or the diplomatic corps, or is the spouse of such a member.

Tax Relief for Insurance for Waiver of Premiums [2.44]

The current practice of granting tax relief for insuring against the inability to pay contributions by taking the premium out of the pension contribution is to end on 5 April 2001. At present, personal pension contributions can only be paid out for reasons of ill health, but this is to be broadened to include unemployment or other reasons. From 6 April 2001, providers will claim back tax at the basic rate for contributions paid out under the waiver insurance.

Income Withdrawals and Phased Vesting   [2.45]

Current rules normally require all the benefits from a personal pension to be taken at the same time. The new provisions allow for phased vesting, which means that people can follow a flexible retirement route and take benefits when it suits them, rather than all together. Members will be able to have more than one pension date and buy annuities at different times.

Approved Employee Share Schemes [2.46]

As is already the case with ISAs, from 6 April 2001 contributions into a stakeholder scheme can be made by transferring shares from an approved employee share scheme. The transfer must take place at market value and will be treated as a contribution paid net of basic rate tax.

Tax Relief on Contributions and Information Provisions [2.47]

All contributions on or after 6 April 2001 will be made net of basic rate tax with the pension provider reclaiming the tax from the Inland Revenue. From 6 April 2001, the information needed to apply for a stakeholder pension can be provided over the telephone, by e-mail or via the Internet. Currently information has to be provided on paper. If information is submitted in a paperless form, the provider must provide confirmation of the details in writing for legal acceptance of the contract.

Life Assurance [2.48]

Life assurance cover can be included within a DC pension, which includes stakeholder pensions, but it should not exceed 10% of contributions paid where the contract for insurance is made after 5 April 2001. Contracts made under existing rules will continue to be subject to the rules that life assurance contributions should be no more than 5% of net relevant earnings. The switch to 10% of contributions paid may mean that lower amounts are available to buy life assurance cover.

Carry Forward and Carry Back Reliefs [2.49]

The complicated provisions for carry forward and carry back provisions have been simplified, with carry forward provisions being abolished. However, there is a new provision on 'earnings holiday' arrangements which mitigates the loss of the carry forward provisions (as detailed at 2.50).

From April 2001, on or before paying a contribution, a member of a DC pension can elect to have it treated as a contribution for the previous tax year. The contribution must be made before 31 January, which is the filing date for returning self-assessment forms.

Contributions After Earnings Cease [2.50]

Contributions above £3,600 can be allowed against an individual's highest level of earnings for the 'basis year' and for the following five years, even where that person's earnings have ceased, provided that evidence of earnings in the basis year has been submitted.

Information About Earnings [2.51]

Information about earnings is only needed if contributions are made above £3,600. This will mean that providers have a reduced administrative burden. Contributions above £3,600 will be possible up to the current personal pension age and earnings related limits into schemes within the new DC regime. From April 2001, if information is provided about higher level contributions for one year, it will be valid for that basis year and the next 5 years (e.g. if a provider already holds a certificate giving information about earnings in 1999/2000, higher contributions will be allowed until 2004/05). If earnings cease and do not recommence within those 5 years, at the end of year 6 the maximum permitted level of contributions would revert to £3,600 or to its current equivalent.

Applications for Approval [2.52]

Providers can apply for approval for a stakeholder pension scheme on or after 1 October 2001. However, the scheme will not be able to accept contributions until 6 April 2001. It can take contributions before that under the existing personal pension tax rules only if it receives approval.

The Child Support, Pensions and Social Security Bill, Part II [2.53]

This Bill was introduced in December 1999, and is due to be enacted later on in 2000. Part II of the Bill provides for the reform of SERPS via the S2P and for reform of occupational and personal pension schemes. Details of the earnings factor from which the S2P will be calculated and the rebates that will be paid to stakeholder personal pension schemes and occupational stakeholder schemes are provided.

State Second Pension (S2P)   [2.54]

Low Earnings Threshold

This provides for the way in which the earnings factors, from which S2P is derived, will be calculated. Those employees with earnings between the prevailing Lower Earnings Limit (LEL) (£3,485 a year in 2000/2001) and the new Low Earnings Threshold (LET) (£9,500 in 1999/2000) will be treated as if they had an earnings factor of £9,500 in that year or the equivalent LET in that year.

In addition, people will be treated as if they had an earnings factor of £9,500 or the equivalent LET in a tax year throughout which they were:

O   entitled to Invalid Care Allowance;
O   paid Child Benefit for a child under six years old and had no earnings or earnings below the Lower Earnings Limit;
O   entitled to long-term Incapacity Benefit and satisfied the labour market attachment test (below);
O   paid Severe Disablement Allowance (SDA) and met the labour market attachment test (below);
O   treated as being precluded from regular employment by responsibilities at home if they:
   ●   received Income Support without needing to be available for work because they were caring for a disabled person; or
   ●   spent at least 35 hours a week caring for a person who received Attendance Allowance or the care component in Disability Living Allowance at the middle or highest rate.

The labour market attachment test will be applied when a person reaches State pension age. Those who were entitled to long-term Incapacity Benefit or SDA must have paid, or been treated as having paid, Class 1 employee National Insurance contributions for at least one tenth of their working life since 1978 (the year when SERPS was introduced). If they meet this test then they will be treated as earning the LET for that year and gain the relevant S2P credits.

Entitlement to S2P **[2.55]**

Entitlement to S2P provides for Additional Pension (the earnings-related part of the State pension) to be the sum of entitlement accrued under SERPS and entitlement accrued under S2P.

People earning between the LEL and the LET and those in the categories listed at paragraph 2.54, will be treated as if they had earned the LET in a qualifying year. Earnings above the annual LEL will be divided into up to three bands and different accrual rates applied to these bands as follows.

- ○ 40% on earnings at or above the annual LEL up to the LET.
- ○ 10% on earnings above the LET up to £21,600.
- ○ 20% on earnings above £21,600 up to £26,000 (the Upper Earnings Limit).

These accrual rates apply to those reaching State pension age after April 2009. Those retiring between the introduction of S2P and April 2009 will have higher accrual rates to reflect those they would have received under SERPS.

Stage two of S2P is to be introduced by order once stakeholder pension schemes have become established. All those earning above the LEL and up to £9,500 will be treated as if they had earned £9,500 in a year (or the prevailing LET at the time), and a 40% accrual rate will be applied.

Increases in the LET **[2.56]**

The Low Earnings Threshold (currently £9,500) is to be increased both before the introduction of the S2P and annually thereafter in line with the rise in national average earnings.

Information requirements **[2.57]**

This provides for regulations to be made for those precluded from regular employment by responsibilities at home to supply the necessary information for this to be taken into account when assessing their pension entitlement. This happens automatically for a person who receives Child Benefit for a child under 16 in any year in which they do not meet the Qualifying Earnings Factor (which is 52 times the weekly LEL).

3 – The Parties To Stakeholder Pensions

This chapter covers the following.

- O   Who will provide stakeholder pensions?
- O   The target customers for stakeholder pensions.
- O   Marketing stakeholder schemes.
- O   Employer access.
- O   The role of affinity groups.
- O   Trustees and authorised stakeholder managers.

Summary [3.1]

Providers of stakeholder pensions will be drawn from both the traditional providers who currently sell pensions and other newcomers to the market, such as schemes sponsored by trade unions and retailers. The key features of their products will have to be easy to understand, with transparent charging structures that do not exceed the 1% annual charge. Providers will need to ensure they have cost effective marketing and administrative procedures in place and comprehensive strategies to reach their target customers.

Potential customers for stakeholder pensions will include those on middle incomes, earning between £10,000 and £20,000. Employees who do not belong to an occupational scheme or who do not have a personal pension, along with the self employed, will find the flexibility and low charging structure of stakeholder pensions attractive. Other target groups include those no longer in the workplace due to caring responsibilities, the unemployed, those suffering from ill health or long term disabilities and spouses of Crown employees and armed forces personnel who have been posted abroad.

Those marketing stakeholder pensions will have to reach disparate groups of people: employees, the self employed and those currently not in the workplace. Consumers will be interested in the way that their funds are going to be invested and the charges that will be deducted from their stakeholder pension fund. Providers of stakeholder pensions will need to communicate effectively with their customers, ensuring that they have all the relevant information and keep them up to date with statements on contributions and fund performance.

Employers are required to designate a stakeholder scheme, having checked that it is registered with OPRA, and provide contact details. The designated scheme must be open to all relevant employees. At the request of the employee, employers have to make deductions from the employee's pay to the designated stakeholder scheme. Employers have to facilitate workplace access for providers to ensure that employees receive the necessary information needed to make an informed choice. This information might be delivered via computer information kiosks, workplace meetings or with payslips.

Affinity groups encompass different ways of grouping people together, for example: trade unions, occupational groupings, leisure and sports interests, professional organisations, shoppers from a certain retail outlet or political and religious groups. Affinity groups have a strong role to play, as they are a useful way of defining a target group for marketing purposes. They provide an alternative route for providers to reach a large number of people, both workers and those currently not earning, with similar needs. Some affinity groups will offer their own stakeholder scheme, whilst others may endorse a particular provider's stakeholder scheme. Affinity group stakeholder schemes must be trust based, as contract based schemes are not permitted to restrict membership to a particular group.

Trustees and authorised stakeholder scheme managers have a duty to ensure that the designated stakeholder scheme complies with the provisions for registration as a stakeholder scheme and continues to do so. They have to ensure that contributions are properly invested and administered on behalf of their members and act in their best interests. The trustees and managers of stakeholder schemes must also comply with all the necessary disclosure requirements and communicate regularly with members.

Who Will Provide Stakeholder Pensions? [3.2]

Stakeholder pensions will be offered by many of the traditional pension providers, along with the new entrants to the pensions market such as Virgin and Marks and Spencer. Some of the larger traditional providers, such as Legal and General and Equitable Life, are using the introduction of stakeholder pensions to offer their products via the new communication media, such as the Internet, as well as the traditional approach via a direct salesforce. This is partly due to the necessity of finding ways to remain within the low annual charge of 1% of the value of a member's fund, but also because direct marketing via technology is seen as the way ahead. Providers will, however, be unable to restrict access to their products to just one medium, such as the Internet.

New providers will include retailers, such as Tesco, who will offer a stakeholder pension to their customers. Affinity groups, like the TUC, aim to launch a scheme for their members, and include family members and friends. Some Independent Financial Advisers (IFAs) have also launched plans for stakeholder pensions, which they will offer direct to their own clients.

IFAs are likely to be wooed by providers of stakeholder schemes as many have close links with small employers, acting as their financial advisers. Small employers generally do not have occupational schemes or group pension plans and so are an ideal target group for providers. Marketing to IFAs is a cost effective route for providers to follow, as it gives them access to many small employers, without having to invest in costly marketing by targeting each employer directly. IFAs will be given details of the stakeholder schemes offered by providers to pass on to employers and will become, in effect, indirect providers of stakeholder pensions. Some IFAs will also wish to promote their own stakeholder schemes, where they have one.

Who Will Take Out a Stakeholder Pension?   [3.3]

Target Customers for Stakeholder Pensions

In the Green Paper 'A New Contract for Welfare: A Partnership for Pensions' (issued in December 1998), the main target group for stakeholder pensions was the 10.75 million people on middle incomes earning between £9,000 and £18,500 (a group whose earnings have now increased to between £10,000 and £20,000). This includes both the employed and the self-employed. However, since the Green Paper, approximately 750,000 people who work for an employer employing 4 or fewer employees have been excluded from the target group, as these small employers have been exempted from the employer access provisions for stakeholder pensions. This exemption will be reviewed in 2004. The government wants to encourage the target group to move to a stakeholder pension as their best second pension option, rather than relying on SERPS (or S2P when it is introduced). This will be achieved by offering a higher rate of rebates from National Insurance contributions (NICs) for those in a contracted-out stakeholder scheme and other privately funded provisions, which at least offers a prospect of producing higher returns than may emerge from S2P.

The other group which will benefit from stakeholder pensions, providing them with access where none has previously been available, are those who are out of the workplace, either due to illness, disability or caring responsibilities, or as spouses of serving members of the forces or of Crown servants posted abroad. They will be able to take advantage of these new provisions as the link with earnings from employment has now been removed. They, their partners or other people may contribute on their behalf to a stakeholder pension up to a maximum of £3,600 per year.

Those who have been in the workplace and have left due to illness, caring responsibilities, unemployment or for other reasons, can continue to make contributions at a higher level for up to 5 years after their earnings cease. Once they have submitted evidence of higher earnings, they can then continue to make contributions within the age and percentage related limits for personal pensions during this period. Thereafter, the £3,600 limit would apply.

One group not specifically targeted by the government who might also take out stakeholder pensions are those earning over £20,000. If they belong to an occupational DC scheme which opts into the new stakeholder regime, or have a personal pension plan, they can also take out a stakeholder personal pension and pay in £3,600 per year, or up to the maximum allowed under the age and salary related personal pension limits, though the Inland Revenue is looking at 'abuse control' measures for these higher earners.

Current Pension Provision Within These Groups [3.4]

Employees

Occupational schemes are generally the best option for those employees who have access to them. The charging structure tends to be lower than for personal pensions and employer contributions are compulsory if the employer wishes to benefit from the tax advantages of offering an occupational scheme. However, not all employers offer occupational schemes.

The next option for employees is to take out a personal pension, but these normally have a 'front-loaded' charging structure. This means that the costs of contacting people, persuading them to take out a personal pension and rewarding the sales force are recouped during the first two or three years' contributions to a pension. Thereafter, annual charges continue to eat into the value of a person's pension fund. According to the 1998 Green Paper 'A New Contract for Welfare: A Partnership for Pensions', a third of people who buy personal pensions stop making contributions within three years and only pay in their National Insurance rebate and make no additional savings. This means in some cases that after charges have been removed, the value of a person's pension fund can be less than the contributions made. If the only further contributions that are added are SERPS (or S2P) rebates then the pot of money available is eaten away by charges. In these cases, personal pensions offer poor value for money.

Personal pensions are perceived as complicated to understand and people find it difficult to compare the different products on offer. Stakeholder pensions, with their transparent charging structures of a maximum of 1% annual charge, should make it easier for people to compare what is on offer. For those employees not in an occupational scheme or without a personal pension, stakeholder pensions are seen as a cost effective solution.

Self Employed [3.5]

The self employed are seen as an ideal target group for stakeholder pensions. Currently they pay into the basic State pension with much reduced rates of NICs, but do not have access to SERPS. There is some discussion taking place as to whether self employed people should be brought within the scope of S2P, but this is still under consideration and there have been no decisions yet.

The self employed top up their basic State pension with private provision for their retirement, as they have no access to occupational pension schemes. The savings vehicles chosen vary from ordinary personal pension plans to ISAs or their predecessors, Personal Equity Plans (PEPs) and a variety of other investment plans. According to the Green Paper, around 50% of self employed people contribute to a personal pension, though more than a third have never contributed to a personal pension.

The self employed also see the charging structures of personal pensions as a disincentive, combined with the fact that the inflexibility of some personal pensions does not reflect the seasonal and fluctuating nature of contract workers. However, some of the newer providers in the market place have launched new personal pension products that allow for people's changing lifestyles.

Stakeholder pensions are seen as an ideal savings vehicle for the self employed, with a constant low charging structure and the flexibility to stop and start contributions. It is envisaged that many might switch from their personal pension to take advantage of the lower charging structure of stakeholder pensions, though market forces may see personal pension plans having to lower their costs.

High Earners [3.6]

At present, many high earners in employment belong either to occupational pension schemes or group pension plans. Some people in occupational schemes also contribute to free standing additional voluntary contribution plans (FSAVCs), which are established separately from occupational schemes. These have administration and management fees, which the member has to meet from his contributions. The total amount of contributions that can be made by a member in an occupational scheme in any tax year is 15% of annual earnings. Those contributing to personal pension plans are restricted by age related percentages of their salary on the amount they can contribute in a given tax year.

Many of those high earners who currently contribute to FSAVCs, which operate on a DC basis, will be attracted by the low charging structure of stakeholder pensions as an alternative. Those in personal pension plans are also likely to be attracted by the lower charging structure of stakeholder plans. Only those high earners that belong to a DC scheme that has opted into the stakeholder tax regime will be able to afford to contribute to a stakeholder pension, up to the limit allowed by the age related salary percentages of the personal pension regime.

Older high earners will be able to benefit from the higher age related allowances under the stakeholder tax regime. Under an occupational scheme contributions are limited to 15% of salary, but under the stakeholder tax regime those aged 56 – 60, for example, could contribute up to a total of 35% of earnings, including employer contributions.

Those Outside the Workplace [3.7]

Carers are those who look after young children, elderly people, the disabled or the infirm and are not active in the workplace. This does not necessarily mean that they have never worked and in many cases they will have given up paid employment to take on caring responsibilities. Equally, some disabled people will have a history of working in the past, as will those unable to work due to illness. The majority of unemployed people will also have had periods of work in the past. Spouses of Crown employees and of members of the armed forces will often have worked before moving abroad to accompany their spouses.

Many of those no longer in the workplace may have left occupational pension schemes or had to stop paying into a personal pension plan, as they no longer had any earnings from employment on which to base their pension contributions. The benefits that have accrued under either private or occupational pension provision are preserved. Contributions to a private pension plan can be restarted at a later date if a carer, unemployed person, disabled or previously ill person goes back into paid employment. If they return to the same employer they are usually able to rejoin the occupational pension scheme, though sometimes this is subject to the trustees' and/or employer's discretion. If they change employment, there could be an opportunity to join a new occupational scheme.

Having left paid employment, carers then rely on the basic State pension, which provides credits for people who have spells of unemployment or are caring for others. They do not earn any credits for SERPS as this is purely for employees. However, under S2P, which is due to be introduced in 2002, carers out of the workplace looking after children under 6 and dependant adults will be treated as though they were earning £9,500 (or the current LET) per year and receive the appropriate credits.

Those with broken work records, who have claimed Special Disability Allowance or long-term Incapacity Benefit, will have to satisfy the labour market attachment test to qualify for the S2P earnings credits. They must have paid, or been treated as having paid, Class 1 employee National Insurance contributions for at least one tenth of their working life since 1978, the date when SERPS was introduced. This will be applied when people reach State pension age.

Carers and the disabled will be helped by the MIG that the government introduced in April 1999. This income related benefit ensures a minimum income in retirement and help with some housing and council tax costs. Pensioners and the disabled receive more than non-pensioners.

As outlined above, many carers, disabled people and those unable to work due to illness have previously been active in the workplace. The removal of the link with earnings from employment for stakeholder pensions will mean that, for contributions up to £3,600, there will be no earnings test and these can continue indefinitely for those no longer in employment. Also, for the first five years after earnings cease, contributions at a higher level can continue to be made under the personal pension limits, which are age linked and allow certain percentages of gross salary to be paid into a personal pension. Thereafter contributions are limited to £3,600 per year unless earnings resume.

This flexibility to keep paying contributions if people wish to do so will make it easier for carers and others to continue to build up their stakeholder pension fund. It will also allow others, such as partners, parents and siblings to make contributions to a carer or disabled person's pension fund on their behalf, if the money is available to do so. As there is no lower age limit for stakeholder pensions, parents could start stakeholder pensions for their children.

It is hoped that these measures will lessen the dependency of carers (mostly women) on the State in later years and increase their independence by giving them the means to build up a stakeholder pension. This also reflects the trend to encourage the individualisation of pension provision. As more and more marriages end in divorce, and fewer people marry, there is a move for each person to have access to their own pension provision rather than a derived right via a partner. Although many occupational pension schemes allow heterosexual unmarried partners to receive a survivor's pension, it is not universal. Provision for homosexual partners in occupational schemes is still rarely found. The move towards individualisation is one that the European Union is keen to encourage – in fact it has already been introduced in the Netherlands.

Marketing Stakeholder Schemes [3.8]

The Financial Services Authority (FSA) will be responsible for regulating the marketing of stakeholder pensions to prospective members. This is dealt with in Chapter 4 on Regulation.

Employers [3.9]

The key for providers is successful low cost marketing to employers as, following designation of their stakeholder scheme, the provider has a right to workplace access to encourage employees to take out one of its stakeholder schemes. Providers will be targeting medium sized employers who do not have an occupational scheme, but have large numbers of employees earning between £10,000 and £20,000. These could be workers in the manufacturing, retail and services sectors, for example.

Providers will have to offer incentives to employers to encourage them to choose their scheme above other stakeholder schemes on offer. Employers are concerned about the possible administrative costs of complying with the access requirements for stakeholder pensions. Therefore, anything that will make this burden easier to bear will be welcome. Possible solutions include bespoke payroll software for easy deduction of contributions to the designated stakeholder scheme and/ or offering assistance with staff training.

Employees [3.10]

Stakeholder schemes are subject to a very tight charging structure of only 1% annual charge on the value of the member's fund, which has to include the costs for basic advice, marketing, administration and information. Although as the years progress the value of the fund, and therefore the charge, will increase, initially this represents a real challenge for providers. They will have to use new ways of marketing their schemes via new communication media. One cost effective marketing method could be via the Internet, using a provider's website, though providers have to ensure that there is more than one communication channel for access to its products.

Some providers have said that they will deliver stakeholder pensions via workplace terminals, where employees can log on and read all the details about stakeholder pensions and other products on offer at the provider's website. This will be supplemented by more traditional methods of selling. By cross-selling other financial products within the provider's portfolio, this will be an effective way of underwriting the start up costs for marketing stakeholder pensions. By 'bundling' the products on offer, for example by offering percentage discounts when another financial product is taken out with the provider, as insurers do with buildings and contents insurance policies, providers will maintain a tight hold on their clients. Equally, the information provided by customers when entering their details on a website will provide future sales opportunities.

Pearl Assurance's usual target market consists of mainly C2, D and E consumers who earn less than £17,500 per year and is similar to the market that stakeholder is trying to reach. It has carried out market research into how many people have access to a computer. In late 1999, in the C2, D and E income brackets, only 30% had Internet access at work and 20% at home. Open access computer booths in the workplace would be an attractive option for the main target group for stakeholder pensions, though it is also likely to benefit from the development of interactive TV.

Alternatively, information could be distributed via workplace meetings and through payslips. These two options would be more costly and time consuming than using the Internet. Workplace meetings would have to be repeated to cover a large workforce and would lack any capacity to deal with each person individually, and would inevitably mean the delivery of generic advice via 'decision trees'. These are flow charts which direct consumers to certain solutions depending on whether their answers to a series of questions are positive or negative. Although communication via the Internet is impersonal, each potential customer could enter his own details and at least have the impression that he was receiving a tailored solution for his needs, though still following a decision tree format.

The Self-Employed [3.11]

The self employed represent a difficult group to target as their needs and income are so diverse and, by virtue of their employment status, they are their own bosses. This means that the suggested route for targeting those who would be interested in signing up for a stakeholder pension, via workplace meetings, is not going to apply to many self-employed people, unless they are under contract to a firm offering workplace access. It seems likely that the self employed will be targeted via their own affinity groups, such as the Builders' Federation and IT industry groupings.

High Earners [3.12]

As a generalisation, high earners tend to be more financially sophisticated than lower paid workers. Providers wishing to target this group will be able to reach them via their websites and advertisements in the financial press. When the benefits of lower charging regimes have been spelt out to those with FSAVCs, they are likely to change over to stakeholder pensions without much further persuasion.

Affinity Groups [3.13]

Targeting affinity groups has the advantage of reaching otherwise disparate groups of people who work for different employers. For large affinity groups, such as members of a trade union like UNISON, which represents large numbers of low paid workers, an endorsement of a particular stakeholder pension will be a powerful marketing tool for a provider.

Affinity groups usually have established channels of communication, so it would be easy to include details of a provider's stakeholder scheme when communicating with the membership or group participants. Using the membership lists of affinity groups, the marketing information that can be extracted from shoppers at a particular store or subscribers to an organisation or publication will be a cost effective way of reaching potential customers for stakeholder pensions.

A provider would probably woo an affinity group with a lower annual charge in return for access to a large pool of potential customers for stakeholder pensions and other financial products. Members of an affinity group stakeholder scheme would pay contributions to the scheme via direct debit or cheque. At present the employer is not under any obligation to provide a payroll deduction facility to any stakeholder scheme other than its designated scheme.

Those Not in the Workplace [3.14]

As with self employed people, there is a problem reaching those not in the workplace. Each group outside the labour market has different characteristics: carers, the unemployed, the disabled, those with ill health and those living abroad with spouses who are members of the armed forces or employed by the Crown. Targeting all these different groups of people and ensuring that they receive adequate information about stakeholder pensions is a complex communications problem. Logically, these groups are not the most cost effective targets for providers, as they cannot be reached via workplace meetings or affinity groups based on one's type of employment.

The government will use its own established channels of communication to publicise stakeholder schemes to those currently not in the workplace and is committed to a widespread information campaign. It has announced its intention to link up with the Post Office, which is installing computerised information booths for its customers. As many people cash their benefit cheques at their local Post Office, be it child benefit, income support, disability benefit or unemployment benefit, this could be a good way to reach potential stakeholder customers. Information about stakeholder pensions could be circulated alongside notifications of changes in rates of benefits or whenever other communications are being issued. TV advertising campaigns, such as those used to publicise the new family credit scheme, will also be used.

Trade unions may also include family members and friends as potential members of their schemes, if they launch their own stakeholder schemes. Details may then be circulated by word of mouth, through marketing material or advertisements. Other affinity groups, such as retailers, will market their products in store directly to their customers, whilst those linked by a common interest will send out details to their members via their normal communication channels.

Providers will be advertising widely in the press and on television so that those not in the workplace can contact them direct. The Internet will be an easy way to contact providers, if potential clients have access to a computer at home. The advent of interactive TV, which also gives access to the Internet, is likely further to revolutionise the way in which providers and retailers can reach consumers. Some figures suggest that by 2003, more people will access the Internet via their interactive televisions than via their computers.

Employer Access [3.15]

The employer has a key role to play in helping to provide access to stakeholder pensions for his 'relevant employees' (defined at 3.16 below). It is the employer who must designate a scheme and provide contact details for the scheme to his employees. Providers are to be allowed workplace access by the employer to market their schemes. If requested to do so by his employees, the employer must arrange a payroll deduction facility to transfer contributions to the designated stakeholder scheme. This is discussed in Chapter 4.

Relevant Employees [3.16]

Definition

The *Welfare Reform and Pensions Act 1999, s 3(9)*, defines the term 'relevant employees'. It states that this means in relation to an employer:

> 'all employees of his employed in Great Britain and also, in the case of an employer resident or incorporated in any part of Great Britain, all employees of his employed outside the United Kingdom, but with the exception, in the case of any employer, of any employees of his whose employment qualifies them for membership of an occupational pension scheme of the employer; whose earnings fall below the LEL as defined in section 181 of the 1993 [Pensions Schemes] Act, or are of such other description as may be prescribed'.

Exemptions [3.17]

Under the *Stakeholder Pension Schemes Regulations 2000, reg 23*, exemptions from the definition of 'relevant employees' are detailed. If all employees fall within one or more of the following categories, then the employer is exempted from having to provide access to a designated stakeholder scheme:

○ employees aged eighteen or over, with more than five years before normal pension age under the employer's occupational scheme who are eligible on completion of twelve months employment to qualify for membership of an employer's occupational pension scheme; or
○ employees who declined to join the employer's occupational pension scheme when eligible and are now excluded; or
○ employees who have worked for the employer for less than three months; or
○ employees that do not satisfy the residency test for the UK and are therefore unable to contribute to a stakeholder pension; or
○ employees whose earnings fell below the NI LEL, (currently £67 per week for 2000/2001) for one or more weeks within the last 3 months.

Exemptions from Employer Access Requirements [3.18]

The *Stakeholder Pension Schemes Regulations 2000, reg 22*, lists exemptions from the requirement for an employer to designate and facilitate access to a stakeholder scheme, if:

○ he employs fewer than five employees; or

○ it is a term of the contract of every relevant employee age 18 or over that:

- the employer will make contributions to a personal pension scheme of at least 3% of employees' earnings (excluding overtime, bonuses, commission or similar payments but before tax, National Insurance and pensions contributions are deducted) each time the employee is paid or at agreed intervals for any period during his employment that the employee is a member of that scheme;

- no exit charges or penalties for stopping contributions (apart from allowable charges and market value adjustments for with profits funds);

- employer will transfer employee contributions, deducted from the employee's salary at his request;

- for GPPs in place before 8 October 2001 an employer can require an employee to match his contributions to the GPP. After 8 October 2001 this condition is optional and an employee can only be required to pay a maximum contribution of 3%; or

○ there is no written term in the employee's contract regarding contributions but there is evidence of contributions continuously made from a date prior to 8 October 2001.

Designating a Scheme [3.19]

If the employer finds that he does not benefit from one of the exemptions listed above, under the *Welfare Reform and Pensions Act 1999, s 3*, he has to comply with the employer access requirements and designate a stakeholder scheme which must be open to all relevant employees. There is no lower age limit for stakeholder pensions, but an upper age limit of 75 for contributions, as with personal pensions.

Under the *Stakeholder Pension Schemes Regulations 2000, reg 22,* an employer has to comply with the access requirements by 8 October 2001. If he employs a fifth employee between 8 July 2001 and 8 October 2001, he has 3 months to select a scheme. After 8 October 2001, if the employer comes within the requirements for the first time or once again he has 3 months to designate a scheme.

A four month period of grace is permitted when the designation of a scheme is withdrawn and more time is needed to designate another scheme. Also when a winding up is taking place, the employer does not need to comply with the workforce consultation requirements, if he chooses to designate the stakeholder pension scheme that the trustees or stakeholder manager have named on the winding up notice.

All stakeholder schemes, both trust based and those managed by an authorised stakeholder manager, have to register with OPRA. The employer must check the register to ensure that the scheme he wishes to designate is registered. Under the *Stakeholder Pension Schemes Regulations 2000, reg 21,* there is a provision for OPRA to charge a fee for the costs of providing a copy of the register. OPRA may publish the register in any way it chooses. It is likely that this will be on the Internet. OPRA's website address is: www.opra.gov.uk

The employer is not required to recommend a scheme, only to designate it. The employer is also not required to seek professional advice when designating a scheme, though he can choose to do so if he wishes. The employer must consult the workforce about the stakeholder scheme he wishes to designate, although it is the employer alone who will decide on the choice of scheme. This can be done at a routine workplace meeting. If employees are dissatisfied with the employer's choice of stakeholder scheme they can choose their own, though employers are not initially obliged to make payroll deductions to stakeholder schemes other than to the designated one.

Workplace Access [3.20]

Once an employer has designated a stakeholder scheme (or several schemes if he wishes to do so, as long as they are accessible to all relevant employees), he must provide his employees with contact details. Typically, these will consist of the name of the provider, an address, a telephone number and a name of a contact at the provider. It is then up to the employee to make contact with the stakeholder provider.

It is likely that providers will publicise the stakeholder schemes via workplace meetings, which the employer will facilitate, or through information provided in payslips. Providers will also make use of their websites, and if employers who have designated their schemes have an intranet, then a link could be provided to the designated provider's website as an easy way to access information. New employees can be provided with details of the designated stakeholder scheme during their induction process.

The Role of Affinity Groups [3.21]

Affinity groups will have a dual role in the provision of stakeholder pensions. One role is to endorse a particular stakeholder scheme that they see as offering value for money and will be of interest to their members. The other role is for them to develop their own stakeholder scheme to offer alongside the retailers' traditional products.

If the affinity group has a defined membership, a stakeholder scheme can be offered to members at workplace meetings. In the case of much looser groupings, such as shoppers at a retail outlet, the stakeholder scheme can be offered along with the retailers' more traditional products.

Potential Providers [3.22]

The Trade Union Congress (TUC) has been active in developing a stakeholder scheme for its members, who include low-paid public sector, manufacturing and service industry workers. These are represented, among others, by the memberships of Unison, GMB and AEEU. It hopes to establish a series of associated schemes from each union, called collectively the TUC/Unison stakeholder. They will share the same administrative, investment and benefits processes to save costs. The TUC estimates that there are around one million trade unionists without any form of pension.

Marks and Spencer is an example of a retailer which is going to offer stakeholder pensions, targeting its cardholders and in-store shoppers in the same way as it markets its current financial services products. It has announced an intention to restrict its costs to a very competitive annual charge of only 0.7%. Its primary target market will be female shoppers. Many of these may well be part time workers with no current pension provision. This group was highlighted in the Green Paper, 'A New Contract For Welfare: Partnership in Pensions' (December 1998), as lacking pension provision as they work part-time for low wages and therefore have little money to put aside. They are unlikely to belong to an occupational pension scheme. The low charging structure will appeal to this group as it reinforces the perception that Marks and Spencer wishes to promote: that it offers value for money.

Possible Cost Savings [3.23]

It is possible that other affinity groups will offer their own stakeholder product rather than endorse a particular provider's scheme. This development of affinity group financial products has already been seen in the development of credit cards. Affinity groups offer credit cards at competitive rates of interest which are then linked to incentive schemes, such as charitable donations linked to the amount spent on the credit card or discount schemes for further products available via the affinity group. Alternatively, affinity groups will be able to negotiate attractive annual charging rates from providers if they endorse a particular scheme.

Trustees and Authorised Stakeholder Managers [3.24]

The day to day management of a stakeholder scheme will be carried out by trustees in the case of a trust based stakeholder scheme and by authorised stakeholder managers for contract based stakeholder schemes. Their roles are examined in detail in Chapter 4 on Regulation and Chapter 5 on Governance.

Trustees and authorised stakeholder managers will have a role to play in ensuring that the stakeholder scheme that they are overseeing continues at all times to comply with the requirements for a stakeholder scheme, as in the *Welfare Reform and Pensions Act 1999, s. 3*. This requirement is a continuing one and is not discharged simply by ensuring that the scheme complies with the minimum standards on registration and is on the register maintained by OPRA.

Decision Trees [3.25]

The following section contains a number of decision trees to aid employers who are trying to assess their own pension provision and decide if they need to establish a stakeholder scheme.

Employers with no Pension Provision [3.26]

	Do you have fewer than 5 employees?	
YES		NO

You do not need to comply with the employer access provisions
(This exemption is to be reviewed in 2004)
N.B. If you take on a fifth employee, you have 3 months to designate a stakeholder scheme and check that it is registered with OPRA, if all 5 employees earn above the LEL and meet the UK residency test.

Do all your employees earn less than or an amount equal to the LEL (Lower Earnings Limit – £3484 in 2000/01) over a continuous 3 month period?

YES	NO

You do not need to comply with the employer access provisions.
N.B. When 5 or more of your employees earn more than the LEL and meet the UK residency test, you have three months to designate a stakeholder scheme and check that it is registered with OPRA.

Do all your employees fail the UK residency test?

YES	NO

You do not need to comply with the employer access provisions.
N.B. When you have 5 or more employees earning above the LEL, who meet the UK residency test, you have 3 months to designate a stakeholder scheme and check that it is registered with OPRA

Do you employ your employees for less than 3 months i.e. for seasonal work only

YES	NO

You do not need to comply with the employer access provisions.
N.B. When you employ 5 or more employees for longer than 3 months, who earn above the LEL and comply with the UK residency test, you have 3 months to designate a stakeholder scheme, and check that it is registered with OPRA.

You must comply with the employer access provisions by 8 October 2001 and offer a designated stakeholder scheme, having checked it is on OPRA's register, to all employees within 3 months of commencing work. Payroll deductions should also be provided (if requested).

Employers with a GPP [3.27]

Do you offer membership of a GPP to all your employees as part of their contract of employment, once they have completed 3 months' employment?

YES   NO

Do you contribute at least 3% of employees' basic pay to the GPP

If you employ more than 5 employees who meet the UK residency test and earn more than the LEL, you must either offer membership of the GPP to all your employees once they have completed 3 months' employment or designate a stakeholder scheme by 8 October 2001 for those employees and provide payroll deductions if requested to do so.

YES   NO

Does your GPP have no exit charges or cessation charges when employees leave the scheme or stop paying contributions?

If you employ more than 5 employees who meet the UK residency test and earn more than the LEL, you must either increase your employer contributions to 3% of employees' basic pay or designate a stakeholder scheme by 8 October 2001 and provide payroll deductions if requested to do so.

YES   NO

You are exempt from the employer access requirements. N.B. This exemption is to be reviewed in 2004.

If you employ more than 5 employees who meet the UK residency test and earn more than the LEL, You must remove exit charges and cessation charges or designate a stakeholder scheme by 8 October 2001 and provide payroll deductions if requested to do.

Employers with a DB Scheme [3.28]

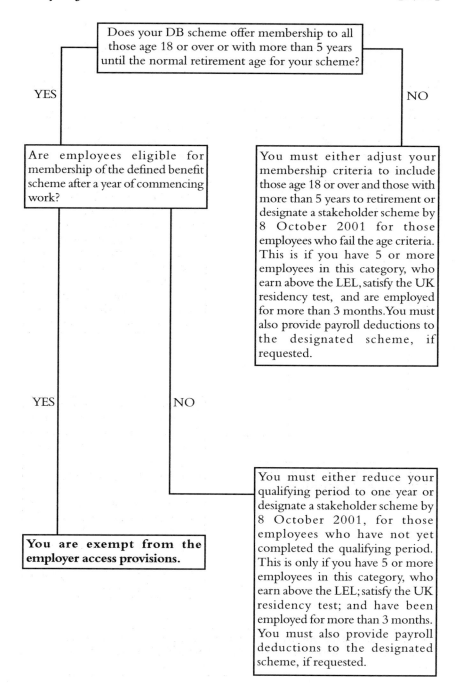

Does your DB scheme offer membership to all those age 18 or over or with more than 5 years until the normal retirement age for your scheme?

YES

NO

Are employees eligible for membership of the defined benefit scheme after a year of commencing work?

You must either adjust your membership criteria to include those age 18 or over and those with more than 5 years to retirement or designate a stakeholder scheme by 8 October 2001 for those employees who fail the age criteria. This is if you have 5 or more employees in this category, who earn above the LEL, satisfy the UK residency test, and are employed for more than 3 months. You must also provide payroll deductions to the designated scheme, if requested.

YES

NO

You are exempt from the employer access provisions.

You must either reduce your qualifying period to one year or designate a stakeholder scheme by 8 October 2001, for those employees who have not yet completed the qualifying period. This is only if you have 5 or more employees in this category, who earn above the LEL; satisfy the UK residency test; and have been employed for more than 3 months. You must also provide payroll deductions to the designated scheme, if requested.

Employers with a DC Scheme   **[3.29]**

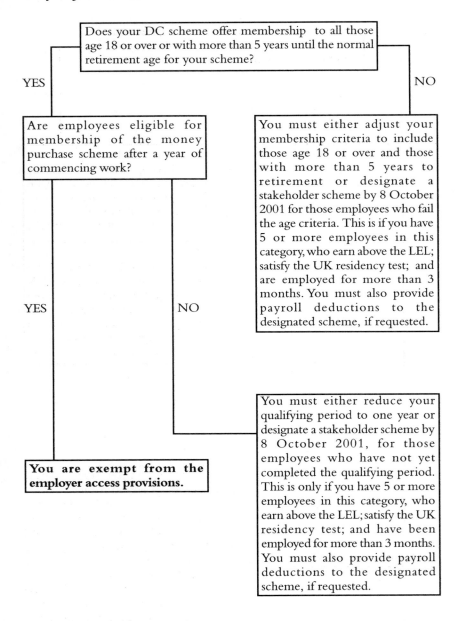

Does your DC scheme offer membership to all those age 18 or over or with more than 5 years until the normal retirement age for your scheme?

YES   NO

Are employees eligible for membership of the money purchase scheme after a year of commencing work?

You must either adjust your membership criteria to include those age 18 or over and those with more than 5 years to retirement or designate a stakeholder scheme by 8 October 2001 for those employees who fail the age criteria. This is if you have 5 or more employees in this category, who earn above the LEL; satisfy the UK residency test; and are employed for more than 3 months. You must also provide payroll deductions to the designated scheme, if requested.

YES   NO

You must either reduce your qualifying period to one year or designate a stakeholder scheme by 8 October 2001, for those employees who have not yet completed the qualifying period. This is only if you have 5 or more employees in this category, who earn above the LEL; satisfy the UK residency test; and have been employed for more than 3 months. You must also provide payroll deductions to the designated scheme, if requested.

You are exempt from the employer access provisions.

N.B. As an alternative approach, you may wish to consider opting into the new DC tax regime. This would bring your scheme within the stakeholder tax regime.

4 – Regulation

This chapter covers the following.

O   The role of the Occupational Pensions Regulatory
    Authority (OPRA).
O   The role of the Financial Services Authority (FSA).
O   Key points on advice.
O   Complaints.
O   Penalties.

Summary [4.1]

The regulation of stakeholder schemes is to be split between the
Occupational Pensions Regulatory Authority (OPRA) and the Financial
Services Authority (FSA). Each regulator will deal with its own areas of
expertise and provide clear information for members and schemes with
co-ordination and dialogue between the regulators.

OPRA is to regulate the registration of stakeholder schemes and the
operation of trust based stakeholder schemes. It will be responsible for
monitoring the information that is supplied to those who are already
members of stakeholder pension schemes and ensure that employers
and providers comply with the requirements for handling members'
contributions and payroll deductions.

The FSA is to regulate the marketing of stakeholder schemes and their
sale as an investment. It will also regulate the provision of advice and
information to prospective members of stakeholder schemes. The FSA
will supervise the firms responsible for managing the funds invested
and also regulate contract based stakeholder schemes.

Nobody has to take advice before purchasing a financial product, but
those that do should be subject to a 'fact find' to ensure that the product
they purchase is appropriate to their needs. Advice must be given by
an authorised adviser. Employers will be able to give generic advice to
employees. Simply designating a stakeholder scheme will not be
perceived as giving investment advice.

The Pensions Advisory Service (OPAS) will deal with complaints about
stakeholder occupational and personal pensions, while the Pensions
Ombudsman will adjudicate on complaints about maladministration

by trustees of trust based stakeholder schemes. Where individuals have complaints relating to misleading literature, inappropriate advice or investment management, these can be referred to either the Financial Services Ombudsman or arbitration. The alternative route is to pursue a complaint through the courts.

If the FSA believes that product literature is misleading or that stakeholder managers are offering inappropriate advice then it can impose sanctions. Equally, OPRA will impose sanctions on trustees who fail to hand over contributions on time, provide misleading information when registering stakeholder schemes, or do not inform members that schemes have been removed from the register. Sanctions will include requiring providers to compensate individuals who have acted on misleading information or advice and the imposition of financial penalties.

OPRA [4.2]

OPRA is the statutory regulator for UK occupational pension schemes. It was set up under the *Pensions Act 1995*, which was introduced in the wake of the Maxwell scandal, and the Goode Committee report in September 1993 which concluded that the regulation of pension schemes needed new safeguards. OPRA's function is to regulate trust based occupational pension schemes against fraud and the misuse of pension scheme assets and ensure that beneficiaries' interests are protected. This role will be widened to include the regulation of trust based stakeholder schemes and the registration of all stakeholder schemes. The Pension Schemes Registry comes within OPRA's remit.

Registration of Stakeholder Schemes [4.3]

Stakeholder schemes, both contract based and trust based, must be registered with OPRA. This registration can commence from 1 October 2000 but schemes cannot begin to operate until 6 April 2001. OPRA is to keep a register of stakeholder pension schemes and it is envisaged that OPRA will make the register of stakeholder schemes available via the Internet as well as via conventional forms of communication. This will provide an easy route for employers seeking to comply with the employer access requirements to check that their designated stakeholder scheme is on the register.

To be able to register with OPRA, providers of stakeholder schemes will have to demonstrate that their product complies with the minimum standards for stakeholder. These include a requirement that annual charging levels are 1% or less of the value of the member's fund and that there are no charges for transfers in or out of the fund. Basic information and explanatory material are to be provided within the 1% charge. Schemes have a choice between providing advice within the charge or charging a separate fee, providing that this is the subject of a separate contract in writing. Schemes must also accept minimum contributions of £20 and cannot specify any minimum level of frequency for contributions e.g. every month. One-off and regular payments must also be accepted. Schemes must nominate a default investment option for those members who do not wish to make a choice.

The legal requirements for registration are detailed in Chapter 2. In essence, trustees and stakeholder managers must declare that their scheme meets all the minimum standards when applying for registration. OPRA can refuse to register a scheme at its discretion if the scheme does not meet the minimum standards and can fine or imprison trustees or stakeholder managers who supply misleading information.

Payroll Deductions [4.4]

One of the employer access criteria is that the employer provides a payroll deduction facility for those employees who request it. Although the employer may make contributions to other pension arrangements, he is under no compulsion to make contributions to the designated stakeholder pension scheme. However, he must deduct and record the amount requested from the employee's pay and pass the contribution to the designated scheme within 19 days of the end of the month in which the contribution was deducted. This is in line with current practice for occupational schemes and employees will be able to check this by looking at their annual statement. OPRA will oversee compliance with the access requirements and the timeliness of payments.

The *Welfare Reform and Pensions Act, s 9,* applies where the employer makes contributions to a stakeholder or personal pension scheme on behalf of his employees or passes on the payroll deductions made at the employees' request. The same provisions for contributions that have been deducted from the payroll for payment to occupational schemes are to apply to personal pension schemes, including stakeholder schemes.

A Record [4.5]

The employer must prepare a record and keep it up to date. It must show the rates and due dates of contributions payable under the payroll deductions. There can be a separate record for each employee or a single record for all employees contributions to an arrangement.

The Due Date for Contributions [4.6]

The due date by which deductions from employees' earnings must reach the trustees or managers of the designated stakeholder scheme is by the nineteenth day of the month following the month in which the deduction was made. For example, if the deduction from earnings is made in March, it must reach the trustees or managers of the stakeholder scheme by 19 April. For convenience, the due date for employer payments can be the same as for employee payments. This can be settled by agreement between the provider and employer.

The Rate of Contributions [4.7]

Employees can contribute a percentage of their salary, or a variable amount as agreed between employer and employee. Employers' contributions to the pension and the rate of deduction from the employee's earnings must be shown separately on the record. All contributions will be made net of basic rate tax, with the provider (or employer/scheme administrator in a self-administered scheme) reclaiming the relevant amount from the Inland Revenue.

Changes to Payroll Deductions [4.8]

Under the *Stakeholder Pension Schemes Regulations 2000, regs 24* and *25*, employees may change their deductions via the payroll every six months. In effect this could mean an alteration to the payroll run each month, as each employee could request an alteration during a different pay period.

The first time that an employee makes a request to start or vary his deductions to the designated stakeholder scheme, the employer must inform him in writing within two weeks:

❍ how the employer will accept requests to make, vary or cease such deductions;

❍ that if he requests an alteration to his deductions within six months of a previous request, the employer does not have to comply with the request;

❍ that he may at any time ask the employer to cease deductions immediately; and

❍ that any request will be complied with as soon as possible but no later than the end of the pay period following that in which the request was made.

If the request is made within six months of the previous request, the employer must give notice to the employee in writing stating:

❍ that he is not complying with his request;

❍ when he can make a new request to make or vary contributions (no sooner than six months after the last request to make, vary or cease contributions);

❍ that the employer can cease deductions by the end of the pay period in which the request was made, though he is not required to reinstate them for a further six months following cancellation; and

❍ that the employee can contribute directly to the designated scheme.

If an employer is informed that his designated stakeholder scheme has commenced winding up, he must immediately stop deducting employee contributions and notify the employee in writing as soon as possible.

Although payroll deductions are currently only envisaged to the designated scheme, and any stakeholder scheme previously designated by the employer, later regulations may allow deductions to other stakeholder schemes. Employees can contribute via direct debit to other stakeholder schemes. If they choose this route then they will be able to alter the rate of contribution more frequently than once every six months, if they wish to do so. Employees can also make top up payments within the percentage and age related limits for contributions to stakeholder personal pension plans.

Reporting Late Payments to OPRA [4.9]

When a payment has not been received by its due date, a report must be sent to OPRA. The report has to reach OPRA within a time limit of 30 days. The starting point for the 30 day period is the day after the due date. The provider must also send a report to the member within ninety days of the due date if payments have not been received by 60 days after the due date. Reports to OPRA need not be made if:

○ the payment is received by the trustees or managers by the tenth day after the due date; and

○ in the preceding 12 months there has been at most one other late payment (a late payment consisting of an employer contribution and a deduction from earnings counts as a single default if the due date for employer and employee contributions is the same).

However, if trustees or managers do have to make a report to OPRA about a late or non-payment, then any late payment not reported by virtue of the above exemption in the previous 12 months must also be notified to OPRA.

Contents of Report [4.10]

The report to OPRA must contain the following information:

○ Name of employee and identifying details e.g. National Insurance number;

○ Name, address and phone number of the employer;

○ Payroll month;

○ Late payment information should include:

   ● amount and date the payment was due; and
   ● if paid late, the date it was actually paid; and
   ● whether the payment was an employee contribution, employer contribution or both.

Charging Regime [4.11]

One of the aims of stakeholder is to have a clear and transparent charging structure. This will be reflected in the cost structure of a stakeholder pension scheme as providers will need to ensure that the costs of marketing, administering and managing the schemes can be contained within the overall maximum annual charge of 1% of the value of the client's fund.

Many providers see the cheapest way of delivering stakeholder schemes within the 1% limit is by providing a self service facility for potential customers via the Internet, backed up by traditional methods of delivery via IFAs and dedicated salesforces. This would enable clients to enter personal details and set up accounts themselves. This saves on administrative costs, as input clerks would not be required to put the details onto the computer. Queries will also be dealt with on-line via e-mail, or if this fails to resolve a query or problem, then through a telephone helpline. Up-to-date valuations of customers' accounts and the ability to put in different scenarios if payments are increased or decreased will all help customers plan more effectively for their retirement.

Details of Allowable Charges [4.12]

The *Stakeholder Pension Schemes Regulations 2000, regs 13* and *14* detail the charging principles and allowable payments from the stakeholder scheme. All contributions to the scheme and the investment returns produced are to be used to provide benefits for the scheme members and beneficiaries. The maximum annual charge of 1% of the value of the member's fund is to cover all the costs associated with membership of the scheme.

The maximum daily charge of 1/365% of the value of the member's rights under the scheme the fund is to be calculated net of any dealing costs in the following ways:

❍ where a member has a personal fund value allocated to him, the charge is deducted from the value of the fund;

❍ where members hold a share in a general fund, charges are applied to that member's share;

❍ in with-profits funds, where individual rights may be allocated according to the actuarial principles that underpin the operation of the with-profits arrangement, charges may be deducted from the overall fund value.

Members' rights can also be valued weekly or monthly on a day or date specified in writing by the trustees or stakeholder managers of the scheme. The specified day or date can only be altered once every 12 months.

No payments in addition to the 1% charge may be made from the scheme funds other than a payment:

- of benefits under the scheme;
- made to cover dealing costs;
- to cover costs incurred in providing an annuity;
- to cover costs incurred in the provision of income drawdown facilities;
- to discharge the trustees' or managers' liability under the *Welfare Reform and Pensions Act 1999, s 46,* concerning a pension credit under a pension sharing agreement;
- to recover costs and to cover charges for pension earmarking orders;
- made in compliance with a court order to return excessive pension contributions made by a member; or
- to discharge any monetary obligation due from the member to the scheme because of a criminal, negligent or fraudulent act or omission by him, or if a trust scheme, due to breach of trust by a trustee.

Provision of Other Services [4.13]

According to the provisions of the *Stakeholder Pension Schemes Regulations 2000, reg 16,* schemes may only make additional charges for services, on top of the annual charge, if they are for services separate from the management of the scheme and its funds. Any such additional services must be the subject of a written contract, setting out the amount of any charge and the terms on which it is to be paid. This could be the case when there is a request for detailed individual advice, separate from the membership contract, when additional charges would apply.

Schemes cannot make it a condition of stakeholder scheme membership that a member enters into any other contract, such as a life assurance policy, with the scheme provider. Where schemes wish to make such additional benefits a condition of membership, and these would normally be subject to an additional charge, they must charge for them within the 1% maximum annual charge limit.

With-profit Funds [4.14]

Stakeholder schemes may offer investment via with-profits funds but these must comply with the stakeholder requirements, including the 1% maximum annual charge on the value of the member's fund. All money accumulated from members' contributions must be ring-fenced (remain in the fund), so that all the money goes back to the members.

Further requirements are detailed in the *Stakeholder Pension Schemes Regulations 2000, reg 15*.

The trustees or stakeholder manager of a stakeholder scheme must obtain a written contract from the insurance company offering the with-profits fund in which they wish to invest stakeholder scheme assets, stating that the insurance company will:

○ provide the information to allow trustees or stakeholder managers to comply with the minimum standard of 1% annual charge on the value of the fund;

○ ensure that the members of the contracting stakeholder fund will not be treated any less favourably than members of other stakeholder pension schemes who have assets invested in the with-profits fund;

○ provide certificates to allow the stakeholder pension scheme's auditor or reporting accountant to certify that the charging provisions have been complied with and no extra expenses have been deducted from the with-profits fund; and

○ ensure that only stakeholder pension scheme assets are invested in the fund.

At least once a year, the insurance company must provide the trustees or managers of the stakeholder pension scheme with a certificate from their actuary to certify that the insurance company has systems and controls:

○ to maintain proper accounting records for all income and expenditure;

○ to ensure that no expenditure is charged to the with-profits fund that is contrary to the 1% charging limit; and

○ stating that the terms of the contract have been met.

If the insurance company does not comply with the agreement, the trustees and managers of the stakeholder schemes must take steps to ensure that they do so.

Disclosure of Information to Members [4.15]

Self employed people, those outside the workplace and those employees who either wish to make contributions to a stakeholder scheme other than their employer's designated scheme or whose employer is exempt from the access requirements will make contributions either via direct debit or cheque. Providers will have to accept minimum contributions of £20 and lump sums whenever people wish to contribute. Providers may accept contributions below £20 and some have already indicated that they will do so.

The *Welfare Reform and Pensions Act 1999, s 1(6),* makes compliance with the disclosure requirements of the *Pensions Act 1995, s 113,* a condition of qualifying as a stakeholder scheme. One of the minimum standards in the Green Paper 'A New Contract for Welfare: Partnership in Pensions', was a requirement for stakeholder schemes to provide members with, as a minimum, annual information about:

O   the value of their pension savings;
O   the contributions that have been paid in; and
O   the charges deducted by the scheme.

The intention is that disclosure requirements for stakeholder pension schemes will mirror the current models for defined contribution (DC) occupational schemes and personal pension schemes. Generally speaking, most information need only be provided on request from a member, prospective member, beneficiary, or trade union. However, the basic scheme information, including details of the scheme's documentation, must be provided regardless of whether or not a request is made. Disclosure requirements for prospective members will be set out in the FSA conduct of business rules for stakeholder pensions.

Annual Declaration   [4.16]

At least once a year, the trustees or manager of a stakeholder scheme must make a signed declaration within three months of the end of a previous 12 month period that:

O   the charging provisions have been complied with;
O   transactions in securities, property and other assets have been carried out at fair market value;
O   the value of members' rights have been established in accordance with the scheme instruments;
O   adequate accounts and records have been maintained to provide members with an annual statement.

The declaration must also include a statement explaining that the *Stakeholder Pension Schemes Regulations 2000,* impose limits on the amount and manner of charges that can be made and that stakeholder schemes are required to provide an annual benefit statement for each scheme member.

Within three months of the date of the declaration, trustees of a trust based scheme or the stakeholder manager of a contract based scheme, certifying whether or not it was reasonable for the trustees or stakeholder manager to make the statements in the declaration. If the auditor or reporting accountant is unable to express an opinion, the reason why he is unable to do so must be included. This statement must then be attached to the annual declaration. Trustees and stakeholder managers must make the annual declaration and attached auditor or reporting accountant's statement available to members and beneficiaries of the scheme on request.

Annual Benefit Statement [4.17]

The additional requirements for disclosure for stakeholder pension schemes, to ensure that the minimum standards for member information proposed in the Green Paper are met, are set out in the *Stakeholder Pension Schemes Regulations 2000, reg 18.* They are as follows.

○ Each member is to receive an annual statement within three months of the end of the statement year of the value of their rights at least once a year and the changes in value during the statement year.
○ The statement year is defined as any period of 12 months ending with a date chosen by the scheme trustees or managers.
○ To allow time for adjustment to the new regime, the first due date for such an annual statement is to be twelve months from the date the scheme was first registered or 12 months from a date before the registration. The statement year can be altered in writing if it falls before the end of previous statement year and it has not been altered during the previous 12 months.
○ The first statements will need to be provided within the tax year 2002/03.

The information in the annual benefit statement is to be sent to all members, including those retired members who are no longer accruing pension rights, but who have opted to take advantage of income drawdown facilities. The statement must include the following information:

O   the total value of the member's rights under the scheme at the start and end of the 'statement year', including the value of any protected rights;

O   the effect of investment growth or decline during the 12 months prior to the statement on the value of the member's rights net of contributions made and payments received;

O   the contributions and payments made to the scheme by and on the member's behalf and the date each was received, with each contribution and payment shown separately.

- Contributions by the member and the date received.
- Contributions by an employer and the date received.
- Inland Revenue payments of tax relief.
- Payments of contracted-out rebates
- Payments of age-related rebates and the member's date of birth used to determine this plus contact details in case the date is incorrect.
- Any 'transfer-in' from a previous pension arrangement, the date it was received and the name of the previous scheme.
- Amounts credited or deducted from a member's account under a pension sharing order or agreement.
- Any other deductions.
- The amount debited for the scheme charge (must be within the 1% maximum annual charge limit on the value of the fund).

Where a member's rights are held within a with profits fund, the annual statement is to provide clear details on how the member's rights within the fund are determined.

Within one month of any change in the scheme's rules or practice regarding any alteration to the scheme's charging regime, members (including beneficiaries making income withdrawals) must be sent a statement by post to their last known address. Scheme providers need not make extra efforts to trace members who have not made any contributions to the scheme during the last two years or where correspondence has been returned undelivered. This mirrors the exemption in the *Personal Pension Schemes (Disclosure of Information) Regulations 1987*. Charges to be notified to prospective members will be part of the FSA's disclosure regime.

FSA [4.18]

The FSA is the regulatory body for the financial services industry in the UK. Its statutory powers derive from the *Financial Services Act 1986* and the *Banking Act 1987*, along with other legislation. It aims to maintain confidence in the financial services industry, ensure customers have the right degree of protection, educate the public about the financial system and help reduce financial crime. While doing this it strives to maintain an appropriate balance between the need to protect consumers without imposing too heavy a regulatory burden on providers of financial services. The *Financial Services and Markets Act 2000* consolidates and extends the powers of the FSA.

The management of stakeholder pension schemes will be identified as a regulated activity under an order to be made under the *Financial Services and Markets Act 2000*. Authorisation to act as a stakeholder scheme manager will be in accordance with new FSA requirements. Information requirements for prospective members of stakeholder schemes are to be found in the FSA's conduct of business rules.

Stakeholder pensions are to be investments within the meaning of the *Financial Services Act 1986* and its successor the *Financial Services and Markets Act 2000*. The FSA has conduct of business rules that apply to dealing in investments within the meaning of the legislation. These cover the contents of promotional literature and advertisements, including direct offer advertisements, to ensure that they contain sufficient information and are fair, clear and accurate. There are also rules about the provision of personalised advice which require the advisor to be an authorised person, to have a specific level of training, and give advice which is appropriate to the circumstances and needs of the individual. The rules for marketing stakeholder pension schemes must comply with these guidelines.

Firms that offer stakeholder pensions must be authorised to do so within the meaning of the *Financial Services Act 1986* and its successor the *Financial Services and Markets Act 2000*. They must also comply with the relevant European Directives and with the conduct of business rules. Fund managers must act with due care, skill and diligence and probity and maintain adequate financial resources.

Selling Stakeholder Pensions [4.19]

The FSA will regulate the sale of stakeholder pensions as an investment. The management of stakeholder pensions is to be identified as a regulated activity by an order to be made under the *Financial Services and Markets Act 2000*. When selling stakeholder pensions, the providers will have to ensure that the literature and advertisements used are not misleading, unfair or inaccurate.

Providers must include the following key features of the investment policies that they are aiming to pursue.

○   Is the scheme going for growth, income or a combination of the two?
○   In which markets and sectors the stakeholder scheme will invest and the weighting of holdings within these markets and sectors.
○   The risk profile of the scheme.
○   Which index, if any, the scheme aims to track or the benchmark it will follow.
○   Projections which detail potential benefits assuming certain growth percentages, such as 3%, 5% and 7%.

Investment of Funds [4.20]

The *Stakeholder Pension Schemes Regulations 2000, reg 8* specifies minimum requirements for stakeholder schemes regarding investments. These include the following.

○   Monies held on deposit from a stakeholder scheme must have a return, net of any fee or charges, of not less than the base rate minus 2%, unless monies are being held on temporary deposit for dealing in scheme assets. Any increase to the base rate must be reflected after a month has elapsed.
○   Trustees and managers of stakeholder schemes must not place scheme assets in unit trusts or under a contract of insurance, unless it is a requirement of the contract of insurance or of the collective investment scheme, that there is no spread in the price of the units in the unit trusts or shares in funds held by the insurance company.

Contract-based stakeholder schemes are to invest stakeholder funds in either Pooled Pension Investments (PPIs) or by spreading the scheme's assets in accordance with FSA rules. PPIs will have similar operating structures to Individual Savings Accounts (ISAs) and act as a long term 'wrapper' for units in unit trusts, shares in investment trusts and gilts. The aim is to have one PPI per scheme member with investment options from which scheme members may choose. The stakeholder manager must also offer a default investment choice. The charging structure for PPIs will be the same as for stakeholder pensions and scheme transfers will operate in the same way as ISA transfers. Firms offering PPIs will have to gain prior authorisation from the FSA.

Trustees in trust based stakeholder schemes will invariably appoint fund managers to invest funds on behalf of their members. Fund managers are authorised by the FSA and will also be subject to its rules. It is likely that stakeholder managers will be subject to a similar regime to ISA managers. Delegation of investment management activities to an authorised person avoids the need for trustees to gain authorisation themselves, unless they take day-to-day investment decisions while supervising fund managers.

Key Points on Advice [4.21]

Providers must provide basic information and explanatory material within the 1% annual charge on the value of the fund. However, scheme providers can choose whether they wish to provide advice within the 1% charge or separately. If advice is charged for separately, it has to be subject to a separate written contract between the provider and the client.

Levels of Advice [4.22]

There is no requirement for individuals to seek advice before taking out any financial services product. The FSA aims to ensure that where people seek advice, the advice they receive is appropriate to their circumstances. Advisers must be appropriately qualified, seek sufficient information about the potential buyer's circumstances and demonstrate that any advice or recommendation to the client is suitable for them and properly reflects their own needs and circumstances.

Execution Only – No Advice [4.23]

Sometimes a customer approaches a pension provider direct and does not want advice. He simply wishes to start a personal pension. Under these circumstances, a pension may be sold on an 'execution only' basis. Group personal pensions with an employer contribution can be offered to employees without advising each potential member on the merits of the scheme. This is referred to as 'direct offer'.

Generic Advice [4.24]

It is intended that generic advice on stakeholder pensions can be provided to demonstrate its suitability for a certain group of people. This can be done by giving initial information, for example in a workplace meeting, with some explanation and guidance. The government and FSA information leaflets on pensions are to include details of stakeholder pensions; although these are to help people decide whether stakeholder is suitable for them, rather than advise on particular schemes.

Those people who do not need individual advice about joining a scheme can use decision trees to help guide them through the decision process, to a clearly defined outcome. Further advice can be provided by an IFA.

The information to be provided for prospective members of a scheme would need to include:

○ information about the scheme's key features;
○ 'generic' advice about the suitability of the scheme for people in particular groups;
○ projections of potential benefits; and
○ an indication that consumers who are uncertain about the suitability of the scheme for themselves should seek more specific advice.

Prospective members of stakeholder schemes can be supplied with an information pack detailing scheme charges, investment options and the terms of any additional benefits offered by the scheme. This would be similar to the scheme booklet which employers generally supply for occupational pension schemes and personal pension plan product details. Contact details for the organisations and individuals involved in running the scheme so that further information can be found should also be supplied. The pack could include a decision tree to help prospective members decide whether joining the particular stakeholder scheme would be a reasonable choice for them, how much to contribute, and whether or not they should contract out of the S2P/SERPS.

Individual Advice [4.25]

When advising on an investment product, there are three main ways in which advice can be given:

O   Full financial health check

This is the most expensive option and involves a comprehensive examination of an individual's financial circumstances. Both present and future needs and priorities are considered and a full range of products, including pensions, is discussed.

O   Filtered fact find

This focuses on a narrower range of priorities, filtering out those products which are not, and are unlikely to become, a priority. Only those products that fulfil a need are examined.

O   Focused fact find

This is where an individual is already interested in a particular product, such as a pension. The adviser can then just focus on the most suitable type of pension arrangements. This can involve different levels of advice depending on the complexity of the person's financial arrangements. A focused fact find tends to be quicker and cheaper than a full or a filtered fact find.

Cooling-off Rights [4.26]

Under the current FSA rules, anyone receiving advice on a personal pension scheme has 14 days to cancel the arrangement (after receipt of a cooling-off notice from the provider). This gives a prospective member an opportunity to reconsider. These rules would be extended to everyone considering joining a stakeholder pension scheme, including those who join solely on the strength of information and generic advice.

Employers [4.27]

Under the provisions of the *Welfare Reform and Pensions Act 1999, s 3(8)*, employers are not required to recommend a scheme to their employees, only to designate a scheme and provide employees with sufficient information to enable them to contact the provider. Employers will not normally be classed as 'introducers', those who introduce clients to a financial services provider for financial reward, by complying with the employer access requirement. This will only occur if they actively recruit members for a scheme.

Employers can give employees factual information about their designated stakeholder scheme without infringing the FSA's rules. It is also possible for employers to give general advice on pensions providing that they do not focus on the merits of any particular scheme. It is only if they recommend the designated stakeholder scheme that this would be classed as investment advice and they would then need to seek authorisation from the FSA. Simply designating a stakeholder scheme is not classed as investment advice. Guidance for employers which clearly explains how they can give information and general advice to their employees without infringing FSA rules is to be supplied.

Complaints [4.28]

FSA Ombudsman

For any complaints that relate to the selling and marketing of stakeholder pensions, a member or prospective member of a stakeholder pension should contact the FSA Ombudsman. He will also deal with complaints about the provision of advice and the conduct of the investment firms and stakeholder managers of contract based schemes regulated by the FSA.

Before contacting the Ombudsman, the best approach is to complain to the firm marketing the stakeholder pension. If the response is not satisfactory, it is usual to lodge a complaint following the formal complaint procedure which most firms will have. If this is still unsuccessful, the next step is to ask the firm whether the FSA Ombudsman or arbitration scheme applies.

Most investment product providers' websites have a complaint form that can be downloaded. Some may supply this with the original product details. Particulars of the complaint, together with copies of original correspondence and all relevant documents, should be sent to the Ombudsman or the arbitration scheme as appropriate. If the decision from the Ombudsman is not positive then the matter can be taken to court. However, if the arbitration route is chosen, the arbitrator's decision must normally be accepted and it is then not possible to pursue the complaint via the courts. It is wise to check the scheme rules before commencing arbitration to see if this is the case. The other route is to pursue the matter through the courts, which is the most expensive option.

OPAS [4.29]

The first step for complaints relating to occupational and personal pension schemes is to contact the scheme trustees or authorities. If this fails the next step is to contact the Pensions Advisory Service (OPAS). The alternative route is to go to an industrial tribunal or pursue the matter throughout the courts. OPAS provides help for people who have a dispute concerning occupational and personal pension schemes. Their remit will also include stakeholder pensions. They have a nationwide team of volunteer advisers. They also operate a telephone helpline to give immediate advice on pension problems. Alternatively, contact with an OPAS adviser can be made via the local Citizens Advice Bureau.

OPAS can explain the benefits to which a member is entitled and ensure that the member receives these benefits. It can also obtain information from the pension scheme or plan if this has not been available. OPAS cannot deal with problems relating to employment or where a member wishes to change the rule of a scheme, nor can it give advice on the best pension scheme to join or on investment. Complaints can only be accepted from individuals, provided that legal proceedings have not already been started or the Pensions Ombudsman (see below) has not investigated the complaint.

OPAS Procedure [4.30]

The *Pensions Act 1995, s 50,* requires all occupational pension schemes to have an internal dispute resolution (IDR) procedure for resolving disputes between scheme trustees and 'prescribed persons'. This requirement is extended to stakeholder schemes under the *Welfare Reform and Pensions Act 1999, Schedule 1.* 'Prescribed persons' include members, surviving spouses and dependants of deceased members and those eligible to become members subject to the employer's consent or to serving a waiting period. It also includes those claiming to be in one of the relevant categories and people who were in one of the categories within 12 months of applying for a decision. OPAS will try to resolve the problem without following the IDR procedure.

It is possible to contract with the scheme's nominated person directly or via a nominated representative such as an OPAS adviser. Within two months of the first application a decision should be received. If not, there should be an explanation for the delay and a forecast of when the decision should be expected. Once the decision is received, and if it is unsatisfactory, a second application must be made within six months of the first application for a review by the trustees or the scheme's authorities. The decision of the review must be issued within two months and if still not acceptable then the matter may be referred to the Pensions Ombudsman if it concerns an occupational stakeholder scheme.

The Pensions Ombudsman [4.31]

The Pensions Ombudsman investigates complaints and disputes concerning occupational schemes, which will include trust based stakeholder schemes. He is appointed by the Secretary of State and is independent. Any decision he makes is final and binding on all the parties to the dispute and can be enforced in the courts. It is only possible to change one of his decisions by appealing against it on a point of law in the appropriate court.

Any complaint will be dealt with in writing and if the dispute concerns the scheme trustees or authorities, the Ombudsman will only investigate if the IDR procedure has already been exhausted. Complaints must be brought within 3 years of the occurrence of the dispute, or within 3 years of the time that knowledge of the problem was first encountered or ought to have been known about. This time bar can be extended at the Ombudsman's discretion, if the delay in bringing the complaint to his attention has been due to using the IDR procedure or dealing with OPAS.

Penalties [4.32]

FSA

Powers

The FSA has investigation and enforcement powers under the *Financial Services and Markets Act 2000*, the *Financial Services Act 1986*, the *Banking Act 1987* and the *Insurance Companies Act 1982*. Amongst other activities, it checks that firms are not conducting investment business without authorisation and deals with issues of misconduct or abuse by authorised institutions. It also ensures that unfit persons are not employed in investment business under the *Financial Services Act 1986, s 59*.

It is also important to note for those providers who will be selling stakeholder pensions via the Internet that, broadly speaking, the provisions of the *Financial Services Act 1986* must be taken into account when carrying on investment business in the UK or issuing investment advertisements in the UK. The exclusions and exemptions apply to investment business and investment advertisements over the Internet, as they do to more traditional media.

Penalties [4.33]

Contraventions of the investment business and investment advertisement provisions are criminal offences. In addition, any investment contracts entered into that do not comply with the provisions of the *Financial Services Act 1986* become unenforceable and the FSA has the power to seek restitution if investors suffer loss. The penalties for these offences could be a maximum of two years in prison, a fine, or both.

OPRA [4.34]

Powers

Under the *Pensions Act 1995,* OPRA has a wide range of powers and functions. These include powers to remove or suspend a trustee from acting or to appoint a new trustee to replace one that has been removed or disqualified. OPRA also has the power to wind up schemes in certain circumstances and to modify schemes. It can apply to the court for an injunction to prevent the misuse or misappropriation of a scheme's assets or apply for an order to require the restitution of the scheme's assets. It can also direct trustees to make payment of benefits in certain circumstances.

Whistle Blowing [4.35]

Anybody may report to OPRA an irregularity which has occurred or is about to occur (e.g. if someone misappropriates a scheme asset). Scheme auditors and actuaries are under a duty to report apparent breaches of the relevant regulatory provisions to OPRA and have statutory protection against a claim for breach of professional conduct. Trustees with knowledge of an apparent breach of regulatory provisions have the power to report this to OPRA, but they are not under a duty to do so. Legal advisers are not under a duty to report breaches of the provisions, but if they do so they also have statutory protection, unless they have disclosed legally privileged documents. OPRA will investigate reports and seek to resolve any reported breaches of statutory provisions by making enquiries and obtaining information on a voluntary basis.

Penalties [4.36]

Civil Penalties

Fines up to a maximum of £5000 and/or imprisonment can be imposed on trustees and stakeholder managers who have supplied misleading information when applying to register their stakeholder scheme with OPRA and declaring that their scheme complies with the minimum standards.

Employers may be subject to civil penalties from OPRA if under the payroll deduction arrangements, they fail to:

- O prepare a record of the direct payment arrangement or to keep it up to date;
- O send the record to the provider;
- O make correct payments by the due date.

Providers may be subject to civil penalties from OPRA if they fail to:

- O notify OPRA of late or missed payments from the employer following payroll deduction;
- O notify the member of late or missed payments; or
- O send the member an annual statement containing dates of payments and amounts.

Criminal Penalties [4.37]

Employers will be subject to criminal penalties if they knowingly and fraudulently evade the direct payment arrangements concerning deductions from salary.

5 – Governance

This chapter covers the following:

○ Trust based schemes.
○ Contract based schemes.
○ Requirements for instruments establishing stakeholder schemes.
○ Governance requirements for stakeholder schemes.
○ Winding-up procedures.

Summary [5.1]

Stakeholder schemes can be established as a trust-based or contract-based scheme according to the *Stakeholder Pension Schemes Regulations 2000, reg 2*. Trust based schemes will be subject to a similar regulatory regime as that currently applied to occupational schemes and they will be supervised by the Occupational Pensions Regulatory Authority (OPRA). One third of the trustees must be independent, though there is no requirement to appoint Member Nominated Trustees (MNTs).

Contract-based stakeholder schemes are to be run by authorised stakeholder scheme managers, with a contract between the managers of a scheme and its members. The Financial Services Authority (FSA) is to include management of stakeholder pension schemes within the definition of regulated activities under the *Financial Services and Markets Act 2000*, when it is enacted. Stakeholder managers will be authorised by the FSA to carry out stakeholder pension business.

The documentation to establish a trust based stakeholder scheme will be a trust deed and rules, as is the current practice for occupational schemes. The documentation to establish a contract based stakeholder scheme is to be specified by the FSA. The documents must comply with certain common requirements for both contract based and trust-based schemes, which are detailed in the *Stakeholder Pension Schemes Regulations 2000*.

Trust based schemes must appoint an auditor and contract based schemes are to appoint a reporting accountant, though they are under no duty to appoint any other professional advisers, such as actuaries and lawyers. Trustees and stakeholder managers who are not authorised to give advice, who have investments as part of their funds must take advice from authorised persons for UK investment business or someone with wide pension fund management experience for advice on other types of investment. Trustees can contract with investment managers and providers of administration services for as long as they see fit, though they should review the appointment from time to time.

Trustees and authorised stakeholder managers are under a duty to ensure that the stakeholder scheme complies with the required minimum standards when they apply to register the scheme with OPRA. This duty is a continuing obligation, and should the scheme fail to meet the minimum standards for stakeholder pensions then the trustees and authorised stakeholder managers have to inform OPRA who will remove the scheme from the register. Winding up procedures will then commence, and are dealt with in detail in the *Stakeholder Pension Schemes Regulations 2000*. Both trust based and contract based schemes must commence winding up on the date OPRA notifies them that it has ceased to be registered as a stakeholder scheme and the members' rights must be transferred to another scheme within 12 months.

Trust Based Stakeholder Schemes [5.2]

Trust law provides a comprehensive framework for the operation of trusts and the duties of trustees. However, the specific powers and duties of trustees are detailed in the trust deed and rules that establish the pension scheme. Personal pension schemes can also be set up under a trust but, in general, the trust deeds for personal pensions provide very few powers for the trustees, especially for investment. They often require that the trustees only invest in funds managed by the provider of the scheme.

Under general trust law, trustees are under a duty to act in the best interests of the beneficiaries of the trust. This ensures that the interests of members are protected and represented by the trustees and that the benefits under the scheme are delivered to the members within the scheme rules. Trustees are involved in the investment of the trust assets and hold them in a custodial role. There is currently no requirement for separate custodians (as in the United States).

Trustees are not allowed to profit from the trust, except where there are provisions in the trust deed. There is neither a provision for, or a prohibition against, stakeholder schemes providing remuneration for trustees. This will allow schemes that wish to do so to appoint professional trustees and allow lay trustees to be paid for the time spent on trustee duties, though this will have to be covered within the 1% annual charge.

Trustees need administrative support and training to assist them in carrying out their duties. Under the *Welfare Reform and Pensions Act 1999, ss 6(1)* and *6(2)* the provisions of the *Employment Rights Act 1996* are extended to permit trustees of a scheme to take time off for training without having a detrimental effect on their employment. Both the training and administrative support will be paid for from the annual charge of 1% on the value of members' funds. There has been comment that this will be very expensive for schemes with a small number of members, but it is likely that stakeholder schemes will be established for a certain minimum number of members to enable providers to cover these costs.

In Stakeholder Consultation Brief no. 5 on Governance, the costs of trustees in a stakeholder scheme were not expected to exceed £150,000 a year. Over time, the percentage of the annual charge taken up by stakeholder trustee costs should fall, in line with mature occupational pension schemes, where trustee costs can be as low as 0.001% of total fund value. Initially, any shortfall in the costs of trustees, when receipts from charges may be lower, will have to be met by the provider or sponsoring employer of the scheme.

Those Who May Not Act As Trustees [5.3]

The *Pensions Act 1995* sets out who may or may not act as a trustee. These provisions will also apply to trustees of stakeholder schemes. OPRA maintains a register of disqualified trustees. Employers and providers establishing a stakeholder scheme should check this before any trustee appointment is made. Those who may not act as trustees include:

O   a trustee (and any person who is connected with or an associate of the trustee) cannot also act as a scheme auditor or actuary under the *Pensions Act 1995, ss 27* and *28,* and he commits an offence if he does so. Under the requirements for trust based stakeholder schemes, there is no obligation to appoint an actuary, though an auditor must be appointed;

O   anyone who has been convicted of an offence involving dishonesty or deception;

O   anyone who is an undischarged bankrupt or has had his estate sequestrated;

O   a company where any director of the company is disqualified to act;

○ anyone who has made an Individual Voluntary Arrangement (IVA) with his or her creditors and has not been discharged;

○ anyone who has been disqualified from acting as a company director; and

○ anyone removed as a trustee of a scheme by OPRA or by the High Court may be disqualified by OPRA from being a trustee of any scheme under the *Pensions Act 1995, ss 3–5* and *s 29*.

Criminal Penalties [5.4]

Acting as a trustee while disqualified or at the same time as acting as the auditor or actuary to a scheme is a criminal offence. Those convicted are liable to a fine of up to £5,000 or up to 2 years imprisonment, or both, under the *Pensions Act 1995, s 6*.

Trustee Requirements for Stakeholder Schemes [5.5]

The *Stakeholder Pension Schemes Regulations 2000, reg 4* requires that at least one third of the trustees of a stakeholder scheme must be independent from the providers of services to the scheme or scheme managers. Where a company is a trustee of the scheme, at least one of the directors of that company, and at least one third of the total number of directors, must not be connected with nor an associate of any person providing services or managing the scheme (other than as a trustee). The route that has been followed mirrors the requirements for industry-wide schemes, which are required to have a minimum number of independent trustees.

There is no requirement at present for Member Nominated Trustees (MNTs) for stakeholder schemes. MNTs are a requirement for occupational pension schemes under the *Pensions Act 1995* and the provisions for these are currently being revised in the Child Support, Pensions and Social Security Bill. At present, occupational schemes with over a hundred members must have two MNTs and at least one third of the scheme trustees elected by the membership, while schemes with under a hundred members must have at least one. MNTs for stakeholder schemes were rejected as it was felt that in the early days of starting up the schemes, it would impose an additional administrative burden to attempt to consult all of the members of stakeholder schemes and carry out elections. However, this is an area that could be revisited in due course. Occupational schemes that opt into the stakeholder DC tax regime will still need to meet the MNT requirements.

There is no requirement to appoint professional trustees with relevant qualifications. These would include lawyers, actuaries or accountants.

Some of the provisions of the *Pensions Act 1995* have been extended to include stakeholder schemes that are trust based, under the *Welfare Reform and Pensions Act 1999, Schedule 1*. Under limited circumstances, OPRA can appoint trustees to the scheme where it has removed a trustee or a trustee has been disqualified under the *Pensions Act 1995, s 7*. It can also appoint a new trustee to secure 'proper administration of the scheme' or 'the proper use or application of the assets of the scheme' and under other circumstances prescribed by regulations. In occupational schemes that have opted into the stakeholder regime, payments made to trustees appointed by OPRA from the scheme's resources will be treated as a debt due from the employer under the *Pensions Act 1995, s 8*.

Trustee Powers and Duties [5.6]

The *Pensions Act 1995* updated trustee powers and duties to ensure that they are suited to modern pension trusts. The *Welfare Reform and Pensions Act 1999, Schedule 1,* amends provisions of the *Pensions Act 1995* to apply them to trust-based stakeholder pension schemes. The provisions that will apply, amongst others, to stakeholder pension schemes are:

O   liability of trustees;
O   trustee meetings and decisions; and
O   internal dispute resolution procedures.

Liability of Trustees [5.7]

Trustees cannot exclude their liability for breach of their duty of care to beneficiaries of the scheme in carrying out their investment functions, even where that function has been delegated to another person under the *Pensions Act 1995, s 33*. Nor can they be reimbursed out of scheme assets for fines for offences or OPRA penalties under the *Pensions Act 1995, s 31*.

However, under the *Pensions Act 1995, s 34*, trustees have the power to make any investment as if they were absolutely entitled to the assets of the scheme and to delegate investment decisions to a fund manager authorised by the FSA for UK investment business or to someone with wider experience of managing pension funds for other types of investment. As long as the trustees take reasonable steps to ensure that the fund manger has the appropriate knowledge and experience to manage investments and is carrying out his work competently and in accordance with the *Pensions Act 1995, s 36* by considering the need for diversification and suitability of the investments proposed, they are not responsible for any act or default of the manager in the exercise of his delegated discretion.

Decisions [5.8]

Decisions taken by the trustees of a trust based stakeholder scheme must be taken by a majority of trustees unless the scheme provides otherwise as under the *Pensions Act 1995, s 32.*

Internal Dispute Resolution [5.9]

Trustees have to ensure that they establish and operate procedures for resolving internal disputes between the scheme beneficiaries and the trustees or scheme managers. Complaints and the decisions reached must be in writing. Beneficiaries include active members, pensioners, deferred members and their dependants and prospective members, waiting to join a scheme. The provisions in the *Pensions Act 1995, s 50,* on internal dispute resolution procedures will apply to all trust based stakeholder schemes. Members will also be able to contact the Pensions Advisory Service (OPAS) and the Pensions Ombudsman as explained in Chapter 4.

Contract Based Stakeholder Schemes [5.10]

The government has decided to allow two types of governance arrangements for stakeholder pension schemes. Trust based, as described above, and contract based. The contract based schemes will be managed by an authorised stakeholder manager. The term 'contract based' refers to the fact that the schemes will be a contract between the authorised stakeholder manger and the members (or someone who contracts on behalf of someone else in a third party arrangement, for example a parent or grandparent on behalf of a child).

Regulated Activity [5.11]

The management of stakeholder pension schemes will be identified as a regulated activity under an order to be made under the *Financial Services and Markets Act 2000*. A regulated activity is defined in the *Financial Services and Markets Act 2000*, as:

> 'an activity of a specified kind which is carried on by way of business and relates to an investment of a specified kind or is carried on in relation to property of any kind'.

Authorisation Procedures [5.12]

Regulated activities include dealing in investments, buying, selling, subscribing for or underwriting investments either as a principal or as an agent on someone's behalf. Arranging deals in investments, managing them and offering investment advice are also regulated activities. Safeguarding and administering assets also fall within the definition. Managing a stakeholder pension scheme will be a regulated activity as it will include most if not all of these elements.

An application to carry on a regulated activity may be made to the FSA by an individual, a firm, a partnership or an unincorporated association. Regulated activities may only be carried out by an authorised or exempt person. For the purposes of stakeholder scheme management, stakeholder managers will have to gain authorisation from the FSA to carry out a regulated activity.

Authorisation to act as a stakeholder scheme manager will be in accordance with new FSA requirements. In Consultation Brief no. 4 on Regulation, it was announced that these are likely to follow in general terms the current arrangements for individual savings account (ISA) managers.

As general requirements, following those in the *Financial Services and Markets Bill Act 2000,* firms wishing to be authorised will have to ensure that:

❑ both their registered office and their head office is in the UK; or both offices are in an European Economic Area (EEA) state; or both offices are in a state outside the UK or EEA; or they have a head office in the UK and carry on business there;

○ if there are close links between the firm and another business, the FSA will have to be satisfied that these links will not impede its ability to supervise the firm and that the other business is not subject to a regime that would jeopardise this;

○ there is adequate provision for liabilities and risk management connected with the proposed business; and

○ the firm acts in a fit and proper manner and undertakes business in a sound and prudent way, with no untoward connections.

Instruments Establishing Stakeholder Pension Schemes [5.13]

The *Stakeholder Pension Schemes Regulations 2000, regs 3 and 4* list the requirements for instruments establishing stakeholder pension schemes and state that none of the provisions in these two regulations can be modified or disapplied by trust instruments. Most of the requirements are common to both contract based and trust based schemes.

Contributions From 6 April 2001 [5.14]

The trust deed, rules and the equivalent instruments for contract based schemes must include a provision that prohibits the scheme from accepting contributions, transfer payments and pension credits to the scheme before 6 April 2001. However, schemes may register as stakeholder schemes from 1 October 2000 and market themselves from that date. It is not necessary to include this provision if schemes are registering as stakeholder schemes after 5 April 2001.

Default Investment Option [5.15]

All stakeholder schemes must include a default investment option. This will mean that those members who do not wish to exercise their investment choice do not need to do so. The *Stakeholder Pension Schemes Regulations 2000, reg 3*, states that members must not be required to make any investment choice regarding any payment made to the scheme, including a pension credit, or any income or capital gain resulting from the investment of the payment.

Investment [5.16]

Trust based schemes cannot include a condition in their deed and rules that trustees must obtain any person's consent before making a decision about scheme investments. The trust instruments must not prohibit the trustees from amending the investment provisions to allow different investments to be held for the purposes of the scheme.

Charging Provisions [5.17]

The charging provisions for stakeholder schemes are dealt with in detail in Chapter 4 on Regulation. The instruments establishing a stakeholder scheme must prohibit the use of contributions, investment growth or value of members' rights in any way that does not result in the provision of benefits to members.

Winding Up Provisions [5.18]

The winding up of stakeholder schemes is dealt with in detail below from paragraph 5.25. The instruments establishing stakeholder schemes must include certain provisions on winding-up procedures, including:

○ a scheme must begin winding up procedures on the date it ceases to be registered as a stakeholder scheme under the *Welfare Reform and Pensions Act 1999,* s 2 or if being wound up for another reason this must be commenced as soon as possible;

○ once the scheme has started winding up procedures (whether it has ceased to be registered as a stakeholder scheme or under other circumstances), it must be wound up within 12 months or if this deadline is not met, the trustees or stakeholder managers must inform OPRA within a month of failing to complete the winding up;

○ within two weeks of the start of winding up procedures, the trustees or stakeholder manager must inform the employers who have designated the scheme the reason why it is being wound up and also, if it has been de-registered, why this has happened;

○ any member contributions made to a scheme after the date of commencement of winding up must be repaid and the remainder paid to the employer;

○ the rights of all members of the scheme must be transferred on winding up to other stakeholder pension schemes or schemes registered under the *Welfare Reform and Pensions (Northern Ireland) Order 1999, Article 4* or to other schemes in accordance with requests by members or beneficiaries under the terms detailed in the *Stakeholder Pension Schemes Regulations 2000, regs 6 and 7;*

○ transfer payments must be the cash equivalent of a member's rights under the scheme on the date the transfer is made, calculated in accordance with the *Pension Schemes Act 1993, s 97;*

○ where the member's rights include any protected rights (contracted out SERPS rebates) within the meaning of the *Pension Schemes Act 1993, s 10,* the transfer must be made subject to the nominated scheme including provisions for a member's protected rights to be used to provide a pension from the scheme or via an annuity; and

○ The provisions on transfer payments do not apply to rights under the scheme for payment of an annuity (though do apply to deferred annuities where payment commences in the future) or lump sum to the member or after his death to another person.

Eligibility [5.19]

Trust-based schemes are to be allowed to restrict eligibility for membership of a scheme to a particular group. This could be to cater for a particular employer, an affinity group or exclusively for members of a particular trade union. It has been decided, however, that contract based schemes, run by authorised stakeholder managers may not restrict eligibility criteria in this way as specified in the *Stakeholder Pension Schemes Regulations 2000, reg 4.*

For all stakeholder schemes there is to be no restriction on membership with reference to a member's financial status. Members cannot be tied to an agreement on the number of contributions that they will make or how they will make them, though both contract and trust based schemes can refuse to accept contributions paid by cash or credit card. In particular, there is to be no requirement for contributions to be made via a certain medium, e.g. via the Internet. This is to ensure that there is accessibility for all those who wish to contribute to a stakeholder scheme.

Restrictions on Contributions [5.20]

Under *Stakeholder Pension Schemes Regulations 2000, reg 17,* the rules of a stakeholder pension scheme may provide that trustees or stakeholder managers may refuse to accept any contribution:

○ of less than £20, though any tax relief, reduced rates of National Insurance contributions (NICs) for those who have contracted out of SERPS and rebates will not fall within this rule;
○ if it might affect the stakeholder scheme's tax status.

Overriding Provisions [5.21]

Scheme rules will be overridden wherever there is a conflict with any requirement of the *Welfare Reform and Pensions Act 1999, Part I.*

Governance Requirements for Stakeholder Schemes [5.22]

Appointment of an Auditor or Reporting Accountant

Trust based stakeholder schemes are required to appoint an auditor. The *Pensions Act 1995, s 47* imposes a duty on trustees to appoint professional advisers, including auditors. This requirement is extended to stakeholder trust based schemes by the *Welfare Reform and Pensions Act 1999, Schedule 1*, though there is no requirement to appoint a scheme actuary.

Auditors are under a 'whistle blowing' obligation to inform OPRA if they believe that trustees, an authorised stakeholder manager, an employer or professional adviser are not complying with their duties in relation to a scheme under the *Pensions Act 1995, s 48.*

The managers of contract based schemes are to appoint a reporting accountant as specified in the *Stakeholder Pension Schemes Regulations 2000, reg 11,* subject to the following conditions.

○ The reporting accountant must not be a member of the scheme or connected with or an associate of the manager of the scheme;
○ The appointment must be in writing and specify the date on which it take effects; to whom the reporting accountant should report and from whom he should take instructions.

○   Within a month of his appointment, the reporting accountant must acknowledge receipt of his notice of appointment to the manager of the stakeholder scheme and confirm in writing that he will notify the manager of any conflict of interest regarding the scheme as soon as he becomes aware of it.

○   As a condition of appointment, the reporting accountant must agree that if he resigns he will specify in his statement of resignation if there are any circumstances connected with his resignation that significantly affect the interests of members or prospective members or beneficiaries or alternatively make a declaration that he knows of no such circumstances.

○   Where the reporting accountant is removed by the manager or resigns or dies, the manager must appoint another reporting accountant within three months from the date of the removal, resignation or death.

Investment Advice from 'Authorised Persons'   [5.23]

Trustees must appoint a fund manager if they hold assets which consist of or include investments under the *Pensions Act 1995, s 47*. This is extended to apply to trust based stakeholder schemes under the *Welfare Reform and Pensions Act 1999, Schedule 1*. Trustees are responsible for selecting and monitoring an appropriate fund manager and must not take professional advice except from an adviser formally appointed by them. Trustees have to have regard to the spread of investments and the risk involved in each type of investment vehicle. Trustees must send a statement of matters of significant interest to their members on the removal or resignation of their professional adviser.

Trustees are free to contract with service providers for administration and investment management services for as long as they see fit. They must make sure that they provide adequate information to their professional advisers. There was concern that trustees might terminate their contracts with providers before the providers had time to recoup their initial start-up costs. On balance though, it was felt that trustees must have the freedom to change service providers if members' interests were being adversely affected, without being tied to a set contract length. Trustees will be able to exercise their own judgement in this matter.

Managers of contract based schemes are also required to have regard to the need for diversification and suitability of investments and to take proper advice from a person authorised under the *Financial Services Act 1986*.

Where the manager of the stakeholder pension fund or those managing the fund on his behalf are authorised persons, then they may consider different investment options and make investments. The selection of investments is to be consistent with the provisions in the statement of investment principles and the advice given is to be recorded in writing. The full details of the requirements are in the *Stakeholder Pension Schemes Regulations 2000, reg 10*. It appears unlikely that managers of contract based schemes are to have the same degree of independence from the investment or administration provider as trustees. Members of contract based schemes will therefore not be afforded the same level of protection as members of trust based schemes.

Statement of Investment Principles   **[5.24]**

Trust based stakeholder schemes are subject to the requirements of the *Pensions Act 1995, s 35*, which requires trustees to maintain a written statement of the principles governing their investment decisions, covering the kinds of investment held, the balance between the different kinds of investment and the risk. The S*takeholder Pension Schemes Regulations 2000, reg 31*, brings stakeholder trust based schemes within the scope of the *Occupational Pension Schemes (Investment) Regulations 1996*.

A new section of the *Occupational Pension Schemes (Investment) Regulations 1996* came into force on 3 July 2000. From this date, trustees must include in their statement of investment principles (SIP) details of the scheme's policy on Socially Responsible Investment (SRI). Members can request a copy of this. SRI has a broad scope, but in essence if one follows a SRI policy then one does not invest in companies associated with armaments, tobacco, alcohol and environmentally damaging activities. In some cases investments in such activities are maintained with a view to using shareholder pressure to deliver changes to companies' policies and practices.

The SIP should include:

❍   the extent (if at all) to which social, environmental or ethical considerations are taken into account in the selection, retention and realisation of investments; and

❍   their policy (if any) in relation to the exercise of the rights (including voting rights) attaching to the investments.

There is no requirement to follow a policy of socially responsible investment, but simply to note that the issue has been considered.

The managers of contract based stakeholder schemes will also have to maintain a SIP under the *Stakeholder Pension Scheme Regulations 2000, reg 9*. This mirrors the requirements for trust based schemes. Managers must have a written statement that is revised 'from time to time' detailing the principles governing decisions about investments for the purposes of the scheme. The statement must cover the manager's policy on:

O   the kinds of investments to be held;
O   the balance between different kinds of investment;
O   risk;
O   the expected return on investments;
O   the realisation of investments;
O   the extent (if at all) to which social, environmental or ethical considerations are taken into account in the selection, retention and realisation of investments; and
O   the exercise of the rights (including voting rights) attaching to investments.

Both members and beneficiaries of the contract based stakeholder schemes can request a copy of the latest SIP. It must be provided within two months of the request, either free of charge or a charge may be made to cover the costs of copying, posting and packaging expenses. Copies of the SIP only have to be provided on request once every twelve months unless it has been amended during that period.

Winding Up Procedures [5.25]

How Long Does an Occupational Pension Scheme Last?

Occupational pension schemes are designed to continue for many years, although there are limitations on the duration of trusts under the *Perpetuities and Accumulations Act 1963*. Pension schemes are exempted from these limitations where they are either contracted-out of SERPS or have received exempt approval (and benefit from the tax advantages) from the Inland Revenue under the *Pension Schemes Act 1993, s 163*. These exemptions will also apply to stakeholder schemes which can apply for tax exempt approval under the Finance Bill 2000, Schedule 1 at any time on or after 1 October 2000.

What Triggers the Winding Up of a Scheme? [5.26]

Generally a scheme will be wound up in accordance with the scheme rules, which list a number of set events which will trigger the winding up of the scheme. The most common winding up events for occupational pension schemes are:

○ the employer giving notice of intention to terminate contributions (to qualify for the tax advantages of an exempt approved scheme, an employer has to make contributions to the scheme);

○ the employer going into liquidation other than for the purposes of amalgamation and reconstruction;

○ the trustees deciding that the objects of the scheme when it was established no longer exist; and

○ the trustees giving notice of the failure of the employer to rectify a serious breach of obligations.

OPRA's Powers to Wind Up Schemes [5.27]

Trust based stakeholder schemes may also be wound up by OPRA. The *Welfare Reform and Pensions Act 1999, Schedule 1*, applies the *Pensions Act 1995, s 11* to trust based stakeholder schemes. This gives OPRA the power to direct or authorise the winding up of schemes in specified circumstances to protect the interests of the members of the scheme.

Disclosure of Information on Winding Up [5.28]

Trustees and stakeholder managers are to inform all members, except an excluded person (i.e. someone who is not known at his last address and mail is returned and from whom no contribution has been received for the past two years):

○ within two weeks of de-registration as a stakeholder scheme, that the scheme is no longer a stakeholder scheme and must be wound up;

○ within four months, or sooner if possible, each member must have information about the value of the member's rights (and the cash equivalent transfer value if different) and what options the member has for his fund; and

O   within four months, or sooner if possible, if the scheme cannot meet its liabilities, the trustees must give members information about the amount by which their rights have been reduced and what action they can take to restore the value of those rights.

Terms For Transfers In A Winding Up [5.29]

The *Stakeholder Pension Schemes Regulations 2000, reg 6 and 7* detail how members' and beneficiaries' rights accrued under a stakeholder scheme should be transferred when the scheme is being wound up. Winding up procedures must be included in the stakeholder scheme documentation and must be followed as soon as a winding up is commenced. The aim is to ensure that members' rights are protected and transferred across to another suitable scheme as soon as possible.

Within four months of the commencement of winding up, trustees and stakeholder managers must write to each member giving notice:

O   that they propose to make a transfer payment to a named stakeholder pension scheme chosen by the trustees unless the member elects an alternative scheme;
O   detailing the current value of his rights, an amount not less than the cash equivalent of these rights on the date the winding up commenced; and
O   stating that if members do not notify trustees or stakeholder managers within four months of the date of the notice that they wish to go ahead with a transfer payment to a scheme of his choice, then a transfer payment will be made without the scheme member's consent to the scheme named by the trustees or stakeholder managers in the notice.

Where a member applies to have his rights transferred to a stakeholder scheme of his choice, the trustees or stakeholder manager must take steps to arrange this unless:

O   it is not possible to carry out the member's request within 12 months of the date of commencement of the winding up; or
O   to do so would contravene the scheme's tax exempt status; or
O   the member withdraws his application before the trustees or manager have carried out the member's instructions.

In circumstances where the trustees or manager cannot carry out the member's instructions they must write promptly to the member explaining why they cannot carry out his instructions. If the member does not make a further request for alternative arrangements, within a month of the notice from the trustees or manager that the member's first request was not possible, then the member's rights will be transferred to the trustees' or manager's chosen scheme within one month. The same procedure will be followed if no request for an alternative arrangement is made or the member withdraws his application for a transfer to an alternative arrangement.

Within one month of making the transfer payment, the trustees or stakeholder manager must give notice in writing to the member (or beneficiary) at his last known address of the amount of payment, the name and address of the scheme and the date of payment. It is not necessary to give notice to an excluded person either before or after the transfer payment is made.

Protected Rights [5.30]

Where the member's rights include any protected rights, these will also be transferred following the procedure detailed above. An amendment to the *Occupational Pension Schemes (Preservation of Benefit) Regulations 1991* has been made by the *Stakeholder Pension Schemes Regulations 2000, reg 27* and to the *Protected Rights (Transfer Payment) Regulations 1996* by the *Stakeholder Pension Schemes Regulations 2000, reg 29* to allow the transfer payments of protected rights without the consent of the member. The transfer of protected rights must be made subject to the nominated scheme including provisions for a member's protected rights to be used to provide a pension from the scheme or via an annuity.

Scheme rules may specify otherwise, but protected rights are a member's rights to DC benefits under the stakeholder scheme. Protected rights usually include:

O SERPS rebates;
O protected rights transferred to the scheme from another arrangement; and
O DC benefits guaranteeing a minimum pension, or post-1997 contracted-out rights deriving from a transfer made to a scheme from a contracted-out DB scheme or an annuity contract.

6 – The Stakeholder Tax Regime

This chapter covers the following.

- O The new Defined Contribution (DC) tax regime that will apply to stakeholder pensions.
- O Opting-in to the new stakeholder regime.
- O The eligibility criteria for membership of a stakeholder pension.
- O Contributions to stakeholder schemes.
- O The tax treatment of contributions.
- O Benefits from stakeholder schemes.

Summary [6.1]

A new integrated and simplified tax regime for Defined Contribution (DC) pensions is being created by modifying the existing personal pensions legislation. Stakeholder pensions will be classed as a type of personal pension under the tax legislation, subject to the specific rules for stakeholder pensions in the *Welfare Reform and Pensions Act 1999, Part I*. The tax regime for stakeholder and personal pensions will come into effect from 6 April 2001, the date from which stakeholder schemes can receive contributions. The relevant tax legislation is in the Finance Bill 2000, Schedule 1 and related tax regulations.

Occupational DC schemes may also opt into this new DC regime, though those that chose not to do so will continue to be subject to the current regime for occupational schemes. DB schemes cannot opt into the new regime and will continue with their current tax arrangements.

For the first time non–earners will be able to make some pension provision as the link with earnings has been removed on contributions up to the earnings threshold, which is currently £3,600. Those with income from earnings who contribute to a DC scheme within the new DC tax regime will be able to contribute to a stakeholder scheme subject to the age and salary percentage related limits of personal pensions. Under current proposals, members of Defined Benefit (DB) schemes, and those occupational DC schemes that have not opted in to the stakeholder regime, will not be able to contribute to stakeholder schemes. All contributors will need to meet the new residency requirements, apart from those abroad on Crown duties and their spouses.

Contributions to stakeholder schemes above the earnings threshold will be earnings related and once evidence of one year's earnings has been submitted (the 'basis 'year'), this level of contributions can be allowed for the following five years. Those who have previously had earnings at a higher level can continue to make contributions at that higher level for the basis year and for five years after earnings cease. This avoids the need to produce evidence of earnings annually (as under current provisions).

All employee contributions from 6 April 2001 will be net of basic rate tax, with the provider reclaiming the payment corresponding to this tax relief from the Inland Revenue. After 6 April 2001, DC contributions may not be used for waiver of contribution insurance and no more than 10% of the DC contribution may be paid towards a life insurance contract.

The benefits under the DC tax regime for stakeholder pensions will follow those currently allowed for occupational schemes and personal pensions. A lump sum of no more than 25% of the value of the fund may be taken at the date an annuity is purchased or purchase is deferred. In line with current practice, the cash lump sum will be tax free while the annuity is taxable.

The New DC Tax Regime [6.2]

Stakeholder pensions are to be classed as personal pensions for tax purposes under the new DC tax regime that is to be introduced by the Inland Revenue from 6 April 2001. Stakeholder pensions must be approved by the Inland Revenue if they wish to benefit from the full range of tax advantages.

Why Apply for Inland Revenue Approval? [6.3]

Gaining approval from the Inland Revenue for a stakeholder scheme brings with it certain tax advantages:

❍ employers, who choose to make contributions to a stakeholder scheme, can set off their contributions against company profits;

❍ employees obtain tax relief on their contributions, which on or after 6 April 2001 will be made net of basic rate tax, with providers reclaiming the corresponding payment for the tax relief from the Inland Revenue;

O employees are not charged on employer contributions as a benefit in kind;

O tax exemption on the income from investments or cash deposits held on behalf of the scheme and from any capital gains tax arising on gains on the sale of investments; and

O part of the pension can be taken as a tax free lump sum.

Applications for Approval [6.4]

First Date for Application

Providers of stakeholder schemes must apply to the Inland Revenue for approval under the *Income and Corporation Taxes Act 1988, Chapter IV of Part XIV.* The application cannot be made before 1 October 2000.

Permitted 'Provider' [6.5]

Under the *Taxes Act 1988, s 632*, approval will only be given to a stakeholder scheme established by a permitted 'provider', which includes an 'authorised person' within the meaning of the *Financial Services Act 1986*. This is a provider authorised to carry on investment business under the *Financial Services Act 1986* and who either issues insurance policies or annuity contracts, or manages unit trust schemes. The *Financial Services and Markets Act 2000* and associated regulations will bring stakeholder managers within the definition of 'authorised persons'.

The Administrator [6.6]

The Inland Revenue requires the scheme administrator, who is responsible for the management and administration of the stakeholder scheme, to be resident in the UK. The administrator can be any individual, including the provider, an employee of the provider or the trustees of the scheme or a corporate body.

The Scheme's Purpose [6.7]

To obtain approval, the Inland Revenue must be satisfied that the sole purpose of the stakeholder pension scheme is the provision of benefits on retirement or death. The scheme must also comply with the Inland Revenue rules on how these benefits are provided.

Model Rules [6.8]

The Inland Revenue has indicated that it intends to publish model rules for stakeholder schemes. These already exist for personal pensions and are easy to use, leading to rapid approval from the Inland Revenue for a new scheme.

Documents to Submit for Approval [6.9]

The Inland Revenue will specify the documents to be submitted for approval as a stakeholder scheme. As a minimum, these include:

○ completed application form;
○ deed and rules for trust based schemes and the appropriate governing documents for contract based schemes, detailing the arrangements between the scheme and the member; and
○ members' booklet or other form of literature.

Restrictions on Approval [6.10]

The Inland Revenue may approve a stakeholder scheme if it accepts contributions only as:

○ monetary sums; or
○ shares from an approved employee share scheme which will be treated as a contribution paid net of basic rate tax.

Existing Approved Schemes [6.11]

The introduction of stakeholder pensions and the reform of the DC tax regime do not mean that existing approved schemes have to change their rules. The changes in the legislation are to be applied to existing approved schemes by the Finance Bill 2000, Schedule 1 when enacted.

Despite the legislation being overriding, schemes will want to incorporate these changes by amendment to their rules at some appropriate point in the future.

Opting-in to the New DC Regime   [6.12]

The trustees of an occupational DC scheme can elect on or after 1 October 2000 (with an effective date from 6 April 2001) that their occupational DC scheme be approved as a stakeholder pension scheme. This is a one-off election and there will be no tax charge if an occupational DC scheme chooses to be treated for tax purposes as a DC stakeholder pension scheme. An occupational scheme can be split in two with one part treated under the DC rules and the other part as a DB scheme.

The detailed rules for allowing an occupational DC scheme to elect to transfer into the new DC tax regime are listed in the draft Finance Bill 2000, Schedule1. A new Schedule 23ZA is to be inserted into the *Income and Corporation Taxes Act 1988* after *Schedule 23*. It is assumed that existing pension scheme rules will cover the transfer of the occupational DC scheme to the DC tax regime.

The information needed to support an application to transfer to the DC regime is to be detailed by the Inland Revenue. It may grant or refuse an application at its discretion and give notice stating the grounds of refusal. It is possible to appeal against a decision by the Inland Revenue not to allow an occupational scheme to transfer into the DC tax regime.

If a scheme is over-funded then the Inland Revenue can refuse an application. The criteria for dealing with such schemes is to be detailed in regulations.

Eligibility for Membership of a Stakeholder Scheme   [6.13]

Age Limits

There is no lower age limit for contributions to a stakeholder pension scheme, but there is an upper age limit of 75. The lack of a lower age limit means that if parents or others wish to contribute to a stakeholder pension on behalf of children, they may do so.

Net Relevant Earnings [6.14]

Members of stakeholder pensions may pay up to the current earnings threshold each year (£3,600 at present) without any reference to 'net relevant earnings'. The earnings threshold can be changed in future by a Treasury Order. However, contributions over this limit must be based on 'net relevant earnings' as defined in *Income and Corporation Taxes Act 1988, s 644*.

'Net relevant earnings' include any earned income which is chargeable to income tax for the year of assessment, less work related expenses, as listed below.

O   Salary or fees chargeable under Schedule E (including any profit-related pay, whether chargeable to tax or not).

O   Earnings from pensionable employment where an occupational DC scheme has opted into the new DC regime.

O   Income from property which is attached to, or forms part of, the salary or fees from an office or employment.

O   Income chargeable under Schedule D derived from a trade, profession or vocation.

O   Income from patent rights and royalties which is treated as earned income.

Those income streams excluded from the definition of 'net relevant earnings' include:

O   monies arising from the buying or selling of shares or an interest in shares or a right to acquire shares;

O   payments on termination of employment e.g. redundancy payments

O   state benefits;

O   pensions in payment;

O   earnings above the 'earnings cap' (in 2000/2001 £91,800); and

O   earnings from international organisations exempt from paying UK income tax.

Residency Requirements [6.15]

As the link with net relevant earnings has been removed for

contributions up to £3,600 to stakeholder schemes, the Inland Revenue has imposed a residency test for those without net relevant earnings. Those outside the workplace can contribute up to £3,600 to a DC pension scheme, including stakeholder schemes, if they:

○ are resident or ordinarily resident in the UK; or
○ have been resident or ordinarily resident at some time during the five years of assessment preceding the relevant year; or
○ were resident or ordinarily resident when the stakeholder pension was first arranged.

If employed abroad on Crown duties or the spouses of those employed abroad on Crown duties, such as members of the armed forces, the diplomatic corps and civil servants, contributions up to the £3,600 limit can be made without having to meet the residency test.

Resident and Ordinarily Resident   [6.16]

The terms 'resident' and 'ordinarily resident' are terms used by the Inland Revenue. Residence is a concept which applies to an individual who is physically present in the UK at some time in a tax year and it can be said to be his home, regardless of whether or not he owns a property in the UK. An individual will generally be treated as resident if he is present in the UK for 183 days or more in the year of assessment, excluding the day of arrival or departure, or if he makes 'habitual and substantial' visits to the UK. These are treated by the Inland Revenue as visits averaging 3 months a year over 4 years – a person would then be treated as resident in the UK from the fifth year.

The Inland Revenue has put forward its view on the meaning of 'ordinarily resident' in the booklet IR20 (1993) as:

> 'If you are resident in the UK year after year, you are treated as ordinarily resident here. You may be resident but not ordinarily resident in the UK for a tax year if, for example, you normally live outside the UK but are in this country for 183 days or more in the year. Or you may be ordinarily resident but not resident for a tax year if, for example, you usually live in the UK but have gone abroad for a long holiday and do not set foot in the UK during that year.'

Loss of Eligibility [6.17]

Concurrent Membership

Under existing legislation, a person may not be a member of both a personal pension scheme and an occupational scheme, subject to some limited exceptions. It is currently proposed under the new DC regime, people may contribute both to a stakeholder personal pension and to a stakeholder occupational scheme, which has opted into the new DC regime.

Under the draft Personal Pension Schemes (Relief At Source) (Amendment) Regulations 2000 a declaration is required as to whether or not a contributor belongs to an occupational pension scheme. This is to be made when the pension is opened and when a year is specified as a basis year. A member must tell the scheme administrator if his circumstances change so that he is ineligible, or will become ineligible, to make contributions because he has:

O   joined an occupational pension scheme that is either a DB scheme or a DC scheme that has not opted into the new DC regime;
O   become non-resident;
O   resigned as a Crown servant or is no longer the spouse of a Crown servant working abroad; or has
O   ceased to have 'net relevant earnings'.

The Inland Revenue must be notified of a change of circumstances and the consequent loss of eligibility to pay into a stakeholder scheme when a member joins an occupational scheme outside the new DC tax regime and/or becomes non-resident by the later date of:

O   April 5 in the year of assessment that it occurs; or
O   30 days after the change of circumstances;

Contributions [6.18]

Information Requirements for Contributions

Under the draft Personal Pension Schemes (Relief At Source) (Amendment) Regulations 2000, the requirement for a member to provide the scheme administrator with personal details in writing has been removed. When declarations and certificates are not submitted in writing, the scheme administrator will note down the details and send a copy to the member. This mirrors current arrangements in place for telephone applications for Individual Savings Accounts (ISAs).

The details required for an application to make pension contributions are:

○ a post code and full postal address;
○ a National Insurance number if the member has one (all but minors under 16 are expected to have one);
○ a declaration of the member's status (employed, self employed, outside the workplace) at the time of joining the scheme to help monitor the take up of stakeholder pensions; and
○ evidence of earnings needed to support contributions above the earnings threshold (such as a P60 and a copy of a tax return) if this is appropriate.

Limits on Contributions [6.19]

Members of occupational DC schemes that opt-into the new DC regime will have to comply with the contribution limits of the personal pension regime. These contributions are limited to a percentage of net relevant earnings that can be contributed to the scheme, depending on the member's age. The amount of contributions paid into a stakeholder occupational pension and personal pension by a member (and if applicable by his employer) must not exceed the appropriate percentages:

Age on 6 April	Percentage of net relevant earnings
35 or less	17.5%
36 to 45	20%
46 to 50	25%
51 to 55	30%
56 to 60	35%
61 or more	40%

The net relevant earnings of a member are subject to the 'earnings cap', imposed by the *Income and Corporation Taxes Act 1988, s 590C*, which has a permitted maximum level of earnings to which the appropriate percentage of net relevant earnings may apply. In 2000/2001 this was set at £91,800. It generally increases annually in line with the retail prices index. Any earnings above the earnings cap must be disregarded for the purposes of calculating a member's net relevant earnings.

Life Assurance and Other Insurances [6.20]

Waiver of Contribution Insurance

On or after 6 April 2001, no part of a DC pension scheme contribution may be used to buy a waiver of contribution insurance. This is insurance against non-payment of pension contributions due to ill health, unemployment or for another reason and can currently be set up within personal pensions and attract tax relief on contributions. After 6 April 2001, such a policy must be outside the DC pension scheme. If a claim is made, the amounts paid into a stakeholder or other DC pension will be treated as net of tax, as though they were normal contributions. Tax relief is therefore switched from the time of payment of the waiver of contribution premium, as under the current regime, to the later point in time, if and when a payout under the policy is used to maintain pension contributions.

Life Assurance Contracts [6.21]

Where contracts are made on or after 6 April 2001, no more than 10% of a DC pension contribution can be paid towards a life insurance contract. For those contracts taken out before 6 April 2001, the limit remains at 5% of net relevant earnings. The insurance will pay out a lump sum in the event of a member's death. This will be in the form of term assurance with the maximum term being to age 75.

Contribution Bands [6.22]

Contributions Up To the Earnings Threshold

Under the new stakeholder pension regime, anyone up to the age of 75 will be able to contribute up to the limit known as the earnings threshold limit (currently £3,600) into a stakeholder pension without any reference to earnings. They must fulfil the criteria for residency, or the exception to the residency criteria, for those people or their spouses who are posted abroad on Crown duties.

For the first time, those outside the workplace on career breaks, such as carers and mature students will be able to make contributions to a pension. In the past, the link with earnings has meant that this was impossible to do. Spouses of those posted abroad on Crown duties will also be able to contribute to a pension, in some cases for the first time if they have been stationed abroad for lengthy periods of time.

Contributions in Excess of the Earnings Threshold [6.23]

Evidence of earnings submitted for the 'basis year' of assessment can be used to support contributions above the current earnings threshold of £3,600 for the basis year, and the following five years, without the requirement to submit any further information. Those providers who already hold a certificate giving information about earnings relating to a year before 2001/02 will not need to obtain further information. For example, if the certificate relates to 1998/1999 they will not need to obtain further information until 2003/2004.

Under the draft Personal Pension Schemes (Relief At Source) (Amendment) Regulations 2000, if at some point in the five years following the basis year the contributor wishes to make higher level contributions as his earnings have increased, then new evidence of earnings will have to be submitted if:

O   contributions are to exceed the earnings threshold (currently £3,600) in a year of assessment; or
O   contributions in a year will exceed the permitted maximum based on the basis year assessment; or
O   the year is more than five years past a basis year; or
O   a basis year has not been set.

More detail on the evidence that needs to be submitted to support contributions above the earnings threshold and what further information is needed when the contributor wishes to increase the level of contributions will be available from the Inland Revenue.

Contributions When Net Relevant Earnings Cease [6.24]

When someone who has been making contributions in excess of the earnings threshold ceases to have 'net relevant earnings', they can continue to make higher level contributions for a further five years. This means that someone who takes a career break, for example to care for children or to study, will be able to continue to make contributions at the higher level without a requirement to provide further information. If he or she does not return to work within the following five years then contributions will revert to the earnings threshold limit in the sixth year.

Tax Treatment of Contributions [6.25]

Member and Employer Contributions

Members of both occupational and personal stakeholder pension schemes will receive tax relief at their highest marginal rate for the contributions made to a personal pension. This will be either 22% or 40%, corresponding to the current tax bands. From 6 April 2001, under the draft Personal Pension Schemes (Relief At Source) (Amendment) Regulations 2000, all contributions to stakeholder pension schemes and other DC schemes will be made net of basic rate tax, with the provider recovering the payment corresponding to this tax relief from the Inland Revenue on behalf of its members. The draft regulations amend the *Personal Pension Schemes (Relief at Source) Regulations 1988* to reflect the fact that stakeholder pension contributions can be made by employees, the self employed and those outside the workplace.

Contributions paid by an employer to a stakeholder scheme (though he is under no obligation to do so), will normally be allowable against the profits of the business, unless the Inland Revenue decides otherwise. Contributions made by an employer on an employee's behalf are not treated as part of the employee's earnings and are therefore not subject to income tax.

Some details on the information requirements for submitting claims for tax relief on contributions have been supplied alongside the draft Personal Pension Schemes (Relief At Source) (Amendment) Regulations 2000. The requirements follow much of the existing requirements for submitting claims in respect of employees paying personal pension contributions. The requirements may change if full concurrency is permitted for members of those occupational DB and DC schemes that cannot or do not opt into the new DC regime. This would allow people to have different concurrent types of pension provision subject to the personal pension age and salary related limits.

Information Requirements [6.26]

Statistical Returns

The annual returns of information, and the detailed information on individuals provided to the Inland Revenue, will be used for statistical monitoring and compliance purposes. Interim returns during the tax year will request aggregate statistical information to help monitor the take-up of stakeholder pensions. The detailed records provided at the end of the year in respect of each member will be used to monitor smaller contributions, and to ensure that evidence of earnings is held for those contributing above the earnings threshold.

The Inland Revenue would like to bring forward the time for submission of the annual statistical return of information, and the end of year details on individuals, and have asked for pension providers' views on this suggestion. The current deadline for submission of the annual return is 6 October, but they wish to bring this forward to 5 June to bring it into line with the timetable adopted for ISAs. This allows statistics based on actual data to be produced earlier. It also accelerates the timetable for checking contribution limits and any corrective actions needed by providers, which may be of greater relevance to providers under the new tax regime, which allows partial concurrency, than it was in the past.

The in-year statistical return required when submitting claims for tax relief, and the annual statistical return, will both need to include the following information for the Inland Revenue:

○ name of scheme administrator;
○ stakeholder pension reference number; and
○ period of claim: from/to.

If the stakeholder scheme is employer sponsored then it should also include the amount and number of employer and employee contributions, or in the case of a personal pension, details of the member's contributions. Any FSAVC Contributions, or contributions to other arrangements, should also be included. In addition, stakeholder approved personal pensions with State Earnings Related Pensions (SERPS) (to be replaced by State Second Pensions (S2P)) rebates or contracted out stakeholder occupational schemes should include the number and amount of DSS contributions.

If a member belongs to more than one stakeholder scheme, the contributions to these arrangements should be aggregated into the various appropriate categories (DSS, individual and employer) and returned as if they were a single arrangement. Arrangements that have not received a contribution in a year should be ignored. This mirrors the current requirement for personal pensions. The amount should always be the cumulative amount from the beginning of the year in question so that returns in support of an interim claim will show the total contributions from the DSS, individuals and the employer for the year to date.

Individual's Details [6.27]

The Inland Revenue requires the following details about each member to be submitted.

- ○ Administrator reference number.
- ○ Pension Schemes Office approval number (given to each scheme by the Inland Revenue when it receives 'exempt approved' status).
- ○ National Insurance Contributions Office Contracted Out Scheme number.
- ○ Tax year.
- ○ Title, forenames and surname.
- ○ National Insurance number.
- ○ Date of birth.
- ○ Full Address including post code.
- ○ Employment status.

Contribution Information [6.28]

Where applicable the following figures should be rounded up to the nearest pound.

◯ Employee contributions.
◯ Employer contributions.
◯ DSS contributions.
◯ Total amount for life assurance premiums.
◯ Current basis year (if appropriate).
◯ Net relevant earnings for basis year.
◯ Carry back indicator (if appropriate).
◯ Amount carried back.

Other Information [6.29]

If relevant the following information should also be supplied.

◯ Whether the applicant is a member of another scheme.
◯ Details of transfer payment(s) received.
◯ The total amount of the transfer payment(s).

Reliefs [6.30]

Carry Forward Relief

It has been decided to abolish carry forward relief with effect from 6 April 2001. This permitted people who had not made the maximum contribution allowed within the age and salary related percentage limits to a personal pension scheme in any previous tax year, to carry the tax relief forward to use in any of the following six years. This was a provision that was used primarily by the self employed and contract workers, who tend to have an unpredictable earnings pattern.

Although carry forward relief is to be abolished, the provisions allowing contributions at a high level of earnings in any one year to be made for the following five years will mitigate the effect of the withdrawal of this relief. If at any time within the five year period the member has higher earnings then evidence can be submitted to the Inland Revenue and contributions at the revised higher level can then be made for the following five years until earnings rise again or revert to a lower level. On the other hand, the facility to make substantial single premium payments to mop up past years' relief will not be available.

Carry Back Relief [6.31]

Carry back relief allows members to elect to have a contribution, or part of a contribution, paid in the tax year immediately preceding the year in which it was paid, or carried back to the previous year if there are no net relevant earnings in that year. If contributions are carried back they must be within the allowable percentages in the year to which they are carried back.

The existing arrangements for carry back relief are to be changed with effect from 6 April 2001. When a member is submitting his self assessment tax form by 31 January, he can elect for a contribution up to that date to be treated as paid in the previous year of assessment. The election to treat the contribution in this way can only be made at or before the time of payment.

Benefits Under DC Schemes [6.32]

DC Schemes

Stakeholder schemes, as has previously been explained, are DC schemes. This means that the amount of pension that a member will ultimately receive is related to the amount of money that he (and his employer where relevant) pays into the pension fund. There are no guarantees on the level of final pension. The benefits provided are dependent on contributions paid in and the investment growth on the contributions. The pension will also depend on the type of annuity purchased on retirement and the annuity rates prevailing at that time.

The benefits that can be paid out under a DC scheme comprise annuities for the member on his retirement, or to his spouse or dependants on his death. Income may also be available in drawdown while annuity purchase is deferred. A tax free cash lump sum may be payable on retirement or on death. On retirement, this may not exceed one quarter of the accumulated fund, while the lump sum on death may equal the entire accumulated fund. The Inland Revenue imposes conditions on the type of annuity that can be purchased and limits on the amount of the fund that can be taken as a lump sum.

Pension Date [6.33]

The rules of a pension scheme will usually allow a member to choose the date on which he retires. This is generally not before 50 nor after 75, though there are cases where people may retire earlier on grounds of ill health or if they are in occupations, such as sports, that are recognised as having a shorter working life. These dates are distinct from the State retirement dates, which are currently 60 for women and 65 for men. The women's State retirement age of 60 is due to equalise gradually with the men's retirement age of 65 between 2010 and 2020. The government is currently contemplating raising the tax-efficient early retirement age for private pensions from 50 to 55 over the same time frame.

Annuities [6.34]

As a member approaches retirement, he has to decide how much of the fund he wishes to take as a tax free lump sum, subject to the 25% limit imposed by the Inland Revenue, with the remainder being used to purchase an annuity, taxable at the member's marginal rate. Single life annuities can be purchased on the basis that payments will continue to pay out to the spouse and/or other dependants on the pensioner's death.

Currently only a minority of people seek advice on purchasing annuities on retirement from the open market. The annuity must satisfy the following conditions:

O   it must be payable by an authorised insurance company situated within the EU;

O   it must start on the member's retirement date and be payable for life;

O   it may be guaranteed for a specified term not exceeding ten years (five years is a more common choice) to continue to pay out at the full rate in the event of the member's death during the specified term;

O   the annuity may not be assigned (unless it has a guarantee period which can be assigned by a member's will) or surrendered;

O   it may increase in line with the retail prices index, or at a fixed rate each year, or be investment linked; and

O   it may be payable in advance or in arrears monthly or annually.

Some personal pension schemes currently provide for multiple annuities by having multiple or cluster pension policies. This is a complex approach, though the only way to achieve a measure of flexibility. On and from 6 April 2001, a single pension arrangement may have more than one pension date. This means that benefits can be taken at different times. In turn, this provides for multiple annuities, which might allow people to benefit from more advantageous annuity rates as they delay purchase or if interest rates alter.

Under new proposals in the Child Support, Pensions and Social Security Bill, occupational pension schemes, including stakeholder occupational schemes will have greater flexibility to offer their members investment-linked annuities. The current indexation rules for personal pensions allow schemes to offer investment-linked annuities to any members who might wish to choose this option as an alternative to a traditional indexed annuity. Investment-linked annuities benefit from the growth in a range of underlying investments after retirement, though this goes hand in hand with a risk of possible falls in pension income if investment performance is poor.

Tax Free Cash Lump Sum [6.35]

Members of stakeholder pension schemes will be able to elect to take part of their pension fund as a tax free lump sum. The member must make this election before his pension date and the tax free lump sum must:

❍ be paid at the same time as the balance of the fund is used to purchase an annuity or an election to defer purchasing an annuity is made;
❍ not exceed one third of the value of the portion of the stakeholder pension fund used to purchase the annuity i.e. not exceed 25% of the value of the fund; and
❍ not include any protected rights element of the fund for the purposes of calculating the lump sum.

Income Withdrawal [6.36]

Annuity purchase may be deferred to 75 if the scheme rules allow, although income must be withdrawn from the fund throughout the period of deferral, but not in the year the annuity is purchased or the member dies. The maximum that can be withdrawn is roughly equivalent to the payments from a single life annuity and the minimum level is 35% of the permitted maximum. Members can choose how much they wish to withdraw within the limits and can alter the amount each year. This method is generally not recommended to members with smaller accumulated funds and little other income.

The cash lump sum can still be taken but only on the date that the election to defer the purchase of an annuity is made. Income withdrawal is treated as a payment of income and is taxed under Schedule E in the same way as earnings from employment.

Funds from a single arrangement subject to income drawdown may, from April 2001, be used to buy annuities at different times. This is a consequence of allowing arrangements to have multiple pension dates and will also apply to existing arrangements such as personal pensions.

7 – Special Situations

This chapter covers the following.

- ○ Divorce and pension sharing.
- ○ Bankruptcy.
- ○ Equal treatment and part timers.
- ○ Early leavers.
- ○ Redundancy and dismissal.
- ○ Life assurance.

Summary [7.1]

Under the provisions of the *Welfare Reform and Pensions Act 1999, ss 16–47*, the government is due to introduce pension sharing for all divorces and nullity proceedings begun after 1 December 2000. From their introduction in April 2001, stakeholder pension schemes will be subject to the pension sharing provisions. Pension sharing is being introduced to try and achieve a fairer distribution of matrimonial assets on divorce and to reach a 'clean break' settlement. It also aims to provide a more secure retirement income for those who receive a share of their ex-spouse's pension rights.

Statutory protection for a bankrupt's pension rights in occupational pension schemes in the *Pensions Act 1995* are to be extended to occupational stakeholder schemes by the *Welfare Reform and Pensions Act 1999, Schedule 1*. Statutory protection on bankruptcy for pension rights in 'approved pension arrangements', which will include personal stakeholder pensions, is included in the *Welfare Reform and Pensions Act 1999, s 11*. These latter provisions came into effect on 29 May 2000, apart from *s 11(12)* which covers bankruptcy and pensions sharing rights on divorce which comes into effect on 1 December 2000. Prior to these new provisions, a bankrupt's personal pension rights were included in the assets that vest in the trustee in bankruptcy for all bankruptcies dating back to 1986.

All stakeholder pension schemes will be subject to the equal treatment provisions to ensure that there is no sex discrimination in providing access to stakeholder schemes. Employers are required to provide access to a designated stakeholder scheme if they have five or more employees, within three months of commencing employment, unless they benefit from one of the exemptions. The definition of employees is not restricted in any way and therefore includes both part time and full time workers, contract and seasonal workers. Under the *Part-time Workers (Prevention of Less Favourable Treatment) Regulations 2000*, in force from 1 July 2000, part timers are to be entitled to the same benefits as other employees on a pro rata basis unless there is an objective reason, unrelated to sex discrimination, for not doing so.

Early leavers include both those that leave an occupational stakeholder scheme as they leave their employment and those that may have to leave if they belong to an affinity scheme and no longer meet the membership criteria, for example if they leave a union. Stakeholder schemes allow the transfer of pension rights both in and out of the schemes, so it should be much easier for early leavers to transfer from a former scheme if they wish to do so. An early leaver will only be disadvantaged if the new stakeholder scheme does not offer the employer contributions he previously enjoyed, so his own contributions have to be increased to reflect this loss.

Redundancy and dismissal will have less effect on pension rights than would have been the case before the introduction of stakeholder pensions. If a member is made redundant or dismissed, either unfairly or wrongfully and is not immediately re-employed, stakeholder pension contributions can continue to be made to a stakeholder pension at the previous level for the year of redundancy or dismissal and for the following five years, even if the member is not earning or is earning but at a lower level than in the previous employment.

Under the draft Finance Bill 2000, Schedule 1, the amount of a pension contribution that goes towards a life assurance contract made on or after 6 April 2001 is 10% of the pension contribution. At present, under the personal pension provisions, 5% of earnings can be put towards a life assurance contract. The new amount is a much lower sum and stakeholder members should check their level of life assurance provision.

Divorce and Pension Sharing [7.2]

Pension sharing provisions are detailed in the *Welfare Reform and Pensions Act 1999, ss 16–51*. As already explained in Chapter 1, the *Welfare Reform and Pensions Act 1999* contains the framework legislation for stakeholder pensions, which will be subject to the pension sharing provisions. These will apply to all divorce and nullity proceedings commenced on or after 1 December 2000. These provisions will apply to stakeholder pensions from their first introduction on 6 April 2001.

Since the 1970s, the courts have had to take account of the value of pension rights in divorce and nullity of marriage settlements (where marriages are annulled for legal reasons) so that these can be offset against other assets in financial settlements. 'Earmarking' provisions in the *Pensions Act 1995* allow courts:

O   in England and Wales (and Northern Ireland under a separate order), to require occupational and personal pension schemes to pay maintenance from a member's pension to their former spouse; and
O   throughout the United Kingdom to order part or all of a lump sum payable on the death or retirement of a member to be directed to their former spouse.

The current practice of 'earmarking' pension rights has proved unsatisfactory. The pension rights remain with the spouse in whose name they have been accrued, so no clean break settlement is achievable. It is not possible under the current arrangements to transfer the pension rights that have been earmarked to a pension scheme of the ex-spouse's choice. Earmarking is especially problematical in unfunded public sector schemes, which have no funds to earmark.

Further problems arise if the ex-spouse remarries, or her former spouse dies before he starts drawing his pension. The ex-spouse loses then all rights to the pension rights that were earmarked on her behalf. Equally, problems can arise if the former spouse decides to delay taking his pension, which he can do up to the age of 75. This could leave the ex-spouse with no pension provision at a time when she most needs it.

The aims of pension sharing are to:

O   allow the courts to achieve the fairest overall settlement of assets in each divorce case, with pension rights being treated in a flexible manner;
O   provide a more secure retirement income for those receiving a share of pension rights; and
O   increase the opportunity for divorcing couples to achieve complete financial independence through a 'clean break' settlement.

With the growth of private pension provision, which includes occupational and personal pensions, pension rights can be the second most valuable asset in a marriage after the matrimonial home. For the first time, the pension sharing provisions will allow pension rights to be transferred from one party to another and be dealt with in the same way as property transfers. Published figures from ONS (Office for National Statistics) Publications show that there were 168,900 divorces in England/ Wales in 1996. Further figures from ONS show that among full-time employees, 75% of men and 65% of women were members of an occupational or personal pension scheme. Among women who worked part-time, however, only one third belonged to some form of pension scheme. Among the self-employed, men were almost twice as likely as women to belong to a personal pension scheme.

The pension sharing provisions will apply equally to both men and women, so in practice it will be possible for pension rights to be transferred from the woman to the man as part of the divorce settlement as well as the more standard scenario. However, the current distribution of pension rights means that the main beneficiaries of pension sharing are expected to be women. This will help with the government's longer term aim of increasing individual non-state pension entitlement.

In announcing the government's aim to introduce pension sharing by the end of 2000, the minister, Jeff Rooker, said:

> 'Pension sharing is fair — it recognises the contribution of both spouses to family income. It encourages independence and will enable some divorcing couples to achieve a fairer settlement than is possible through offsetting or earmarking pension assets.'

It is important to note that pension sharing will not be compulsory. It will still be possible to offset the value of the pension rights against other assets. Where appropriate earmarking orders can also be made.

How Pension Sharing Will Operate in Practice [7.3]

If divorcing couples opt for pension sharing then they will rightly expect that once the pension rights have been shared that the sum of the two parts is roughly equivalent to the value of the overall 'pot' of money available. The legislation provides that the divorcing couple will bear the costs of the pension share, and that no expenses should fall on other scheme members or employers (in occupational stakeholder schemes). The *Welfare Reform and Pensions Act 1999* uses the term 'scheme member' for the person in whose name the pension rights have been accrued and 'former spouse' for the person who may acquire pension rights under a pension share.

At the stage of the divorce proceedings when the court requests a statement of financial affairs from the divorcing couple, the scheme member (but not his spouse) can submit a request to the 'person responsible for a pension arrangement' to provide information on the value of his accrued pension rights. For stakeholder schemes, the responsible person will be the trustees or stakeholder managers of the scheme. They will have to check the provisions within the scheme rules for pension sharing and provide the necessary information within three months beginning with the date that the trustees or stakeholder manager receive the request or not less than six weeks prior to the hearing date.

No charge can be made for a valuation if a cash equivalent valuation has not been provided in the previous 12 months. Scheme members will also need to approach the DSS for a valuation for their State Earnings Related Pension Scheme (SERPS) accrued rights (and from 2002 for their State Second Pension (S2P) accrued rights) in stakeholder schemes that have not opted out of SERPS.

How Stakeholder Schemes Should Deal with Pension Sharing Requirements [7.4]

Stakeholder schemes need to consider how they will handle the pension sharing requirements. These need to be clearly stated in the rules and a copy of the policy statement should be made available to divorcing couples. Schemes must offer external transfers and some occupational schemes may also wish to consider offering scheme membership as an alternative. If schemes do decide to offer scheme membership then they must also decide on the benefits package that will go with it.

Copies of the divorce order and the pension sharing order will be sent to the trustees and stakeholder managers of the stakeholder scheme, so that they have specific details of what they are required to do. The effective date will not be before the date of the divorce or the date of the order, whichever is later. The pension share will be expressed as a percentage of the scheme member's cash equivalent transfer. At the same time, the divorcing couple also has to provide sufficient information about themselves so that the scheme can identify and contact them. The stakeholder scheme will have four months in which to implement the pension share.

Steps to Follow When the Pension Sharing Order is Received [7.5]

○ First, stakeholder schemes must value the member's accrued rights as a cash equivalent transfer on the date the agreement came into effect, or in the case of a divorce, 21 days after the date of divorce (this is to allow for any appeal);

○ Next, the scheme must create a debit on the scheme member's rights and a credit for the same amount for the former spouse – in most schemes the credit and debit amounts will directly reflect the percentage of the cash equivalent transfer specified in the sharing order, though in some occupational schemes this will be a more complex calculation. All rights, including contracted-out rights, will be reduced by the same percentage.

○ The scheme must then transfer the pension credit to the destination chosen by the former spouse. This could be simply to create rights in the member's own scheme. However, where the former spouse chooses an external transfer, the pension credit may be transferred to one of the following three destinations:

● the former spouse's own occupational scheme;
● a new or existing contract with a personal pension scheme (stakeholder personal pension schemes could prove a popular destination for external transfers); or
● an insurance policy or annuity contract.

The trustees and stakeholder managers will be responsible for ensuring that the pension credit is transferred as the former spouse requests. However, if the former spouse fails to notify the trustees or stakeholder mangers of her choice, then they may operate a default option, such as scheme membership, purchase of an annuity contract or an insurance policy.

SERPS rights (and from April 2002, S2P rights) will be shared out in the same way, using the pension debit and pension credit system. However, it will not be possible for the former spouse to transfer the pension credit out of the scheme. Instead, entitlement to an 'additional shared pension' will be given.

Any reasonable administrative costs for implementing a pension share can be recovered from the divorcing couple in cash. If this is not forthcoming then a deduction on the pension rights can be imposed. Once the pension share is complete the trustees or stakeholder manager must inform the former spouse and the scheme member.

If stakeholder schemes decide in their rules to offer membership to former spouses, then they should consider establishing a new category of membership for former spouses with pension credit rights. Former spouses' credits will give them future benefits based purely on their own circumstances and the scheme rules and not the circumstances of the scheme member. Schemes must ensure that former spouses' credits can be separately identified and that their benefits are clearly set out.

Rebuilding Scheme Members' Rights [7.6]

When scheme members have had their pension rights reduced due to a pension sharing order, they will wish to rebuild their pensions. The benefits transferred to a former spouse by pension credit will continue to be treated as though they were the scheme member's, though scheme members will be able to rebuild their rights within the benefit rules. Members of stakeholder schemes will be subject to the Inland Revenue rules for personal pension contributions based on age and salary related percentage limits.

Bankruptcy and Stakeholder Pensions [7.7]

Protecting Pension Rights From Creditors

When a person becomes bankrupt, his assets generally vest in the trustee in bankruptcy. Under the provisions that are in force for occupational schemes within the *Pensions Act 1995, ss 91–95,* pension rights (as opposed to pension payments) are not counted as an asset in bankruptcy. The provisions in the *Pensions Act 1995* are extended to occupational stakeholder schemes by the *Welfare Reform and Pensions Act 1999, Schedule 1,* which is expected to come into effect by April 2001.

Pension rights in 'approved pension arrangements', such as personal pensions are given statutory protection on bankruptcy by the *Welfare Reform and Pensions Act 1999, s 11,* which came into effect on 29 May 2000, apart from *s 11(12)* which covers bankruptcy and pension sharing on divorce and comes into effect on 1 December 2000. 'Approved pension arrangements' are those pension arrangements recognised for tax purposes under the *Income and Corporation Taxes Act 1988, Part XIV,* which includes stakeholder personal pensions.

If approval for a pension arrangement is still pending on the date that a bankruptcy order is made against a person, and the Inland Revenue subsequently decides not to grant approval, then the bankrupt's pension rights in the scheme vest in the trustee in bankruptcy. If a bankrupt has rights in a scheme and the Inland Revenue issues a notice withdrawing its approval after a bankruptcy is made, and the effective date for the withdrawal of approval is before the date of the bankruptcy, then any rights that the bankrupt has in the pension scheme vest in the trustee in bankruptcy.

Pensions schemes of all kinds will no longer be allowed to forfeit a member's benefits to the scheme under the *Welfare Reform and Pensions Act 1999, s 14,* (expected to come into effect by April 2001). This was a method used by occupational schemes in the past to protect a member's benefits and then to pay them on a discretionary basis to the member's family. Pension benefits will be protected from creditors under the *Welfare Reform and Pensions Act 1999, s 11* although the statutory provisions will allow creditors to recover assets from the pension where these are the result of excessive contributions.

Recovery of Excessive Pension Contributions   [7.8]

The aim of the provisions outlined above is to protect people's pension rights when they become bankrupt. It is possible that large amounts of assets could be paid into pensions to keep them out of the reach of creditors. The *Welfare Reform and Pensions Act 1999, ss 15 and 16* contain a power for the trustee in bankruptcy to apply to the court for an order to recover excessive contributions.

When deciding whether or not contributions have been excessive the court must consider:

O   whether any contributions were made for the purpose of putting assets beyond the reach of creditors;
O   whether the total amount of contributions was excessive in the light of the bankrupt's circumstances when the contributions were made.

If the court is satisfied that excessive contributions have been made, then it can make an order to restore the pension to its original position prior to the excessive contributions having been made. The order may also include provision:

O   for the pension scheme to pay an amount to the trustee in bankruptcy;

O   to reduce any pension benefits that the individual and his family are entitled to; and

O   for recovering the costs incurred by the scheme in supplying information for the trustee in bankruptcy's application to the court and complying with the order.

The amount that the pension scheme can be required to pay to the trustee in bankruptcy is limited to the lesser of:

O   the amount of excessive contributions; or

O   the current value of the bankrupt's pension rights under the scheme.

The order must provide for a corresponding reduction in the bankrupt's rights under the scheme. The order is binding on the trustees and stakeholder managers of the scheme and overrides the scheme rules.

In due course, regulations will give guidance concerning the calculation of the value of an individual's rights under the pension scheme and how schemes should calculate the reduction in the scheme's liabilities regarding that person.

Pension Sharing and Bankruptcy   [7.9]

Pension sharing has already been discussed in detail above. A situation may arise where, prior to a person's bankruptcy, his pension rights were subject to a pension sharing agreement. If a court subsequently rules that the bankrupt's pension rights are based on excessive contributions which can be shown to have unfairly prejudiced the bankrupt's creditors, then the pension share awarded to the former spouse, or a portion of it, may in limited circumstances be available to the trustee in bankruptcy. These are if:

O   the pension sharing order had the effect of defeating creditors;

O   the pension rights transferred to the former spouse could not have been made without excessive contributions; or

O   some of the former spouse's pension share is derived from excessive contributions.

If the court finds that the pension scheme must pay out part of the former spouse's pension share, the amount repayable is limited to the least of:

O the amount of the former spouse's pension share which represents excessive contributions and is recoverable;
O the value of the former spouse's pension share; and in Scotland
O so much (if any) of the excessive contributions as is not recoverable out of the bankrupt's share.

As mentioned above, where the bankrupt's pension rights are reduced due to excessive contributions, in the case of the former spouse's pension share being reduced a corresponding reduction in the former spouse's rights under the scheme must also take place. Regulations will provide guidance on how to calculate the rights and reductions.

Equal Treatment and Part Timers   [7.10]

The employer access requirements for stakeholder pensions require all employers with five or more employees earning above the annual lower earnings limit (£3,484 in 2000/01) who satisfy the UK residency test, to provide access to a stakeholder scheme within three months of employment with the company unless:

O the employer has an occupational pension scheme which the employee is eligible to join after a year, though schemes are allowed to exclude those employees who are under eighteen or within five years of retirement; or
O the employer contributes at least 3% of an employee's earnings to a group personal pension plan which has no exit charges and no penalties for stopping contributions.

These requirements apply equally to male and female employees, whether working full time, part time, or as seasonal or contract workers.

Equal Treatment   [7.11]

The principle of equal treatment is enshrined in the *EU Treaty, Article 141 (formerly Article 119)*. This deals with equal pay and this principle has been upheld in many cases before the European Court of Justice. Employers must ensure that equal access for men and women is provided for membership of an occupational stakeholder pension scheme and for any employer designated stakeholder scheme.

Part Timers [7.12]

In order to implement the requirements of the *Part Time Workers Directive 97/81/EC,* the *Part Time Employees (Prevention of Less Favourable Treatment) Regulations 2000* (the *Regulations*) came into force on 1 July 2000. In the past, part timers could be excluded from an occupational scheme if employers had been able to show objective reasons for doing so (such as factors connected with the running of their business, administrative costs and better productivity). With the introduction of the new regulations, employers must not discriminate between full-time and part-time employees over access to pension schemes, unless different treatment is justified on objective grounds unrelated to discrimination on the grounds of sex. Where full and part time employees are employed on similar contracts, objective grounds will be very difficult to establish.

Benefits [7.13]

A consequence of the *Regulations* is that the calculation of benefits under the pension scheme for part-time staff should be on a pro rata basis of those for full-time employees. Although in some schemes this has been the case for some time, it does not always follow and this provision will give a legal basis for the way in which the calculation of benefits should be made. Also, if any part time employee feels he or she has been discriminated against, under the provisions in the *Regulations* he or she will be able to make a claim based directly on that less favourable treatment, rather than having to go through the longer and more complicated indirect sex discrimination procedure.

Early Leavers [7.14]

Early leavers are those scheme members who leave an occupational pension scheme before their normal pension age. This is the earliest date on which a member has an unqualified right to retire on an unreduced pension without needing the consent of the trustees or the employer and without any actuarial reduction. People usually leave an occupational scheme before normal pension age because they leave the employer. However, under the new provisions for stakeholder schemes, which allow affinity groups to set up stakeholder schemes, there may be members of these stakeholder schemes who become early leavers by default as they no longer belong to the affinity group.

This could be the case where a stakeholder scheme run by a union has a member who either decides to leave the union or moves to a new job which precludes membership of that union.

Options [7.15]

In order to ensure that the pension rights of early leavers are protected when they leave an occupational scheme, there is legislation to cover the preservation of pension rights if the member has had two years 'qualifying service' in the pension scheme. This can either be a continuous period of time (with permitted breaks e.g. for maternity leave) or can include 'linked qualifying service' where the scheme has accepted a transfer payment from another occupational pension scheme. Members may transfer their rights to a personal pension or to their new employer's scheme. Alternatively, their pension rights are preserved within the occupational scheme and benefits can be taken at normal retirement age, or sometimes earlier with the consent of the trustees and/or the employer (depending on the scheme rules).

Those members who do not have two years qualifying service will have options that depend on the scheme's rules. They may have the value of their contributions less tax refunded to them without the employer's contributions, or they may apply to have their pension rights transferred to their new employer's scheme or, to a personal pension with no tax deducted.

Transfer to New Employer's Stakeholder Scheme [7.16]

The provisions that apply for early leavers from occupational schemes have to be considered in the light of the minimum standards for stakeholder schemes. These include provisions that members are able to transfer their funds to another scheme at any time without any additional charge on their funds. Another minimum standard is that schemes should accept transfers of members' pension rights from other schemes. Many occupational schemes currently exclude transfers-in in their scheme documentation. For those schemes wishing to opt into the new DC regime, this is something that they will have to adopt.

Those employees who leave an employer with a stakeholder occupational scheme will be faced with a dilemma. Under the current arrangements for employer access, an employer is only obliged to remit employee payroll deductions to his designated stakeholder scheme if requested to do so by the employee. It is also likely that the employer will only pay his contributions, if he makes any on the employee's behalf, to his designated stakeholder scheme.

The employee moving to the new employer will have to weigh up these considerations and either arrange to set up a direct debit arrangement to his current scheme or ask for his rights to be preserved and become a deferred member. Alternatively, he could transfer his pension rights to his new employer's designated stakeholder occupational scheme. In later years, as more people move around and are contributing to different occupational stakeholder schemes, there may be an obligation for employers to agree to transfer employee payroll contributions to the stakeholder scheme of the employee's choice as well as to the employer's designated stakeholder scheme. The employer may also be obliged to pay his contributions, if he makes any, to any stakeholder scheme nominated by the employee.

Redundancy and Dismissal [7.17]

Redundancy

On redundancy some employees are entitled to a statutory redundancy payment, which is based on age, length of continuous employment and gross average pay, subject to a statutory maximum. However, they are not entitled to any element relating to an employer's contributions to a pension scheme. This means that an employee's entitlement on redundancy will depend upon the wording of the scheme documentation. In some instances, where a pension is payable immediately on redundancy, the employer can reduce or not pay a redundancy payment.

These provisions will need to be borne in mind when employers consider which stakeholder scheme they are going to designate to comply with the employer access requirements. Employers must ensure that they and their advisers check the scheme documentation.

Unfair Dismissal [7.18]

When an employee establishes that he has been dismissed unfairly, i.e. without a fair reason or where a fair procedure has not been followed, then he is entitled to compensation. This may include a basic award based on his weekly pay, age and length of service, and also a compensatory award including any loss of pension benefits. This could include situations where an employee fails to find another job, where the new employer operates a less beneficial scheme or does not have a pension scheme at all.

With the introduction of the employer access requirements to designate a stakeholder scheme, it is unlikely that a new employer will not have a pension scheme, unless the new employer has fewer than five employees. The new employer's designated stakeholder scheme would be unlikely to be less beneficial than the previous employer's designated scheme. An exception would be if the new employer does not make employer contributions whilst the former employer did. For an employee unfairly dismissed from an employer with an occupational stakeholder scheme, and moving to another employer with an occupational stakeholder scheme, the amount of the compensatory award for the pension element will be minimal in most instances. Clearly the situation would be different if considering occupational schemes that have not opted into the stakeholder regime.

Wrongful Dismissal [7.19]

When an employee is dismissed without proper notice, he is entitled to damages for the loss of earnings and other contractual benefits up to the date on which the employment contract could have been terminated had the correct notice been given. Under a DC scheme, such as an occupational stakeholder scheme, compensation for the pension element of the employee's damages claim will be based on the employer contributions that would have been made during the notice period. This will only apply for stakeholder schemes where employers make contributions. The damages will also include an assumed investment return and an allowance for salary increases if appropriate.

The employee will be able to transfer his accrued pension rights from the employer's stakeholder scheme into a personal stakeholder scheme, or to his new employer's stakeholder scheme where one is available. If he remains out of work, he will be able to continue making contributions to his former employer's occupational stakeholder scheme for the year of his wrongful dismissal and for the following five years at his current contribution level.

Life Assurance   [7.20]

One special situation that we will all eventually reach is death. Even if we manage to avoid the pitfalls of bankruptcy, divorce, redundancy and dismissal, reaching the end of one's life is a certainty. Under the personal pension tax regime, a member had the option to decide what amount of his contribution, subject to a maximum of 5% of net relevant earnings, he wished to go towards life assurance. In the event of death before the end of the policy term, which could extend to age 75, the insurance company pays a lump sum for the amount assured.

The draft Finance Bill 2000, Schedule 1 has altered this provision and states that for life assurance contracts taken out on or after 6 April 2001, no more than 10% of the contribution to a stakeholder pension scheme, or to other DC schemes, can be paid towards a life assurance contract. For earlier insurance contracts the limit remains at 5% of earnings.

This is a subtle change, as it appears that the percentage has increased. However, a closer examination reveals that there has been a switch from a percentage of earnings to a percentage of contributions. This means that a much lower monetary amount can be paid towards a life assurance contract. This is because the government wants as much of the value of the contribution as possible to go towards a future pension and has reduced the extent of the tax relief that the member receives on purchasing life assurance. Those employees starting to pay into a stakeholder pension for the first time will be well advised to consider the amount of life cover that they have and the level that might be appropriate.

8 – Stakeholder – The Wider Picture

This chapter covers the following.

- ○ Will stakeholder pensions be successful?
- ○ Pensions policy in Europe.
- ○ The global experience of low cost DC savings plans.
- ○ The effect of stakeholder on other pension provision and savings vehicles.

Summary [8.1]

The success of stakeholder pensions rests with middle earners, the main target group for stakeholder pensions. They should be attracted by the low charging regime and enhanced rebates if they choose to opt-out of the State Earnings Related Pension Scheme (SERPS) (or the State Second Pension (S2P) from 2002). High earners who belong to an occupational defined contribution (DC) scheme that has opted into the new DC regime will also be attracted by the low charging regime of stakeholder pensions. They will be a viable alternative to free standing additional voluntary contributions (FSAVCs). For older contributors, the advantage of higher contribution levels under the new DC tax regime is also a significant plus point. On the other hand, low earners would be better off relying on the Minimum Income Guarantee (MIG), rather than attempting to accumulate sufficient capital for a pension, the value of which is then deducted in assessing the MIG payment. Those outside the workplace will have the opportunity to contribute to a pension for the first time if they have sufficient spare income or if a partner, friend or parent gives them money to make contributions to a stakeholder pension.

Stakeholder pensions must be considered within the broader context of European pension policy. Member States, like the UK, are all facing the same demographic crisis of an ageing population and shrinking workforce. In many Member States this problem is aggravated by their unfunded pension systems whereby the current generation of workers support pensioners under the Pay-As-You-Go (PAYG) systems and reform is urgently needed.

The Americas and Australia have all had individual retirement savings plans for at least 20 years. The key features of these are similar to some aspects of stakeholder pensions, but there are some clear differences. In Chile there is compulsion on the employers to deduct a percentage of employee's earnings. In Australia employers have to contribute 7% of the employee's salary. The US has a more flexible approach to its plans, allowing them to be used as a source of loans and borrowing when contributors fall on hard times.

Stakeholder pensions have been decried by some as the final nail in the coffin for defined benefit (DB) schemes. Although some employers may choose to switch their pension provision in its entirety to a stakeholder occupational scheme, many others may view stakeholder schemes as a viable alternative to offering membership to their DB schemes to all employees and operate the arrangements in parallel. A stakeholder scheme can be reserved for those employees starting their employment with the company and for seasonal and contract workers, providing other employees are eligible to join either an occupational scheme or a GPP that complies with the employer access exemptions. The low charging levels will force down the charges for Group Personal Pension Plans and for other personal pensions. Additional voluntary contribution (AVC) providers will also have to become more competitive.

Aims for Stakeholder Pensions [8.2]

The government's aims for stakeholder pensions are to ensure that those people who can afford to save for their retirement do so, whilst those who cannot are given greater levels of support. Stakeholder pensions are aimed primarily at those people on middle incomes, defined by the government as those earning between £10,000 and £20,000, both employed and self employed. They will be encouraged to contribute to a stakeholder pension by receiving enhanced rebates if they opt out of SERPS (or S2P from 2002).

As a stated policy aim, the government wishes to switch the current proportions of State and private pension provision from 60% State/ 40% private to a scenario where privately funded pensions account for 60% of the provision. This drive towards a smaller percentage of State provision is motivated both by economic necessity and an increasing elderly population. Recent figures have shown that before the end of this decade, retired people will outnumber young people in the UK for the first time and, by 2040, a quarter of the population will be pensioners while fewer than half will be age 45 or under.

Due to improvements in health care, people live longer and place an increasing burden on the already overstretched National Health Service. This longevity creates additional problems as people fail to make adequate provision for their retirement. This is either because they do not have the means to do so, or because the products on offer have been tainted by scandal, such as the Maxwell affair and personal pensions mis-selling. People are worried that their money, and their futures, will not be safe. The effect of possible future inflation on deposit based savings is also a risk factor.

This combination of circumstances has forced the government to re-examine how pension provision is delivered in the UK. In its Green Paper, entitled the New Insurance Contract for Welfare: Partnership in Pensions a new approach was announced. This three pronged approach consists of the basic state pension together with a new second state pension (S2P to replace SERPS in April 2002), a minimum income guarantee and stakeholder pensions.

High Earners [8.3]

For the purposes of stakeholder pensions, high earners are defined as those people earning above £20,000. Generally speaking, if people in this group contribute to a pension, they are already either in an occupational scheme or a personal pension scheme. They are able to contribute up to the personal pension limits, which are age and salary related, if they have a personal pension and up to 15% of their salary above their employer's contribution if in an occupational scheme. Voluntary contributions in addition to those required under scheme rules qualify for relief at the member's highest marginal rate of income tax, subject to the overall 15% of salary limit. Free Standing Additional Voluntary Contributions (FSAVCs) tend to be subject to a higher charging regime than basic contributions and scheme AVCs so the low charging regime of stakeholder pensions will be attractive to high earners.

Those employees in occupational schemes who currently make AVCs, or have an FSAVC plan and wish to contribute to stakeholder pensions, will have to belong to an occupational scheme that opts into the new DC regime. Concurrency for those in DB schemes and for those occupational schemes that have not opted into the new DC regime is under discussion. In addition to the low charging regime, older members will also benefit from the higher percentage of earnings that they can contribute to a stakeholder scheme, which is treated for tax purposes as a personal pension. The lowest maximum contribution level to a personal pension is 17.5% of earnings for those aged 35 and under rising to a maximum of 40% for those aged 61 and above. In opted in DC schemes, the employer contribution will count towards these percentages.

For high earners who meet the necessary criteria, stakeholder pensions will be a very cost effective savings vehicle. Some may be deterred from taking out a stakeholder pension by the announcement of recent government proposals to raise the tax efficient early retirement age for private pension provision from 50 to 55, although this will be unlikely to affect anyone retiring before 2010. The tax advantages of using a stakeholder pension (or any AVC arrangement) to help fund early retirement will seem less attractive if the proposals are adopted. Therefore, non-pension savings vehicles such as Individual Savings Accounts (ISAs) may become more popular for longer term savings.

Middle Earners [8.4]

Despite the incentive of enhanced rebates for middle earners who opt out of SERPS (or S2P), whether or not they will be persuaded to keep contributing to a stakeholder pension as the years roll on remains to be seen. At present, many people stop contributing to their personal pensions within the first three years due to other commitments. This is very expensive and wasteful. One approach considered in the Green Paper on pensions and then rejected by the Government was compulsory contributions to pensions, though it has not been removed from the agenda for future consideration. Compulsion would deprive people of a percentage of their disposable income if they decided that they wished to provide for their retirement via other means such as buying property, shares or savings products.

Those on middle incomes, earning between £10,000 – £20,000, will receive enhanced rebates if they opt out of SERPS (and from 2002, S2P), take out a stakeholder pension and then remain as members of a stakeholder pension scheme. The rebates from S2P are scheduled to become flat rate five years after its introduction, although there are proposals that those who are members of stakeholder schemes will continue to receive an enhanced rate.

Low Earners [8.5]

Low earners have been classified by the government as those earning less than £10,000 per year but more than the lower earnings level (currently £3,484 in 2000/01). They will benefit from enhanced SERPS (and subsequently S2P) rebate levels, which will give them the same level of rebates as those earning £9,500 per year if they opt out of SERPS. Those remaining within SERPS will also be treated as though they earned £9,500 (or the prevailing LET) per year, although they will not be given the enhanced rebate rates.

It is difficult to see why low earners might decide to contribute to a stakeholder pension due to their low level of disposable income. As such, they are not viewed as a prime target group for stakeholder pensions by the government and providers. The fact that they will all be treated as though they had higher levels of earnings up to the LET (currently £9,500) under SERPS (and S2P from 2002) will mean that there is little incentive to contribute to their own funded private pension.

Another factor for low earners is the Minimum Income Guarantee (MIG). This ensures that everyone will have a basic minimum income, if his or her basic state pension falls below the MIG. This is provided via Income Benefit and is currently around £78 per week for a single person and £121 for a married couple for 2000/01. Housing Benefit and Council Tax Benefit can also be paid on top of this. If they have a pension, however small, the MIG falls each week by the amount of the pension. On current figures, a person would need to have a pension fund of around £70,000 before they would be better off relying on their own pension than the MIG. It is unlikely that a low earner could accumulate the necessary sum of £70,000 or so over their lifetime so as to provide income comparable with MIG levels. Relying on the MIG seems the best approach for low earners as benefits stand at the moment, though there is no guarantee that successive governments will maintain the MIG in future.

Those Outside the Workplace [8.6]

Stakeholder pensions offer the first opportunity for those who have ceased earning to continue to contribute to a pension. Under the current tax legislation, those without any earnings cannot make any contributions into a pension beyond the end of the tax year that they leave employment. The new stakeholder tax regime will allow a member of a pension plan to continue to make contributions at the level of their previous earnings for the year in which they cease employment and for the following five years. If they go back into employment during those five years at a higher rate of pay, then they can increase their contributions accordingly. Conversely, if they return to work at a lower rate of pay and they are able to afford it, they can maintain their contributions at the higher level. If they do not go back into employment then they are still able to contribute indefinitely up to the earnings threshold, currently £3,600, without any reference to earnings.

Equally, those who have never been able to contribute to a pension will also benefit from the stakeholder tax regime as they, or someone on their behalf, will be able to contribute to a pension and benefit from the tax relief. This will include those caring for children under school age and dependant adults, the disabled, the unemployed and mature students. As with low earners, it is debatable whether or not this group would be better off relying on the MIG rather than contributing to a pension. Money could be saved in an ISA providing that they made sure they did not breach the capital limits, currently £8,000 increasing to £12,000 in April 2001, for receiving the MIG. An ISA is more flexible than a stakeholder pension as one is not tied to taking an annuity, but there is no tax relief on contributions. However, any income and capital gains are tax exempt.

EU Pensions Policy [8.7]

Demographics

The plans for pension provision in the UK for the beginning of the twenty-first century need to be seen in a wider European context, particularly in terms of our membership of the European Union (EU). Member States are facing a demographic time bomb of an ageing population, supported by a shrinking number of workers. This means an ever increasing bill for governments to cover the old age pensions of the new millennium's pensioners, whose life expectancy is increasing due to developments in healthcare and awareness of diet.

State pensions currently account for 10% of the EU's annual GDP and 88% of pension payouts. Member States must encourage the growth of funded schemes, to ensure adequate pension provision for future generations and that they remain within the budgetary constraints for membership of the euro. Only the UK, Ireland and the Netherlands have well developed funded pensions systems. Most of the other Member States, especially France and Italy, rely heavily on the Pay As You Go (PAYG) system where those in work support those who have retired. This system operates well when workers outnumber pensioners by a large margin.

Although there are currently 4 people of working age to support each pensioner in the EU, by 2040 this ratio will have halved. The average number of births per European woman has declined from 2.5 in 1965 to 1.8 in France and the UK and to less than 1.5 in Germany, Italy and Spain. This means that over the next few decades, the base of people in employment will shrink as the numbers of people aged 80 and over increases.

The EU wants to ensure that less of Member States' Gross Domestic Product (GDP) is taken up with retirement provision. In some cases, some Member States will require 200% of GDP to fund their PAYG system by 2010. Pre-funding pensions is the route that the UK government also wishes to follow by encouraging the growth of personal pension provision via stakeholder pensions, to ensure less dependency on the state.

The EU is keen to promote the growth of funded pensions, to help spur capital market growth. Pension funds could play an important role in the development of pan-European risk capital markets, as the investment of new monies on the market could be used for the smaller and more innovative companies in the new technologies which constantly need venture capital. One suggestion from the European Commission has been that if all European pension funds had only 2% of their assets in risk capital shares, the impact on the growth of small and medium-sized companies would be highly significant. These and other topics relating to investment are currently under review in the UK.

Regulatory framework   [8.8]

Pension funds represent an amount approximately equal to 23% of the EU's annual GDP, but are not covered by a framework of EU legislation. This is in marked contrast to insurance companies whose assets amount to approximately 35% of the Union's GDP and operate in a Single Market based on nearly 30 legislative or regulatory acts. The size of the problems and the sums of money involved demonstrate how large a gap still exists in the regulatory framework for a Single Market in financial services.

However, it is not only a framework for institutions that offer retirement provision that is needed. EU citizens also need encouragement to take out a supplementary pension. The EU has a major role to play in ensuring that supplementary pensions are regulated and structured in such a way as to provide an attractive long-term investment, so that future pensioners can see that supplementary schemes will provide adequate money for them in retirement. Combined with security considerations, there needs to be a more flexible approach to the investment profile of a fund, with greater freedom of investment. This is the subject of much debate between the Member States, as there are different approaches to the way pension fund money is and should be invested. Some favour investment in low yielding but theoretically safe government bonds, whilst other Member States favour greater freedom to invest in equities, traditionally held to be more volatile but historically achieving greater returns over the long term.

The European Commission is due to issue a proposal in summer 2000 on the prudential supervision of pension funds. The Commission wants to ensure the best possible protection for pension fund beneficiaries combined with attractive returns. It aims to achieve this by only limiting investment strategies for prudential reasons and ensuring that pension funds can use the services of any EU approved asset manager or agent. To ensure equal treatment for all occupational pension providers, a prudential framework will be established, leading in time to the mutual recognition of prudential regimes.

Although the mutual recognition of supervisory regimes will go some way to beginning the move towards true cross-border membership of different institutions offering occupational retirement provision, the fundamental right to freedom of movement for EU citizens will still be hindered by lengthy vesting periods and a lack of agreement on transfer values and acquired rights. The lack of tax concessions from some Member States on member contributions to their home state supplementary pension will also have to be tackled. Further work also needs to be done on the co-ordination of social security systems and Member States' social policy if there is ever going to be a coherent approach.

Global DC Plans [8.9]

USA

Social security in the USA only accounts for around 20% of average living expenses and is not adequate for retirement needs. As in the UK and Europe, longevity is increasing in the USA and money for retirement is needed for longer periods of time. Americans are strongly encouraged to save for their retirement through the use of many different savings vehicles. The American retirement schemes most widely recognised in the UK, which are similar to stakeholder, are the so-called '401(k) savings plans'. This name is based on the section of the US Internal Revenue code that contains the details for these plans, which are funded by defined contributions and employer sponsorship.

In US there has been an increase in the number of DC plans over DB schemes as large companies have looked for ways to decrease their overheads and cut costs. DC plans ensure that the investment burden is placed on the individual and that the eventual payout is based on the contributions made and the investment returns achieved on those funds. This avoids the burden which the employer faces in DB schemes where the onus is on the employer to provide the employee's pension.

Key features of 401(k) plans [8.10]

Contributions to a 401(k) plan are made from gross salary and are not taxed until money is withdrawn from the plan, theoretically at retirement when pensioners are in a lower tax bracket. This is a similar approach to the UK, where contributions are tax exempt and, when a pension is paid out from an annuity, the income is taxed at the appropriate rate. As with the planned provisions for stakeholder pensions, there are automatic payroll deductions for contributions to 401(k) plans. There is no compulsion for the employer to contribute to a 401(k) plan, though in many cases they do so, matching contributions up to a certain limit. Legislation encourages employer contributions and higher employee take up rates.

The 401(k) plans are flexible and can be taken from job to job. The amount that an employee has saved in a plan can be:

○ transferred directly to the new employer's 401(k) plan where contributions can continue; or
○ the employee can keep his old 401(k) account and contribute to the new employer's plan; or
○ transfer the money in the old 401(k) account into an individual retirement account (IRA, broadly similar to an ISA) and start a new 401(k) plan with the new employer.

This wide range of options is not available under the proposed stakeholder legislation, which only allows a free transfer of monies accrued in a stakeholder pension into another stakeholder pension, or to contribute to the new employer's designated stakeholder scheme whilst keeping the initial stakeholder pension. This latter option may be chosen where the new employer only contributes to his designated stakeholder scheme. As contributions to a pension in the UK are given tax relief at the highest marginal rate applicable to the contributor, there is no option to move money from a pension scheme into another savings vehicle until retirement, when the maximum tax free lump sum of 25% can be placed elsewhere.

Withdrawals [8.11]

A further aspect of 401(k) plans is that contributors can make a withdrawal from the plan if there is 'hardship' which represents an 'immediate and heavy financial need' for which there are no 'other resources reasonably available'. The US Inland Revenue Service recognises four circumstances for hardship:

○ some medical expenses that cannot be reimbursed;
○ purchase of a primary residence;
○ payment of post-secondary education expenses for the next year;
○ to prevent eviction or foreclosure on your home.

Some plans will allow hardship withdrawals for other reasons, though various withholding taxes and penalties apply. It is also possible to take a loan from the 401(k) account and repay it over a fixed time with interest at an agreed rate, which is deducted via the payroll. There are no penalties or withholding taxes provided the loan is repaid on time. There is no current plan to allow withdrawals and loans from stakeholder pensions, though there has been a proposal to allow mature students to take out a loan against their pension fund to help pay for further education.

Contributors to 401(k) plans are kept up to date on an hourly basis, if they so wish. Many investment houses send out statements every three months with detailed information on the state of the account. Those who wish to access their details on a daily basis, can have access to their account details via the Internet or an automated telephone service with a dedicated free phone number. Some plans also allow transactions to be made via the Internet or automated services. For those who want human contact, representatives from the investment houses are available virtually seven days a week. Many of those providers in the UK who will be offering stakeholder pensions are also investing heavily in information systems and will also be able to offer personalised access to stakeholder pension plans, mirroring developments in the USA.

Retirement options [8.12]

When contributors to 401(k) plans retire they have three options:

◯ they can leave their money in the employer sponsored plan;
◯ they can move their money into a rollover IRA or purchase an income annuity; or
◯ withdraw the money in cash.

Although on the face of it these options look broadly similar to the options available to people who retire with a stakeholder pension, there are differences. In the first option, if the money is left with the employer, it must be taken out by the time the employee reaches 70½ under a 401(k) plan (as opposed to 75 under a stakeholder plan). In the UK, those with a stakeholder pension will have to purchase an annuity with the monies remaining if they choose to take the maximum 25% tax free cash sum. There is no option to transfer the money to an ISA. On the other hand, in the USA there are stiff tax penalties via withholding, state and local taxes for taking money out of a 401(k) plan as cash on that portion of the plan that could have been rolled over into an IRA.

These plans (and other savings vehicles) have been a success in the USA with nearly half of retirement income now deriving from capital based funds. In 1998, figures show that 70% of companies with 100 – 499 employees sponsored a 401(k) plan, an almost 100% increase on 1994 figures. It will be interesting to note whether stakeholder can match this level of market penetration in the UK.

Chile [8.13]

Historically, Chile has led pension reform in South America. It was the first country in the western hemisphere to follow the example of Bismarck's Prussia and introduce a PAYG social security system. This was replaced in 1980 with the introduction of a privately administered national system of Pension Savings Accounts (PSA). This radical approach was introduced under the military regime (when it could be argued that such a step was easier to take than with a democratically elected government for whom pensions would have been a very political issue). However, other South American countries have followed suit during the 1990s.

Key features [8.14]

By removing pensions from the government's control, an individual's future retirement income depends on investment returns on the amount invested. There is a welfare pension for those who are in extreme poverty at retirement. Saving is compulsory, with the employer depositing 10% of the employee's earnings each month in his individual PSA. This percentage of earnings was calculated on a 4% average net yield during a worker's life, allowing him theoretically to retire on 70% of salary. Workers may also contribute up to an additional 10% of salary each month from their gross income. This element of compulsion is missing from the proposals for UK stakeholder pensions, as it was felt that this would lead to claims of government intervention in people's financial affairs. The total amount that a Chilean worker can contribute to his PSA does not increase with age as with British personal pension allowances.

The PSAs are managed by regulated investment companies, though there are no minimum standards imposed for charges. Instead, competition between the investment companies means that they try to achieve higher investment returns, better customer service and lower charges than their competitors. Insurance against premature death and disability is provided by the investment companies via group policies from private life insurance companies. This is subject to an additional worker contribution of 3% of his salary, including the commission for the investment company. This approach differs from stakeholder pension provisions, which allow 10% of the pension contribution, rather than earnings, to benefit from tax relief for life assurance premiums for contracts taken out after April 2001.

On retirement, at 65 for men and 60 for women, an employee can either purchase an annuity from any private insurance company, indexed to inflation plus survivors' benefits for the employee's dependants or can leave the funds in his PSA and make programmed withdrawals equal to 70% of his final salary. If the employee dies, the remaining funds in his account form part of his estate. This is not the case in the UK.

The new pension system in Chile has given Chileans a personal stake in the economy via the private pension funds who own stocks in all the biggest Chilean companies. They are able to monitor the position of their PSA via workplace computers and quarterly statements. For many, their PSA is their main asset. In time, stakeholder pensions could also become a significant asset for middle income earners in the UK.

Australia [8.15]

The Australian approach to dealing with the burden of pensions has been to introduce compulsory contributions from employers. This approach has ensured that it was not necessary to raise taxes to deal with the familiar problems of an ageing population supported by a declining number of workers. By making employer contributions compulsory, this avoided the need for a democratically elected government taking the unpopular step of imposing compulsory contributions on employees.

Employer Contributions [8.16]

The employer contribution is currently 7% of an employee's salary, rising to 9% by 2002/03. Employers are required to contribute this to an employee pension scheme or a superannuation guarantee charge (SGC) is levied. There is a powerful incentive to avoid the charge, as 'voluntary' contributions are tax deductible, whilst the SGC is not. In addition, employers subject to the SGC have to pay administration fees and interest on arrears. The only exemptions from employer contributions are if the employer has staff:

O   under 18 or over 70;
O   working less than 30 hours a week; or
O   on very low levels of income.

The lack of parity for part-time workers contrasts with UK and European legislation that requires pro-rata pension and other benefits for part-time workers.

Self Employed [8.17]

Self employed people can contribute to a pension scheme on a voluntary basis and claim a tax deduction up to about £1,250, though they obviously do not benefit from employer contributions. There are tax concessions for contributions to a pension on behalf of one's spouse if he or she is on a very low income. This contrasts with the situation for stakeholder pensions where the self employed will receive the same basic rate tax relief as employees and those out of the workplace.

Concerns [8.18]

It is felt by some commentators on Australian pensions, that the maximum level of compulsory contributions, which will reach 9% in 2001 and remain at that level thereafter, is not sufficient to maintain an adequate level of retirement income. Some proposals suggest compulsory contributions of at least 18% of income.

There is also concern in Australia that employees do not choose their own pension scheme. This is decided by agreement between the unions and the employer, though in many instances the majority of employees may not be union members. Under the employer access provisions for UK stakeholder pensions, it is the employer who will make the decision on which scheme to designate, after consultation with the workforce. Where an employee disagrees with the choice of designated scheme, he can take out his own stakeholder pension, though the employer is under no obligation to deduct contributions from the payroll for any scheme other than his designated stakeholder scheme.

Members of Australian pension schemes are rarely directly represented on trustee boards, as the legislation provides for the appointment, rather than election of employee representatives. In many cases these tend to be union officials representing the employees, rather than directly elected members of the pension scheme. This makes it difficult for scheme members to become involved in the management of the scheme. In the UK, it was decided for stakeholder pensions that Member Nominated Trustees (MNTs) would not be compulsory for stakeholder schemes as it would be too difficult to administer the voting procedures for a newly established scheme with a scattered membership. This is likely to be revisited at a later date.

Market Polarisation [8.19]

The compulsion element of Australian pensions has led to a polarisation of the market, with four main providers dominating the scene. As pension scheme contributions are transferred to the scheme chosen by agreement between the union and the employer, with no input from employees, there is little pressure for schemes to perform well. If the choice of scheme were left to the members, with provision to switch funds from an under performing scheme, the competition element would return to the market and encourage better performances. There is legislation proposed to give employees a limited choice between four schemes, or unlimited choice, though in essence this would just push the business back to the main providers on the market.

This scenario of a few providers (maybe 6 or 7) dominating the market is likely to develop in the UK after stakeholder pensions have been in operation for several years and funds have accumulated. Although the maximum 1% annual charge for stakeholder pensions appears to be a very low margin within which funds must operate, as funds accumulate the 1% charge will increase in value year on year. It is at this point that large providers will move in and 'cherry pick' the most valuable funds, building them up to reach a viable mass.

The Effect of Stakeholder Pensions [8.20]

Funded Pension Provision

Stakeholder pensions will have an effect on funded pension provision, including personal pensions, group personal pension plans, occupational pension schemes and FSAVC contracts. If their introduction proves successful, they will also reduce the percentage of the population that has to rely on state pension provision. They will introduce a new dimension into the decision making process for employers, employees, the self employed and those outside the workplace who are considering their pension provision.

Charging Regimes [8.21]

Personal pensions, group personal pension plans and providers offering FSAVC contracts must rethink their levels of charges in the light of the 1% maximum annual charge that can be levied on the value of the stakeholder pension fund. Under current charging structures, there is an initial management charge that can typically be as high as 5.5% and an annual administration charge of around 1–2%. Plans based on smaller contributions may find charges exceed these levels. Customers who are considering their options for a pension plan will not be attracted to such high charges when stakeholder pensions will be offered with annual charges of 0.7% –1%. This has to be good news for consumers and will force personal pensions and group personal pension plans to be more competitive and to justify their level of charges with tailored services or product features.

The End of Defined Benefit Schemes? [8.22]

There has been comment that stakeholder schemes could signal the end of defined benefit schemes as some companies, looking at ways to reduce their costs, could view stakeholder as an ideal vehicle for providing access to retirement provision without the expense of a DB scheme. For those companies who had been considering moving out of a DB scheme, or no longer offering DB membership to new employees and moving to a DC scheme, designating a stakeholder scheme would be a simple solution. However, a significant number of companies will probably continue with their DB scheme, perhaps using the stakeholder scheme for new employees, seasonal and contract workers. Membership of the DB scheme could, following a transition period, become a perk for those employees who remain with the company for a set length of time e.g. 5 years.

It is likely that contract based stakeholder schemes will offer cost savings over occupational stakeholder schemes as they will be able to achieve greater economies of scale. They will also have the infrastructure to offer frequent communications and updates via the Internet to their members. More traditional trust based occupational schemes will need to update their systems in order to meet member demand for more information on the performance of their funds.

AVCs [8.23]

AVC providers will face increasing competition with the introduction of stakeholder pensions and the impact will be particularly sharp in the area of freestanding additional contribution plans (FSAVCs). They will then have to reduce their charges, or advisers will find themselves unable to recommend them when looking at other products in the market place for scheme members. For those scheme members who can profit from the concurrency rules for schemes that have opted into the new DC regime, an FSAVC contract will no longer look attractive.

Members of occupational DC schemes that have opted into the new DC tax regime will be able to take out a stakeholder pension and pay in their current FSAVC contributions. This will of course be subject to the personal pension age and earnings related limits. The older the member, the more valuable this concurrency option will be. At the top end of the personal pension limits he will be able to contribute a total of 40% of salary, including employer contributions at age 61 and above, as opposed to a maximum of 15% of salary excluding employer contributions as a member of an occupational scheme.

Stakeholder Pensions and Other Savings Vehicles [8.24]

Although stakeholder pensions are primarily designed to provide income in retirement, particularly for people on moderate incomes, they will take their place among an increasingly crowded long term savings market. The alternatives that some individuals may consider will include ISAs, Unit Trusts, Investment Trusts, life assurance plans and residential property.

ISAs [8.25]

These are subject to cash limits on the level of annual investment permitted, and contributions must be made from taxed income. Nevertheless, they offer tax free growth on accumulated contributions and benefits may be taken with no further tax payable. While their overall tax status is less efficient than stakeholder pensions, they do offer several advantages to long term savers.

The time at which benefits may be withdrawn is more flexible than for pensions of any description. Furthermore, benefits can be taken wholly in cash. These factors may be attractive to long term savers who are wary of having savings tied up until an age when a pension may be payable. There may also be a strong appeal to savers who intend to use their accumulated savings to provide income in retirement but prefer to retain control over these assets. However, they may wish to avoid being restricted to taking only a quarter of their funds in cash and the remainder being used for an annuity purchase. They may also want to derive income from their savings whilst also retaining the ability for their dependants ultimately to inherit the underlying assets.

Unit Trusts [8.26]

Similar arguments to those in favour of ISAs may motivate a number of savers to prefer regular investment in Unit Trusts. Although the degree of tax shelter is less, accumulated savings may grow free of capital gains tax. The range of investment choice is very wide, and although this may add to the appeal for some savers, the additional risks and costs may make this less attractive for others. Nevertheless, this savings route offers the advantage of potential income provision without encashment. Progressive encashment of units within annual capital gains tax allowances can also provide an income to unit holders with no further tax to pay.

Investment Trusts [8.27]

The degree of tax shelter is also lower with this form of investment, however many Investment Trusts now offer considerable flexibility in the timing and amounts of contributions. They can also be placed within an ISA 'wrapper' to obtain favourable tax treatment. Although less well known than Unit Trusts, they typically offer a similar breadth of investment options with lower charges. They can also be used to provide income directly.

Life Assurance [8.28]

Although the charges on life policies can be higher than for other forms of regular saving, and there is tax levied on the underlying funds, these savings vehicles may still have an attraction to long term savers. The principal advantages might be the high level of life cover that could benefit dependants, the ability to advance life cover payouts via critical illness cover and the availability of tax free cash. On the other hand, these vehicles are still relatively inflexible and can penalise those who find keeping up regular contributions difficult.

Residential Property [8.29]

A more recent phenomenon, particularly in university towns and the South East, has been the growth in the numbers of people exploiting more readily available 'buy-to-let' mortgage finance. The rationale for many is that a relatively small capital investment combined with borrowing that, with adequate rental income, may be better than self-funding, will ultimately produce an asset capable of providing either continuing rental income equivalent to a pension or a source of capital on sale.

While none of these savings alternatives will attract the level of tax reliefs available via a pension, and none is likely to benefit from any degree of employer contribution, they all offer certain advantages. The principal benefits that cannot be duplicated by stakeholder, or any other form of pension, are in the control over timing of enjoyment of the results of the savings made and the control over the underlying assets. While these may only represent minority choices in the long run, they illustrate the degree to which stakeholder pensions will be launched into a competitive long term savings market.

Appendix 1

Welfare Reform and Pensions Act 1999

This Appendix contains *ss 1–51* and *Schedule 1* of the *Welfare Reform and Pensions Act 1999* which are relevant to stakeholder pension schemes.

CHAPTER II
SHARING OF STATE SCHEME RIGHTS

SCHEDULES

Welfare Reform and Pensions Act 1999

1999 Chapter 30

An Act to make provision about pensions and social security; to make provision for reducing under-occupation of dwellings by housing benefit claimants; to authorise certain expenditure by the Secretary of State having responsibility for social security; and for connected purposes. [11th November 1999]

B E IT ENACTED by the Queen's most Excellent Majesty, by and with the advice and consent of the Lords Spiritual and Temporal, and Commons, in this present Parliament assembled, and by the authority of the same, as follows:—

PART I
STAKEHOLDER PENSION SCHEMES

1.—(1) A pension scheme is a stakeholder pension scheme for the purposes of this Part if it is registered as such a scheme under section 2 and each of the following is fulfilled, namely—

    (a) the conditions set out in subsections (2) to (9); and

    (b) such other conditions as may be prescribed.

(2) The first condition is that the scheme is established under a trust or in such other way as may be prescribed.

(3) The second condition is that the provisions made by the instruments establishing the scheme comply with such requirements as may be prescribed.

(4) The third condition is that, subject to such exceptions as may be prescribed, the benefits provided by the scheme are money purchase benefits within the meaning given by section 181 of the Pension Schemes Act 1993 ("the 1993 Act").

(5) The fourth condition is that the scheme complies with such requirements as may be prescribed as regards the extent to which, and the circumstances in which—

    (a) any payment made to the scheme by or on behalf of a member of the scheme,

(b) any income or capital gain arising from the investment of such a payment, or

(c) the value of rights under the scheme,

may be used to defray the administrative expenses of the scheme, to pay commission or in any other way which does not result in the provision of benefits for or in respect of members.

(6) The fifth condition is that the scheme complies with such of the requirements of regulations under section 113 of the 1993 Act (disclosure of information about schemes to members etc.) as are applicable to it.

(7) The sixth condition is that, subject to such minimum contribution levels and other restrictions as may be prescribed, members of the scheme may make such contributions to the scheme as they think appropriate.

(8) The seventh condition is that, except in so far as is necessary to ensure that the scheme has tax-exemption or tax-approval (within the meaning of the 1993 Act), the scheme accepts transfer payments in respect of members' rights under—

(a) other pension schemes;

(b) contracts and schemes approved under Chapter III of Part XIV of the Income and Corporation Taxes Act 1988 (retirement annuity contracts);

(c) annuities and insurance policies purchased or transferred for the purpose of giving effect to rights under pension schemes; and

(d) annuities purchased or entered into for the purpose of discharging liability in respect of pension credits under section 29(1)(b) or under corresponding Northern Ireland legislation.

(9) The eighth condition is that the scheme has such exemption or approval as is mentioned in subsection (8).

2.—(1) The Occupational Pensions Regulatory Authority ("the Authority") shall keep a register of stakeholder pension schemes.

(2) Subject to subsection (3), the Authority shall register a pension scheme under this section if the trustees of the scheme, or any person or persons prescribed in relation to the scheme—

(a) make an application for the purpose and pay such fee as the Authority may determine; and

(b) declare that each of the following is fulfilled in relation to the scheme, namely—

(i)   the conditions set out in subsections (2) to (9) of section 1; and

(ii)   such other conditions as may be prescribed under subsection (1) of that section.

(3)   Where the Authority are satisfied on reasonable grounds that any of those conditions is not fulfilled in relation to a pension scheme, the Authority may—

(a)   refuse to register the scheme; or

(b)   where the scheme is registered under this section, remove it from the register.

(4)   Section 3 (prohibition orders) and section 10 (civil penalties) of the Pensions Act 1995 ("the 1995 Act") apply to any trustee of a pension scheme which is or has been registered under this section, and section 10 of that Act applies to any person prescribed in relation to such a scheme, if—

(a)   he fails to take all such steps as are reasonable to secure that each of those conditions is fulfilled in relation to the scheme or (as the case may be) while the scheme was so registered he failed to take all such steps as were reasonable to secure that each of those conditions was so fulfilled; or

(b)   where the scheme was registered on his application, any of those conditions was not fulfilled in relation to the scheme at the time of the application.

(5)   Any person who, in applying for registration of a pension scheme under this section, knowingly or recklessly provides the Authority with information which is false or misleading in a material particular shall be liable—

(a)   on summary conviction, to a fine not exceeding the statutory maximum;

(b)   on conviction on indictment, to imprisonment or a fine or both.

(6)   Section 115 of the 1995 Act (offences by bodies corporate or Scottish partnerships) applies in relation to an offence under subsection (5) as it applies in relation to an offence under Part I of that Act.

(7)   The Secretary of State may by regulations make provision—

(a)   for the register, or extracts from the register, or for copies of the register or of extracts from the register, to be open to inspection by, and

(b)   for copies of the register, or of extracts from it, to be supplied to, such persons, in such manner, at such times, on payment of such fees, and subject to such other terms and conditions, as may be prescribed.

3.—(1) Except in so far as regulations otherwise provide, it shall be the duty of an employer of relevant employees to comply with the requirements set out below.

(2) The first requirement is that the employer shall ensure that at all times there is at least one scheme designated by him for the purposes of this subsection which is registered under section 2 and offers membership to all his relevant employees (whether or not any other scheme registered under that section which does not offer membership to all those employees is for the time being designated by him for those purposes).

Before designating a scheme for the purposes of this subsection the employer shall consult with his relevant employees and any organisations representing them.

(3) The second requirement is that the employer shall supply his relevant employees with—
    (a) the name and address of the designated scheme or, as the case may be, of each of the designated schemes; and
    (b) such other information as may be prescribed.

(4) The third requirement is that the employer shall allow representatives of the designated scheme or schemes reasonable access to his relevant employees for the purpose of supplying them with information about the scheme or schemes.

(5) The fourth requirement is that, subject to such exceptions and qualifications as may be prescribed, the employer shall, if he is requested to do so by a relevant employee of his who is a member of a qualifying scheme—
    (a) deduct the employee's contributions to the scheme from his remuneration; and
    (b) pay them to the trustees or managers of the scheme or, if regulations so provide, to a prescribed person.

(6) The fifth requirement is that the employer shall, if any scheme designated by him for the purposes of subsection (2) ceases to be registered under section 2, withdraw his designation of the scheme (but this requirement is not to be taken as implying that he cannot withdraw his designation of a scheme in other circumstances).

(7)   Section 10 of the 1995 Act (civil penalties) applies to an employer who fails to comply with any of the requirements set out above.

(8)   An employer is not, whether before designating a scheme for the purposes of subsection (2) or at any time while a scheme is designated by him for those purposes, under any duty—

    (a)   to make any enquiries, or act on any information, about the scheme for any purpose not connected with—

        (i)   ascertaining whether the scheme is for the time being registered under section 2,

        (ii)   ascertaining the persons to whom it offers membership, or

        (iii)   enabling him to comply with subsection (3), or

    (b)   in particular, to investigate or monitor, or make any judgment as to, the past, present or future performance of the scheme.

(9)   In this section—

"employer" means any employer, whether or not resident or incorporated in any part of the United Kingdom;

"qualifying scheme", in relation to an employer, means—

        (a)   the designated scheme or one of the designated schemes; or

        (b)   if regulations so provide, any other stakeholder pension scheme;

"relevant employees", in relation to an employer, means all employees of his employed in Great Britain and also, in the case of an employer resident or incorporated in any part of Great Britain, all employees of his employed outside the United Kingdom, but with the exception, in the case of any employer, of any employees of his—

        (a)   whose employment qualifies them for membership of an occupational pension scheme of the employer;

        (b)   whose earnings fall below the lower earnings limit as defined in section 181 of the 1993 Act; or

        (c)   who are of such other description as may be prescribed.

4.—(1)   Any person appearing to the Authority to be a person who holds, or is likely to hold, information which is relevant to the issue whether an employer is complying, or has complied, with the requirements under—

    (a)   section 3, or

    (b)   corresponding Northern Ireland legislation,

must, if required to do so by the Authority by notice in writing, produce any document which is so relevant.

(2)   To comply with subsection (1) the document must be produced in such a manner, at such a place and within such a period as may be specified in the notice.

(3)   Section 100 of the 1995 Act shall have effect as if references to section 98(1) or 99(1)(b) of that Act included references to subsection (1) or section 5(1)(b).

(4)   Sections 101 to 103 of that Act shall have effect as if references which are or include references to section 98 or 99 of that Act included references to this section or section 5.

(5)   In this section and section 5 "document" includes information recorded in any form, and any reference to production of a document, in relation to information recorded otherwise than in legible form, is to producing a copy of the information in legible form.

5.—(1) An inspector may, for the purposes of investigating whether an employer is complying, or has complied, with the requirements under section 3 or corresponding Northern Ireland legislation, at any reasonable time enter premises liable to inspection and, while there—

(a)   may make such examination and inquiry as may be necessary for such purposes,

(b)   may require any person on the premises to produce, or secure the production of, any document relevant to compliance with those requirements for his inspection, and

(c)   may, as to any matter relevant to compliance with those requirements, examine, or require to be examined, either alone or in the presence of another person, any person on the premises whom he has reasonable cause to believe to be able to give information relevant to that matter.

(2)   Premises are liable to inspection for the purposes of this section if the inspector has reasonable grounds to believe that—

(a)   employees of the employer are employed there,

(b)   documents relevant to the administration of the employer's business are being kept there, or

(c)   the administration of the employer's business, or work connected with that administration, is being carried out there,

unless the premises are a private dwelling-house not used by, or by permission of, the occupier for the purposes of a trade or business.

(3)   An inspector applying for admission to any premises for the purposes of this section must, if so required, produce his certificate of appointment.

(4)   In this section "inspector" means a person appointed by the Authority as an inspector.

6.—(1)   Sections 46 and 102 of the Employment Rights Act 1996 (occupational pension scheme trustees: protection from unfair dismissal and other detriment) shall apply in relation to an employee who is (or is a director of a company which is) a trustee of a scheme designated by his employer under section 3(2) as they apply in relation to an employee who is (or is a director of a company which is) a trustee of a relevant occupational pension scheme which relates to his employment.

(2)   Section 58 of that Act (occupational pension scheme trustees: time off) shall apply to the employer in relation to a designated scheme as it applies to the employer in relation to a relevant occupational pension scheme.

(3)   Schedule 1 (application of the 1993 and 1995 Acts to registered schemes) shall have effect.

(4)   In this section "relevant occupational pension scheme" has the meaning given by section 46 of the Employment Rights Act 1996.

7.—(1)   An order under section 42B(2) of the 1993 Act (determination and alteration of reduced rates of Class 1 contributions, and rebates, for members of money purchase contracted-out schemes) may specify different percentages in respect of earners by reference to whether the money purchase contracted-out scheme of which the earner is a member is or is not for the time being registered under section 2.

(2)   An order under section 45A(2) of that Act (determination and alteration of minimum contributions to be paid to appropriate personal pension schemes) may—
  (a) specify different percentages in respect of earners by reference to whether the appropriate personal pension scheme of which the earner is a member is or is not for the time being registered under section 2; and
  (b) specify different percentages in respect of earners by reference to the time when the earner first became a member of the scheme.

(3)   This section is without prejudice to section 182 of that Act (orders and regulations: general provisions).

8.—(1)   In this Part—
"the 1993 Act" means the Pension Schemes Act 1993;
"the 1995 Act" means the Pensions Act 1995;
"the Authority" means the Occupational Pensions Regulatory Authority;
"designated scheme", in relation to an employer, means a scheme designated by him for the purposes of section 3(2);
"occupational pension scheme" and "personal pension scheme" have the meanings given by section 1 of the 1993 Act;
"pension scheme" means an occupational pension scheme or a personal pension scheme;
"prescribed" means prescribed by regulations made by the Secretary of State;
"stakeholder pension scheme" shall be construed in accordance with section 1.

(2)   The Secretary of State may by regulations make provision for a stakeholder pension scheme which—
    (a)   is of a prescribed description, and
    (b)   would (apart from the regulations) be an occupational pension scheme,
to be treated for all purposes, or for such purposes as may be prescribed, as if it were a personal pension scheme and not an occupational pension scheme.

(3)   This Part applies to a pension scheme managed by or on behalf of the Crown as it applies to other pension schemes; and, accordingly, references in this Part to a person in his capacity as a trustee or manager of, or person prescribed in relation to, a pension scheme include the Crown, or a person acting on behalf of the Crown, in that capacity.

(4)   This Part applies to persons employed by or under the Crown in like manner as if such persons were employed by a private person; and references in this Part to a person in his capacity as an employer include the Crown, or a person acting on behalf of the Crown, in that capacity.

(5)   Subsections (3) and (4) do not apply to any provision of this Part under or by virtue of which a person may be prosecuted for an offence; but such a provision applies to persons in the public service of the Crown as it applies to other persons.

(6)   Nothing in this Part applies to Her Majesty in Her private capacity (within the meaning of the Crown Proceedings Act 1947).

PART II

PENSIONS: GENERAL

Payments by employers to pension schemes

9. In Part VI of the Pension Schemes Act 1993 (further requirements for protection of scheme members), after section 111 there shall be inserted—

"Monitoring of employers' payments to personal pension schemes

111A.—(1)   This section applies where—
    (a) an employee is a member of a personal pension scheme; and
    (b) direct payment arrangements exist between the employee and his employer.

(2) In this section "direct payment arrangements" means arrangements under which contributions fall to be paid by or on behalf of the employer towards the scheme—
    (a) on the employer's own account (but in respect of the employee); or
    (b) on behalf of the employee out of deductions from the employee's earnings.

(3) The employer must secure that there is prepared, maintained and from time to time revised a record of the direct payment arrangements which complies with subsection (4).

(4)   The record must—
    (a) show the rates and due dates of contributions payable under the direct payment arrangements, and
    (b) satisfy prescribed requirements.

(5)   The employer must, within the prescribed period after the preparation or any revision of the record, send a copy of the record or (as the case may be) of the revised record to the trustees or managers of the scheme.

(6) Except in prescribed circumstances, the trustees or managers of the scheme must, where any contribution shown by the record to be payable under the direct payment arrangements has not been paid on

or before its due date, give notice of that fact, within the prescribed period, to the Regulatory Authority and the employee.

(7)   The trustees or managers of the scheme must before the end of prescribed intervals send the employee a statement setting out the amounts and dates of the payments made under the direct payment arrangements during a prescribed period.

(8)   If—
    (a) the employer fails to take all such steps as are reasonable to secure compliance with subsection (3) or (5), or
    (b) a contribution payable under the direct payment arrangements is not paid to the trustees or managers of the scheme on or before its due date,

section 10 of the Pensions Act 1995 (power of the Regulatory Authority to impose civil penalties) applies to the employer.

(9)   If subsection (6) or (7) is not complied with, section 10 of the Pensions Act 1995 applies to any trustee or manager of the scheme who has failed to take all such steps as are reasonable to secure compliance.

(10)   If—
    (a) subsection (6) or (7) is not complied with, and
    (b) the scheme—
        (i)   is established under a trust, and
        (ii) is or has been registered under section 2 of the Welfare Reform and Pensions Act 1999 (stakeholder schemes),

section 3 of the Pensions Act 1995 (power of the Regulatory Authority to remove trustees) applies to any trustee of the scheme who has failed to take all such steps as are reasonable to secure compliance.

(11)   A person shall not be required by virtue of subsection (8)(b) above to pay a penalty under section 10 of the Pensions Act 1995 in respect of a failure if in respect of that failure he has been—

(a) required to pay a penalty under that section by virtue of section 3(7) of the Welfare Reform and Pensions Act 1999 (failures in respect of stakeholder pensions), or

(b) convicted of an offence under subsection (12) below.

(12)   A person is guilty of an offence if he is knowingly concerned in the fraudulent evasion of the direct payment arrangements so far as they are arrangements for the payment by him or any other person of any such contribution towards the scheme as is mentioned in subsection (2)(b).

(13)   A person guilty of an offence under subsection (12) is liable—

(a) on summary conviction, to a fine not exceeding the statutory maximum; and

(b) on conviction on indictment, to imprisonment for a term not exceeding seven years or a fine or both.

(14)   No prosecution shall be brought against the Crown for an offence under subsection (12), but that subsection applies to persons in the public service of the Crown as to other persons.

(15)   In this section "due date", in relation to a contribution payable under the direct payment arrangements, means—

(a) if the contribution falls to be paid on the employer's own account, the latest day under the arrangements for paying it;

(b) if the contribution falls to be paid on behalf of the employee, the last day of a prescribed period.

(16)   Regulations may provide for this section to apply with such modifications as may be prescribed in a case where—

(a) the direct payment arrangements give effect to a requirement arising under subsection (5) of section 3 of the Welfare Reform and Pensions Act 1999 (deduction and payment of employee's contributions to stakeholder scheme), and

(b) in accordance with regulations under that subsection, that requirement is for the employer to pay contributions to a person prescribed by such regulations (instead of to the trustees or managers of the scheme).

(17) Nothing in this section shall be taken as varying the provisions of the direct payment arrangements or as affecting their enforceability.

Obtaining information for purposes of section 111A and corresponding Northern Ireland legislation

111B.—(1) Any person appearing to the Regulatory Authority to be a person who holds, or is likely to hold, information which is relevant to the issue—

(a) whether any provision made by or under section 111A is being, or has been, complied with by an employer or the trustees or managers of a personal pension scheme,

(b) whether, in the case of any direct payment arrangements existing between an employee and his employer, there has been such a failure to pay a contribution as is mentioned in subsection (8)(b) of that section, or

(c) whether an offence has been committed under subsection (12) of that section in relation to any such arrangements,

must, if required to do so by the Regulatory Authority by notice in writing, produce any document which is so relevant.

(2) To comply with subsection (1) the document must be produced in such a manner, at such a place and within such a period as may be specified in the notice.

(3) An inspector may, for the purposes of investigating any of the matters set out in subsection (1)(a) to (c), at any reasonable time enter premises liable to inspection and, while there—

(a) may make such examination and inquiry as may be necessary for such purposes,

(b) may require any person on the premises to produce for his inspection, or secure the production for his inspection of, any document relevant—

(i) to compliance with any provision made by or under section 111A, or with the direct payment arrangements, or

(ii) to the issue whether an offence has been committed under subsection (12) of that section in relation to those arrangements, and

(c) may, as to any matter so relevant, examine, or require to be examined, either alone or in the presence of another person, any person on the premises whom he has reasonable cause to believe to be able to give information relevant to that matter.

(4) An inspector applying for admission to any premises in pursuance of subsection (3) must, if so required, produce his certificate of appointment.

(5) For the purposes of subsection (3) premises are liable to inspection if the inspector has reasonable grounds to believe that—

(a) employees of the employer are employed there,

(b) documents relevant to the administration of—

(i) the employer's business,

(ii) the direct payment arrangements, or

(iii) the scheme to which those arrangements relate, are kept there, or

(c) either of the following is being carried out there, namely—

(i) the administration of the employer's business, the arrangements or the scheme, or

(ii) work connected with the administration of the employer's business, the arrangements or the scheme,

unless the premises are a private dwelling-house not used by, or by permission of, the occupier for the purposes of a trade or business.

(6) Section 100 of the Pensions Act 1995 (warrants) shall have effect as if references to section 98 (1) or 99(1)(b) of that Act included references to subsection (1) or (3)(b).

(7) Sections 101 to 103 of that Act (penalties, savings and reports) shall have effect as if references which are or include references to section 98 or 99 of that Act included references to this section.

(8) In this section—

"direct payment arrangements" has the same meaning as in section 111A;

"document" includes information recorded in any form, and any reference to production of a document, in relation to information recorded otherwise than in legible form, is to producing a copy of the information in legible form;

"inspector" means a person appointed by the Regulatory Authority as an inspector.

(9)   References in this section to, or to any provision of, section 111A include references to corresponding provisions of Northern Ireland legislation; and in this section as it has effect in relation to those corresponding provisions, "employee" and "employer" have the meaning they have for the purposes of those provisions."

10.—(1)   For section 49(8) of the Pensions Act 1995 (offence where deduction from earnings not paid in timely fashion to occupational pension scheme) there shall be substituted—

"(8)   Where on making a payment of any earnings in respect of any employment there is deducted any amount corresponding to any contribution payable on behalf of an active member of an occupational pension scheme, the amount deducted is to be paid, within a prescribed period, to the trustees or managers of the scheme.

(9)   If in any case there is a failure to comply with subsection (8)—
    (a) section 10 applies to the employer; and
    (b) except in prescribed circumstances, the trustees or managers must give notice of the failure, within the prescribed period, to the Authority and the member.

(10)   If in any case subsection (9)(b) is not complied with—
    (a) section 3 applies to any trustee who has failed to take all such steps as are reasonable to secure compliance; and
    (b) section 10 applies to any trustee or manager who has failed to take all such steps.

(11)   If any person is knowingly concerned in the fraudulent evasion of the obligation imposed by subsection (8) in any case, he is guilty of an offence.

(12)   A person guilty of an offence under subsection (11) is liable—

    (a) on summary conviction, to a fine not exceeding the statutory maximum; and

    (b) on conviction on indictment, to imprisonment for a term not exceeding seven years or a fine or both.

(13)   A person shall not be required by virtue of subsection (9)(a) above to pay a penalty under section 10 in respect of a failure if in respect of that failure he has been—

    (a) required to pay a penalty under that section by virtue of section 3(7) of the Welfare Reform and Pensions Act 1999 (failures in respect of stakeholder pensions), or

    (b) convicted of an offence under subsection (11) above."

(2)   In section 88(3) of that Act (civil penalty where contributions by or on behalf of employer to occupational pension scheme not paid by due date), after "by or on behalf of the employer" there shall be inserted "on the employer's own account".

Pensions and bankruptcy

11.—(1)   Where a bankruptcy order is made against a person on a petition presented after the coming into force of this section, any rights of his under an approved pension arrangement are excluded from his estate.

(2)   In this section "approved pension arrangement" means—

    (a) an exempt approved scheme;

    (b) a relevant statutory scheme;

    (c) a retirement benefits scheme set up by a government outside the United Kingdom for the benefit, or primarily for the benefit, of its employees;

    (d) a retirement benefits scheme which is being considered for approval under Chapter I of Part XIV of the Taxes Act;

    (e) a contract or scheme which is approved under Chapter III of that Part (retirement annuities);

    (f) a personal pension scheme which is approved under Chapter IV of that Part;

    (g) an annuity purchased for the purpose of giving effect to rights under a scheme falling within any of paragraphs (a) to (c) and (f);

(h) any pension arrangements of any description which may be prescribed by regulations made by the Secretary of State.

(3) The reference in subsection (1) to rights under an approved pension arrangement does not include rights under a personal pension scheme approved under Chapter IV of Part XIV of the Taxes Act unless those rights arise by virtue of approved personal pension arrangements.

(4) Subsection (5) applies if—

(a) at the time when a bankruptcy order is made against a person a retirement benefits scheme is being considered for approval under Chapter I of Part XIV of the Taxes Act, and

(b) the decision of the Commissioners of Inland Revenue is that approval is not to be given to the scheme.

(5) Any rights of that person under the scheme shall (without any conveyance, assignment or transfer) vest in his trustee in bankruptcy, as part of his estate, immediately on—

(a) the Commissioners' decision being made, or

(b) (if later) the trustee's appointment taking effect or, in the case of the official receiver, his becoming trustee.

(6) Subsection (7) applies if, at any time after a bankruptcy order is made against a person, the Commissioners of Inland Revenue give notice—

(a) withdrawing their approval under Chapter I of Part XIV of the Taxes Act from a retirement benefits scheme, or

(b) withdrawing their approval under Chapter IV of that Part from a personal pension scheme or from any approved personal pension arrangements,

and the date specified as being that from which the approval is withdrawn ("the withdrawal date") is a date not later than that on which the bankruptcy order is made.

(7) Any rights of that person under the scheme or arising by virtue of the arrangements, and any rights of his under any related annuity, shall (without any conveyance, assignment or transfer) vest in his trustee in bankruptcy, as part of his estate, immediately on—

(a) the giving of the notice, or

(b) (if later) the trustee's appointment taking effect or, in the case of the official receiver, his becoming trustee.

(8) In subsection (7) "related annuity" means an annuity purchased on or after the withdrawal date for the purpose of giving effect to rights under the scheme or (as the case may be) to rights arising by virtue of the arrangements.

(9)   Where under subsection (5) or (7) any rights vest in a person's trustee in bankruptcy, the trustee's title to them has relation back to the commencement of the person's bankruptcy; but where any transaction is entered into by the trustees or managers of the scheme in question—

(a)   in good faith, and

(b)   without notice of the making of the decision mentioned in subsection (4)(b) or (as the case may be) the giving of the notice mentioned in subsection (6),

the trustee in bankruptcy is not in respect of that transaction entitled by virtue of this subsection to any remedy against them or any person whose title to any property derives from them.

(10)   Without prejudice to section 83, regulations under subsection (2)(h) may, in the case of any description of arrangements prescribed by the regulations, make provision corresponding to any provision made by subsections (4) to (9).

(11)   In this section—

(a)   "exempt approved scheme", "relevant statutory scheme" and "retirement benefits scheme" have the same meaning as in Chapter I of Part XIV of the Taxes Act;

(b)   "approved personal pension arrangements" and "personal pension scheme" have the same meaning as in Chapter IV of that Part;

(c)   "estate", in relation to a person against whom a bankruptcy order is made, means his estate for the purposes of Parts VIII to XI of the Insolvency Act 1986;

(d)   "the Taxes Act" means the Income and Corporation Taxes Act 1988.

(12)   For the purposes of this section a person shall be treated as having a right under an approved pension arrangement where—

(a)   he is entitled to a credit under section 29(1)(b) as against the person responsible for the arrangement (within the meaning of Chapter I of Part IV), and

(b)   the person so responsible has not discharged his liability in respect of the credit.

12.—(1)   The Secretary of State may by regulations make provision for or in connection with enabling rights of a person under an unapproved pension arrangement to be excluded, in the event of a bankruptcy order being made against that person, from his estate for the purposes of Parts VIII to XI of the Insolvency Act 1986.

(2)   Regulations under this section may, in particular, make provision—

(a) for rights under an unapproved pension arrangement to be excluded from a person's estate—

(i)   by an order made on his application by a prescribed court, or

(ii)   in accordance with a qualifying agreement made between him and his trustee in bankruptcy;

(b) for the court's decision whether to make such an order in relation to a person to be made by reference to—

(i)   future likely needs of him and his family, and

(ii)   whether any benefits (by way of a pension or otherwise) are likely to be received by virtue of rights of his under other pension arrangements and (if so) the extent to which they appear likely to be adequate for meeting any such needs;

(c) for the prescribed persons in the case of any pension arrangement to provide a person or his trustee in bankruptcy on request with information reasonably required by that person or trustee for or in connection with the making of such applications and agreements as are mentioned in paragraph (a).

(3)   In this section—

"prescribed" means prescribed by regulations under this section;

"qualifying agreement" means an agreement entered into in such circumstances, and satisfying such requirements, as may be prescribed;

"unapproved pension arrangement" means a pension arrangement which—

(a)   is not an approved pension arrangement within the meaning of section 11, and

(b)   is of a prescribed description.

(4)   For the purposes of this section a person shall be treated as having a right under an unapproved pension arrangement where—

(a) he is entitled to a credit under section 29(1)(b) as against the person responsible for the arrangement (within the meaning of Chapter I of Part IV), and

(b) the person so responsible has not discharged his liability in respect of the credit.

13.—(1)   This section shall have effect for the purposes of the application of sections 11 and 12 to Scotland.

(2) A reference to—

    (a) the making of a bankruptcy order against a person is a reference to the award of sequestration on his estate or the making of the appointment on his estate of a judicial factor under section 41 of the Solicitors (Scotland) Act 1980;

    (b) the estate of a person is a reference to his estate for the purposes of the Bankruptcy (Scotland) Act 1985 or of the Solicitors (Scotland) Act 1980, as the case may be;

    (c) assignment is a reference to assignation;

    (d) a person's trustee in bankruptcy is a reference to his permanent trustee or judicial factor, as the case may be;

    (e) the commencement of a person's bankruptcy is a reference to the date of sequestration (within the meaning of section 12(4) of the Bankruptcy (Scotland) Act 1985) or of the judicial factor's appointment taking effect, as the case may be.

(3) For paragraph (b) of each of subsections (5) and (7) of section 11 there shall be substituted—

    "(b) if later, the date of sequestration (within the meaning of section 12(4) of the Bankruptcy (Scotland) Act 1985) or of the judicial factor's appointment taking effect, as the case may be."

14.—(1) In the Pension Schemes Act 1993, after section 159 there shall be inserted—

"No forfeiture on bankruptcy of rights under personal pension schemes

159A.—(1) A person's rights under a personal pension scheme cannot be forfeited by reference to his bankruptcy.

(2) For the purposes of this section—

    (a) a person shall be treated as having a right under a personal pension scheme where—

        (i) he is entitled to a credit under section 29(1)(b) of the Welfare Reform and Pensions Act 1999 (sharing of rights on divorce etc.),

        (ii) he is so entitled as against the person responsible for the scheme (within the meaning of Chapter I of Part IV of that Act), and

        (iii) the person so responsible has not discharged his liability in respect of the credit; and

    (b) forfeiture shall be taken to include any manner of deprivation or suspension."

(2)   In section 159(6) of that Act (application of section 159 to Scotland), after "this section" there shall be inserted "and section 159A".

(3)   In section 92(2) of the Pensions Act 1995 (exceptions to the rule preventing forfeiture of rights under occupational pension schemes), paragraph (b) (which allows forfeiture of such rights by reference to a scheme member's bankruptcy) shall cease to have effect.

15.—For sections 342A to 342C of the Insolvency Act 1986 there shall be substituted—

"Recovery of excessive pension contributions

342A.—(1)   Where an individual who is adjudged bankrupt—

(a) has rights under an approved pension arrangement, or

(b) has excluded rights under an unapproved pension arrangement,

the trustee of the bankrupt's estate may apply to the court for an order under this section.

(2)   If the court is satisfied—

(a) that the rights under the arrangement are to any extent, and whether directly or indirectly, the fruits of relevant contributions, and

(b) that the making of any of the relevant contributions ("the excessive contributions") has unfairly prejudiced the individual's creditors,

the court may make such order as it thinks fit for restoring the position to what it would have been had the excessive contributions not been made.

(3)   Subsection (4) applies where the court is satisfied that the value of the rights under the arrangement is, as a result of rights of the individual under the arrangement or any other pension arrangement having at any time become subject to a debit under section 29(1)(a) of the Welfare Reform and Pensions Act 1999 (debits giving effect to pension-sharing), less than it would otherwise have been.

(4)   Where this subsection applies—

(a) any relevant contributions which were represented by the rights which became subject to the debit shall, for the purposes of subsection (2), be taken to be contributions of which the rights under the arrangement are the fruits, and

   (b) where the relevant contributions represented
         by the rights under the arrangement
         (including those so represented by virtue of
         paragraph (a)) are not all excessive
         contributions, relevant contributions which
         are represented by the rights under the
         arrangement otherwise than by virtue of
         paragraph (a) shall be treated as excessive
         contributions before any which are so
         represented by virtue of that paragraph.

   (5)   In subsections (2) to (4) "relevant contributions"
means contributions to the arrangement or any other
pension arrangement—
   (a) which the individual has at any time made on
         his own behalf, or
   (b) which have at any time been made on his
         behalf.

   (6)   The court shall, in determining whether it is
satisfied under subsection (2)(b), consider in
particular—
   (a) whether any of the contributions were made
         for the purpose of putting assets beyond the
         reach of the individual's creditors or any of them,
         and
   (b) whether the total amount of any
         contributions—
             (i) made by or on behalf of the individual
         to pension arrangements, and
             (ii) represented (whether directly or
         indirectly) by rights under approved pension
         arrangements or excluded rights under
         unapproved pension arrangements,
         is an amount which is excessive in view of the
         individual's circumstances when those
         contributions were made.

   (7)   For the purposes of this section and sections
342B and 342C ("the recovery provisions"), rights of
an individual under an unapproved pension
arrangement are excluded rights if they are rights which
are excluded from his estate by virtue of regulations
under section 12 of the Welfare Reform and Pensions
Act 1999.

(8) In the recovery provisions—
"approved pension arrangement" has the same meaning as in section 11 of the Welfare Reform and Pensions Act 1999;
"unapproved pension arrangement" has the same meaning as in section 12 of that Act.

Orders under
section 342A

342B.—(1) Without prejudice to the generality of section 342A(2), an order under section 342A may include provision—
(a) requiring the person responsible for the arrangement to pay an amount to the individual's trustee in bankruptcy,
(b) adjusting the liabilities of the arrangement in respect of the individual,
(c) adjusting any liabilities of the arrangement in respect of any other person that derive, directly or indirectly, from rights of the individual under the arrangement,
(d) for the recovery by the person responsible for the arrangement (whether by deduction from any amount which that person is ordered to pay or otherwise) of costs incurred by that person in complying in the bankrupt's case with any requirement under section 342C(1) or in giving effect to the order.

(2) In subsection (1), references to adjusting the liabilities of the arrangement in respect of a person include (in particular) reducing the amount of any benefit or future benefit to which that person is entitled under the arrangement.

(3) In subsection (1)(c), the reference to liabilities of the arrangement does not include liabilities in respect of a person which result from giving effect to an order or provision falling within section 28(1) of the Welfare Reform and Pensions Act 1999 (pension sharing orders and agreements).

(4) The maximum amount which the person responsible for an arrangement may be required to pay by an order under section 342A is the lesser of—
(a) the amount of the excessive contributions, and

(b) the value of the individual's rights under the arrangement (if the arrangement is an approved pension arrangement) or of his excluded rights under the arrangement (if the arrangement is an unapproved pension arrangement).

(5)   An order under section 342A which requires the person responsible for an arrangement to pay an amount ("the restoration amount") to the individual's trustee in bankruptcy must provide for the liabilities of the arrangement to be correspondingly reduced.

(6)   For the purposes of subsection (5), liabilities are correspondingly reduced if the difference between—
    (a) the amount of the liabilities immediately before the reduction, and
    (b) the amount of the liabilities immediately after the reduction,
is equal to the restoration amount.

(7)   An order under section 342A in respect of an arrangement—
    (a) shall be binding on the person responsible for the arrangement, and
    (b) overrides provisions of the arrangement to the extent that they conflict with the provisions of the order.

Orders under section 342A: supplementary

342C.—(1)   The person responsible for—
    (a) an approved pension arrangement under which a bankrupt has rights,
    (b) an unapproved pension arrangement under which a bankrupt has excluded rights, or
    (c) a pension arrangement under which a bankrupt has at any time had rights,
shall, on the bankrupt's trustee in bankruptcy making a written request, provide the trustee with such information about the arrangement and rights as the trustee may reasonably require for, or in connection with, the making of applications under section 342A.

(2)   Nothing in—
    (a) any provision of section 159 of the Pension Schemes Act 1993 or section 91 of the Pensions Act 1995

(which prevent assignment and the making of orders that restrain a person from receiving anything which he is prevented from assigning),

(b) any provision of any enactment (whether passed or made before or after the passing of the Welfare Reform and Pensions Act 1999) corresponding to any of the provisions mentioned in paragraph (a), or

(c) any provision of the arrangement in question corresponding to any of those provisions,

applies to a court exercising its powers under section 342A.

(3)   Where any sum is required by an order under section 342A to be paid to the trustee in bankruptcy, that sum shall be comprised in the bankrupt's estate.

(4)   Regulations may, for the purposes of the recovery provisions, make provision about the calculation and verification of—

(a) any such value as is mentioned in section 342B(4)(b);

(b) any such amounts as are mentioned in section 342B(6)(a) and (b).

(5)   The power conferred by subsection (4) includes power to provide for calculation or verification—

(a) in such manner as may, in the particular case, be approved by a prescribed person; or

(b) in accordance with guidance—

(i) from time to time prepared by a prescribed person, and

(ii) approved by the Secretary of State.

(6)   References in the recovery provisions to the person responsible for a pension arrangement are to—

(a) the trustees, managers or provider of the arrangement, or

(b) the person having functions in relation to the arrangement corresponding to those of a trustee, manager or provider.

(7)   In this section and sections 342A and 342B—

"prescribed" means prescribed by regulations;

"the recovery provisions" means this section and sections 342A and 342B;

"regulations" means regulations made by the Secretary of State.

(8)   Regulations under the recovery provisions may—
(a) make different provision for different cases;
(b) contain such incidental, supplemental and transitional provisions as appear to the Secretary of State necessary or expedient.

(9)   Regulations under the recovery provisions shall be made by statutory instrument subject to annulment in pursuance of a resolution of either House of Parliament."

16.—For sections 36A to 36C of the Bankruptcy (Scotland) Act 1985 there shall be substituted—

"Recovery of excessive pension contributions

36A.—(1)   Where a debtor's estate has been sequestrated and he—
(a) has rights under an approved pension arrangement, or
(b) has excluded rights under an unapproved pension arrangement,
the permanent trustee may apply to the court for an order under this section.

(2)   If the court is satisfied—
(a) that the rights under the arrangement are to any extent, and whether directly or indirectly, the fruits of relevant contributions, and
(b) that the making of any of the relevant contributions ("the excessive contributions") has unfairly prejudiced the debtor's creditors,
the court may make such order as it thinks fit for restoring the position to what it would have been had the excessive contributions not been made.

(3)   Subsection (4) applies where the court is satisfied that the value of the rights under the arrangement is, as a result of rights of the debtor under the arrangement or any other pension arrangement having at any time become subject to a debit under section 29(1)(a) of the Welfare Reform and Pensions Act 1999 (debits giving effect to pension-sharing), less than it would otherwise have been.

(4)   Where this subsection applies—

    (a) any relevant contributions which were represented by the rights which became subject to the debit shall, for the purposes of subsection (2), be taken to be contributions of which the rights under the arrangement are the fruits, and

    (b) where the relevant contributions represented by the rights under the arrangement (including those so represented by virtue of paragraph (a)) are not all excessive contributions, relevant contributions which are represented by the rights under the arrangement otherwise than by virtue of paragraph (a) shall be treated as excessive contributions before any which are so represented by virtue of that paragraph.

(5)   In subsections (2) to (4) "relevant contributions" means contributions to the arrangement or any other pension arrangement—

    (a) which the debtor has at any time made on his own behalf, or

    (b) which have at any time been made on his behalf.

(6)   The court shall, in determining whether it is satisfied under subsection (2)(b), consider in particular—

    (a) whether any of the contributions were made for the purpose of putting assets beyond the reach of the debtor's creditors or any of them, and

    (b) whether the total amount of any contributions—

        (i) made by or on behalf of the debtor to pension arrangements, and

        (ii) represented (whether directly or indirectly) by rights under approved pension arrangements or excluded rights under unapproved pensions arrangements,

    is an amount which is excessive in view of the debtor's circumstances when those contributions were made.

(7)   For the purposes of this section and sections 36B and 36C ("the recovery provisions"), rights of a debtor under an unapproved pension arrangement are excluded rights if they are rights which are excluded from his estate by virtue of regulations under section 12 of the Welfare Reform and Pensions Act 1999.

(8)   In the recovery provisions—
"approved pension arrangement" has the same meaning as in section 11 of the Welfare Reform and Pensions Act 1999;
"unapproved pension arrangement" has the same meaning as in section 12 of that Act.

Orders under
section 36A

36B.—(1) Without prejudice to the generality of section 36A(2) an order under section 36A may include provision—

(a) requiring the person responsible for the arrangement to pay an amount to the permanent trustee,

(b) adjusting the liabilities of the arrangement in respect of the debtor,

(c) adjusting any liabilities of the arrangement in respect of any other person that derive, directly or indirectly, from rights of the debtor under the arrangement,

(d) for the recovery by the person responsible for the arrangement (whether by deduction from any amount which that person is ordered to pay or otherwise) of costs incurred by that person in complying in the debtor's case with any requirement under section 36C(1) or in giving effect to the order.

(2)   In subsection (1), references to adjusting the liabilities of the arrangement in respect of a person include (in particular) reducing the amount of any benefit or future benefit to which that person is entitled under the arrangement.

(3)   In subsection (1)(c), the reference to liabilities of the arrangement does not include liabilities in respect of a person which result from giving effect to an order or provision falling within section 28(1) of the Welfare Reform and Pensions Act 1999 (pension sharing orders and agreements).

(4)   The maximum amount which the person responsible for an arrangement may be required to pay by an order under section 36A is the lesser of—

(a) the amount of the excessive contributions, and

(b) the value of the debtor's rights under the arrangement (if the arrangement is an approved pension arrangement) or of his excluded rights under the arrangement (if the arrangement is an unapproved pension arrangement).

(5)   An order under section 36A which requires the person responsible for an arrangement to pay an amount ("the restoration amount") to the permanent trustee must provide for the liabilities of the arrangement to be correspondingly reduced.

(6)   For the purposes of subsection (5), liabilities are correspondingly reduced if the difference between—

(a) the amount of the liabilities immediately before the reduction, and

(b) the amount of the liabilities immediately after the reduction,

is equal to the restoration amount.

(7)   An order under section 36A in respect of an arrangement—

(a) shall be binding on the person responsible for the arrangement; and

(b) overrides provisions of the arrangement to the extent that they conflict with the provisions of the order.

Orders under section 36A: supplementary

36C.—(1)   The person responsible for—

(a) an approved pension arrangement under which a debtor has rights,

(b) an unapproved pension arrangement under which a debtor has excluded rights, or

(c) a pension arrangement under which a debtor has at any time had rights,

shall, on the permanent trustee making a written request, provide the permanent trustee with such information about the arrangement and rights as the permanent trustee may reasonably require for, or in connection with, the making of applications under section 36A.

(2)   Nothing in—

(a) any provision of section 159 of the Pensions Schemes Act 1993 or section 91 of the Pensions Act 1995 (which prevent assignation and the making of orders that restrain a person from receiving anything which he is prevented from assigning),

(b) any provision of any enactment (whether passed or made before or after the passing of the Welfare Reform and Pensions Act 1999) corresponding to any of the provisions mentioned in paragraph (a), or

(c) any provision of the arrangement in question corresponding to any of those provisions,

applies to a court exercising its powers under section 36A.

(3)   Where any sum is required by an order under section 36A to be paid to the permanent trustee, that sum shall be comprised in the debtor's estate.

(4)   Regulations may, for the purposes of the recovery provisions, make provision about the calculation and verification of—

(a) any such value as is mentioned in section 36B(4)(b);

(b) any such amounts as are mentioned in section 36B(6)(a) and (b).

(5)   The power conferred by subsection (4) includes power to provide for calculation or verification—

(a) in such manner as may, in the particular case, be approved by a prescribed person; or

(b) in accordance with guidance—

(i) from time to time prepared by a prescribed person, and

(ii) approved by the Secretary of State.

(6)   References in the recovery provisions to the person responsible for a pension arrangement are to—

(a) the trustees, managers or provider of the arrangement, or

(b) the person having functions in relation to the arrangement corresponding to those of a trustee, manager or provider.

(7)   In this section and sections 36A and 36B—
"the recovery" provisions means this section and
sections 36A and 36B;
"regulations" means regulations made by the
Secretary of State.

(8)   Regulations under the recovery provisions may contain
such incidental, supplemental and transitional provisions as
appear to the Secretary of State necessary or expedient."

PART III
PENSIONS ON DIVORCE ETC.
Pension sharing orders

19. Schedule 3 (which amends the Matrimonial Causes Act 1973
for the purpose of enabling the court to make pension sharing orders
in connection with proceedings in England and Wales for divorce or
nullity of marriage, and for supplementary purposes) shall have effect.

20.—(1) The Family Law (Scotland) Act 1985 shall be amended as
follows.
(2)   In section 8(1) (orders for financial provision), after paragraph
(b) there shall be inserted—
"(baa) a pension sharing order."
(3)   In section 27 (interpretation), in subsection (1), there shall be
inserted at the appropriate place—
""pension sharing order" is an order which—
(a) provides that one party's—
(i) shareable rights under a specified pension
arrangement, or
(ii) shareable state scheme rights,
be subject to pension sharing for the benefit of the
other party, and
(b) specifies the percentage value, or the amount, to
be transferred;".

(4)   In that section, after subsection (1) there shall be inserted—
"(1A) In subsection (1), in the definition of "pension
sharing order"—
(a)   the reference to shareable rights under a
pension arrangement is to rights in relation to
which pension sharing is available under
Chapter I of Part IV of the Welfare Reform and
Pensions Act 1999, or under corresponding
Northern Ireland legislation, and

> (b) the reference to shareable state scheme rights is to rights in relation to which pension sharing is available under Chapter II of Part IV of the Welfare Reform and Pensions Act 1999, or under corresponding Northern Ireland legislation."

Sections 25B to 25D of the Matrimonial Causes Act 1973

21. Schedule 4 (which amends the sections about pensions inserted in the Matrimonial Causes Act 1973 by section 166 of the Pensions Act 1995) shall have effect.

22.—(1) Part III of the Matrimonial and Family Proceedings Act 1984 (financial relief in England and Wales after overseas divorce etc.) shall be amended as follows.

(2) In section 18 (matters to which the court is to have regard in exercising its powers to make orders for financial relief), after subsection (3) there shall be inserted—

> "(3A) The matters to which the court is to have regard under subsection (3) above—
>
> (a) so far as relating to paragraph (a) of section 25(2) of the 1973 Act, include any benefits under a pension arrangement which a party to the marriage has or is likely to have (whether or not in the foreseeable future), and
>
> (b) so far as relating to paragraph (h) of that provision, include any benefits under a pension arrangement which, by reason of the dissolution or annulment of the marriage, a party to the marriage will lose the chance of acquiring."

(3) In that section, at the end there shall be added—

> "(7) In this section—
>
> (a) "pension arrangement" has the meaning given by section 25D(3) of the 1973 Act, and
>
> (b) references to benefits under a pension arrangement include any benefits by way of pension, whether under a pension arrangement or not."

(4)   In section 21 (application of provisions of Part II of the Matrimonial Causes Act 1973), the existing provision shall become subsection (1) and, in that subsection, after paragraph (b) there shall be inserted—

> "(bd) section 25B(3) to (7B) (power, by financial provision order, to attach payments under a pension arrangement, or to require the exercise of a right of commutation under such an arrangement);
> (be)   section 25C (extension of lump sum powers in relation to death benefits under a pension arrangement);".

(5)   In that section, after subsection (1) there shall be inserted—

> "(2)   Subsection (1)(bd) and (be) above shall not apply where the court has jurisdiction to entertain an application for an order for financial relief by reason only of the situation in England or Wales of a dwelling-house which was a matrimonial home of the parties.

(3)   Section 25D(1) of the 1973 Act (effect of transfers on orders relating to rights under a pension arrangement) shall apply in relation to an order made under section 17 above by virtue of subsection (1)(bd) or (be) above as it applies in relation to an order made under section 23 of that Act by virtue of section 25B or 25C of the 1973 Act.

(4)   The Lord Chancellor may by regulations make for the purposes of this Part of this Act provision corresponding to any provision which may be made by him under subsections (2) to (2B) of section 25D of the 1973 Act.

(5)   Power to make regulations under this section shall be exercisable by statutory instrument which shall be subject to annulment in pursuance of a resolution of either House of Parliament."

Miscellaneous

23.—(1) The Secretary of State may by regulations—
(a) make provision imposing on the person responsible for a pension arrangement, or on the Secretary of State, requirements with respect to the supply of information relevant to any power with respect to—

      (i) financial relief under Part II of the Matrimonial Causes Act 1973 or Part III of the Matrimonial and Family Proceedings Act 1984 (England and Wales powers in relation to domestic and overseas divorce etc),

      (ii) financial provision under the Family Law (Scotland) Act 1985 or Part IV of the Matrimonial and Family Proceedings Act 1984 (corresponding Scottish powers), or

      (iii) financial relief under Part III of the Matrimonial Causes (Northern Ireland) Order 1978 or Part IV of the Matrimonial and Family Proceedings (Northern Ireland) Order 1989 (corresponding Northern Ireland powers);

(b)   make provision about calculation and verification in relation to the valuation of—

      (i)   benefits under a pension arrangement, or

      (ii)   shareable state scheme rights,

      for the purposes of regulations under paragraph (a)(i) or (iii);

(c)   make provision about calculation and verification in relation to—

      (i)   the valuation of shareable rights under a pension arrangement or shareable state scheme rights for the purposes of regulations under paragraph (a)(ii), so far as relating to the making of orders for financial provision (within the meaning of the Family Law (Scotland) Act 1985), or

      (ii) the valuation of benefits under a pension arrangement for the purposes of such regulations, so far as relating to the making of orders under section 12A of that Act;

(d)   make provision for the purpose of enabling the person responsible for a pension arrangement to recover prescribed charges in respect of providing information in accordance with regulations under paragraph (a).

(2)   Regulations under subsection (1)(b) or (c) may include provision for calculation or verification in accordance with guidance from time to time prepared by a person prescribed by the regulations.

(3)   Regulations under subsection (1)(d) may include provision for the application in prescribed circumstances, with or without modification, of any provision made by virtue of section 41(2).

(4) In subsection (1)—
- (a) the reference in paragraph (c)(i) to shareable rights under a pension arrangement is to rights in relation to which pension sharing is available under Chapter I of Part IV, or under corresponding Northern Ireland legislation, and
- (b) the references to shareable state scheme rights are to rights in relation to which pension sharing is available under Chapter II of Part IV, or under corresponding Northern Ireland legislation.

24. The Secretary of State may by regulations make provision for the purpose of enabling the person responsible for a pension arrangement to recover prescribed charges in respect of complying with—
- (a) an order under section 23 of the Matrimonial Causes Act 1973 (financial provision orders in connection with divorce etc), so far as it includes provision made by virtue of section 25B or 25C of that Act (powers to include provision about pensions),
- (b) an order under section 12A(2) or (3) of the Family Law (Scotland) Act 1985 (powers in relation to pensions lump sums when making a capital sum order), or
- (c) an order under Article 25 of the Matrimonial Causes (Northern Ireland) Order 1978, so far as it includes provision made by virtue of Article 27B or 27C of that Order (Northern Ireland powers corresponding to those mentioned in paragraph (a)).

25.—(1) If any amendment by the Family Law Act 1996 of Part II or IV of the Matrimonial Causes Act 1973 comes into force before the day on which any provision of this Part comes into force, the Lord Chancellor may by order make such consequential amendment of that provision as he thinks fit.

(2) No order under this section may be made unless a draft of the order has been laid before and approved by resolution of each House of Parliament.

26.—(1) In this Part—
"occupational pension scheme" has the same meaning as in the Pension Schemes Act 1993;

"pension arrangement" means
- (a) an occupational pension scheme,
- (b) a personal pension scheme,

> (c) a retirement annuity contract,
> (d) an annuity or insurance policy purchased, or transferred, for the purpose of giving effect to rights under an occupational pension scheme or a personal pension scheme, and
> (e) an annuity purchased, or entered into, for the purpose of discharging liability in respect of a pension credit under section 29(1)(b) or under corresponding Northern Ireland legislation;

"personal pension scheme" has the same meaning as in the Pension Schemes Act 1993;

"prescribed" means prescribed by regulations made by the Secretary of State;

"retirement annuity contract" means a contract or scheme approved under Chapter III of Part XIV of the Income and Corporation Taxes Act 1988;

"trustees or managers", in relation to an occupational pension scheme or a personal pension scheme, means—

(2) References to the person responsible for a pension arrangement are—

> (a) in the case of an occupational pension scheme or a personal pension scheme, to the trustees or managers of the scheme,
> (b) in the case of a retirement annuity contract or an annuity falling within paragraph (d) or (e) of the definition of "pension arrangement" above, the provider of the annuity, and
> (c) in the case of an insurance policy falling within paragraph (d) of the definition of that expression, the insurer.

PART IV

PENSION SHARING

CHAPTER I

SHARING OF RIGHTS UNDER PENSION ARRANGEMENTS

Pension sharing mechanism

27.—(1) Pension sharing is available under this Chapter in relation to a person's shareable rights under any pension arrangement other than an excepted public service pension scheme.

(2)   For the purposes of this Chapter, a person's shareable rights under a pension arrangement are any rights of his under the arrangement, other than rights of a description specified by regulations made by the Secretary of State.

(3)   For the purposes of subsection (1), a public service pension scheme is excepted if it is specified by order made by such Minister of the Crown or government department as may be designated by the Treasury as having responsibility for the scheme.

28.—(1) Section 29 applies on the taking effect of any of the following relating to a person's shareable rights under a pension arrangement—

    (a)   a pension sharing order under the Matrimonial Causes Act 1973,

    (b)   provision which corresponds to the provision which may be made by such an order and which—

        (i)   is contained in a qualifying agreement between the parties to a marriage, and

        (ii)   takes effect on the dissolution of the marriage under the Family Law Act 1996,

    (c)   provision which corresponds to the provision which may be made by such an order and which—

        (i)   is contained in a qualifying agreement between the parties to a marriage or former marriage, and

        (ii)   takes effect after the dissolution of the marriage under the Family Law Act 1996,

    (d)   an order under Part III of the Matrimonial and Family Proceedings Act 1984 (financial relief in England and Wales in relation to overseas divorce etc) corresponding to such an order as is mentioned in paragraph (a),

    (e)   a pension sharing order under the Family Law (Scotland) Act 1985,

    (f)   provision which corresponds to the provision which may be made by such an order and which—

    (i)   is contained in a qualifying agreement between the parties to a marriage,

        (ii)   is in such form as the Secretary of State may prescribe by regulations, and

        (iii)   takes effect on the grant, in relation to the marriage, of decree of divorce under the Divorce (Scotland) Act 1976 or of declarator of nullity,

    (g)   an order under Part IV of the Matrimonial and Family Proceedings Act 1984 (financial relief in Scotland in relation to overseas divorce etc) corresponding to such an order as is mentioned in paragraph (e),

(h)   a pension sharing order under Northern Ireland legislation, and

(i)   an order under Part IV of the Matrimonial and Family Proceedings (Northern Ireland) Order 1989 (financial relief in Northern Ireland in relation to overseas divorce etc) corresponding to such an order as is mentioned in paragraph (h).

(2)   For the purposes of subsection (1)(b) and (c), a qualifying agreement is one which—

(a)   has been entered into in such circumstances as the Lord Chancellor may prescribe by regulations, and

(b)   satisfies such requirements as the Lord Chancellor may so prescribe.

(3)   For the purposes of subsection (1)(f), a qualifying agreement is one which—

(a)   has been entered into in such circumstances as the Secretary of State may prescribe by regulations, and

(b)   is registered in the Books of Council and Session.

(4)   Subsection (1)(b) does not apply if—

(a)   the pension arrangement to which the provision relates is the subject of a pension sharing order under the Matrimonial Causes Act 1973 in relation to the marriage, or

(b)   there is in force a requirement imposed by virtue of section 25B or 25C of that Act (powers to include in financial provision orders requirements relating to benefits under pension arrangements) which relates to benefits or future benefits to which the party who is the transferor is entitled under the pension arrangement to which the provision relates.

(5)   Subsection (1)(c) does not apply if—

(a)   the marriage was dissolved by an order under section 3 of the Family Law Act 1996 (divorce not preceded by separation) and the satisfaction of the requirements of section 9(2) of that Act (settlement of future financial arrangements) was a precondition to the making of the order,

(b)   the pension arrangement to which the provision relates—

(i)   is the subject of a pension sharing order under the Matrimonial Causes Act 1973 in relation to the marriage, or

(ii)   has already been the subject of pension sharing between the parties, or

(c) there is in force a requirement imposed by virtue of section 25B or 25C of that Act which relates to benefits or future benefits to which the party who is the transferor is entitled under the pension arrangement to which the provision relates.

(6) Subsection (1)(f) does not apply if there is in force an order under section 12A(2) or (3) of the Family Law (Scotland) Act 1985 which relates to benefits or future benefits to which the party who is the transferor is entitled under the pension arrangement to which the provision relates.

(7) For the purposes of this section, an order or provision falling within subsection (1)(e), (f) or (g) shall be deemed never to have taken effect if the person responsible for the arrangement to which the order or provision relates does not receive before the end of the period of 2 months beginning with the relevant date—
(a) copies of the relevant matrimonial documents, and
(b) such information relating to the transferor and transferee as the Secretary of State may prescribe by regulations under section 34(1)(b)(ii).

(8) The relevant date for the purposes of subsection (7) is—
(a) in the case of an order or provision falling within subsection (1)(e) or (f), the date of the extract of the decree or declarator responsible for the divorce or annulment to which the order or provision relates, and
(b) in the case of an order falling within subsection (1)(g), the date of disposal of the application under section 28 of the Matrimonial and Family Proceedings Act 1984.

(9) The reference in subsection (7)(a) to the relevant matrimonial documents is—
(a) in the case of an order falling within subsection (1)(e) or (g), to copies of the order and the order, decree or declarator responsible for the divorce or annulment to which it relates, and
(b) in the case of provision falling within subsection (1)(f), to—
(i) copies of the provision and the order, decree or declarator responsible for the divorce or annulment to which it relates, and
(ii) documentary evidence that the agreement containing the provision is one to which subsection (3)(a) applies.

(10) The sheriff may, on the application of any person having an interest, make an order—

    (a) extending the period of 2 months referred to in subsection (7), and

    (b) if that period has already expired, providing that, if the person responsible for the arrangement receives the documents and information concerned before the end of the period specified in the order, subsection (7) is to be treated as never having applied.

(11) In subsections (4)(b), (5)(c) and (6), the reference to the party who is the transferor is to the party to whose rights the provision relates.

29.—(1) On the application of this section—

    (a) the transferor's shareable rights under the relevant arrangement become subject to a debit of the appropriate amount, and

    (b) the transferee becomes entitled to a credit of that amount as against the person responsible for that arrangement.

(2) Where the relevant order or provision specifies a percentage value to be transferred, the appropriate amount for the purposes of subsection (1) is the specified percentage of the cash equivalent of the relevant benefits on the valuation day.

(3) Where the relevant order or provision specifies an amount to be transferred, the appropriate amount for the purposes of subsection (1) is the lesser of—

    (a) the specified amount, and

    (b) the cash equivalent of the relevant benefits on the valuation day.

(4) Where the relevant arrangement is an occupational pension scheme and the transferor is in pensionable service under the scheme on the transfer day, the relevant benefits for the purposes of subsections (2) and (3) are the benefits or future benefits to which he would be entitled under the scheme by virtue of his shareable rights under it had his pensionable service terminated immediately before that day.

(5) Otherwise, the relevant benefits for the purposes of subsections (2) and (3) are the benefits or future benefits to which, immediately before the transfer day, the transferor is entitled under the terms of the relevant arrangement by virtue of his shareable rights under it.

(6) The Secretary of State may by regulations provide for any description of benefit to be disregarded for the purposes of subsection (4) or (5).

(7) For the purposes of this section, the valuation day is such day within the implementation period for the credit under subsection (1)(b) as the person responsible for the relevant arrangement may specify by notice in writing to the transferor and transferee.

(8) In this section—

"relevant arrangement" means the arrangement to which the relevant order or provision relates;

"relevant order or provision" means the order or provision by virtue of which this section applies;

"transfer day" means the day on which the relevant order or provision takes effect;

"transferor" means the person to whose rights the relevant order or provision relates;

"transferee" means the person for whose benefit the relevant order or provision is made.

30.—(1) The Secretary of State may by regulations make provision about the calculation and verification of cash equivalents for the purposes of section 29.

(2) The power conferred by subsection (1) includes power to provide for calculation or verification—
    (a) in such manner as may, in the particular case, be approved by a person prescribed by the regulations, or
    (b) in accordance with guidance from time to time prepared by a person so prescribed.

Pension debits

31.—(1) Subject to subsection (2), where a person's shareable rights under a pension arrangement are subject to a pension debit, each benefit or future benefit—
    (a) to which he is entitled under the arrangement by virtue of those rights, and
    (b) which is a qualifying benefit,
is reduced by the appropriate percentage.

(2) Where a pension debit relates to the shareable rights under an occupational pension scheme of a person who is in pensionable service under the scheme on the transfer day, each benefit or future benefit—

    (a) to which the person is entitled under the scheme by virtue of those rights, and

    (b) which corresponds to a qualifying benefit,

is reduced by an amount equal to the appropriate percentage of the corresponding qualifying benefit.

(3) A benefit is a qualifying benefit for the purposes of subsections (1) and (2) if the cash equivalent by reference to which the amount of the pension debit is determined includes an amount in respect of it.

(4) The provisions of this section override any provision of a pension arrangement to which they apply to the extent that the provision conflicts with them.

(5) In this section—

"appropriate percentage", in relation to a pension debit, means—

    (a) if the relevant order or provision specifies the percentage value to be transferred, that percentage;

    (b) if the relevant order or provision specifies an amount to be transferred, the percentage which the appropriate amount for the purposes of subsection (1) of section 29 represents of the amount mentioned in subsection (3)(b) of that section;

"relevant order or provision", in relation to a pension debit, means the pension sharing order or provision on which the debit depends;

"transfer day", in relation to a pension debit, means the day on which the relevant order or provision takes effect.

32.—(1) The Pension Schemes Act 1993 shall be amended as follows.

(2) In section 10 (protected rights), in subsection (1), for "subsections (2) and (3)" there shall be substituted "the following provisions of this section", and at the end there shall be added—

      "(4) Where, in the case of a scheme which makes such provision as is mentioned in subsection (2) or (3), a member's rights under the scheme become subject to a pension debit, his protected rights shall exclude the appropriate percentage of the rights which were his protected rights immediately before the day on which the pension debit arose.

(5) For the purposes of subsection (4), the appropriate percentage is—

    (a) if the order or provision on which the pension debit depends specifies the percentage value to be transferred, that percentage;

    (b) if the order or provision on which the pension debit depends specifies an amount to be transferred, the percentage which the appropriate amount for the purposes of subsection (1) of section 29 of the Welfare Reform and Pensions Act 1999 (lesser of specified amount and cash equivalent of transferor's benefits) represents of the amount mentioned in subsection (3)(b) of that section (cash equivalent of transferor's benefits)."

(3) After section 15 there shall be inserted—

"Reduction of guaranteed minimum in consequence of pension debit

15A.—(1) Where—

    (a) an earner has a guaranteed minimum in relation to the pension provided by a scheme, and

    (b) his right to the pension becomes subject to a pension debit,

his guaranteed minimum in relation to the scheme is, subject to subsection (2), reduced by the appropriate percentage.

(2) Where the earner is in pensionable service under the scheme on the day on which the order or provision on which the pension debit depends takes effect, his guaranteed minimum in relation to the scheme is reduced by an amount equal to the appropriate percentage of the corresponding qualifying benefit.

(3) For the purposes of subsection (2), the corresponding qualifying benefit is the guaranteed minimum taken for the purpose of calculating the cash equivalent by reference to which the amount of the pension debit is determined.

(4) For the purposes of this section the appropriate percentage is—

(a) if the order or provision on which the pension debit depends specifies the percentage value to be transferred, that percentage;

(b) if the order or provision on which the pension debit depends specifies an amount to be transferred, the percentage which the appropriate amount for the purposes of subsection (1) of section 29 of the Welfare Reform and Pensions Act 1999 (lesser of specified amount and cash equivalent of transferor's benefits) represents of the amount mentioned in subsection (3)(b) of that section (cash equivalent of transferor's benefits)."

(4) In section 47 (entitlement to guaranteed minimum pensions for the purposes of the relationship with social security benefits), at the end there shall be added—

"(6) For the purposes of section 46, a person shall be treated as entitled to any guaranteed minimum pension to which he would have been entitled but for any reduction under section 15A."

(5) In section 181(1), there shall be inserted at the appropriate place—

""pension debit" means a debit under section 29(1)(a) of the Welfare Reform and Pensions Act 1999;".

Pension credits

33.—(1) A person subject to liability in respect of a pension credit shall discharge his liability before the end of the implementation period for the credit.

(2) Where the trustees or managers of an occupational pension scheme have not done what is required to discharge their liability in respect of a pension credit before the end of the implementation period for the credit—

(a) they shall, except in such cases as the Secretary of State may prescribe by regulations, notify the Regulatory Authority of that fact within such period as the Secretary of State may so prescribe, and

(b) section 10 of the Pensions Act 1995 (power of the Regulatory Authority to impose civil penalties) shall apply to any trustee or manager who has failed to take all such steps as are reasonable to ensure that liability in respect of the credit was discharged before the end of the implementation period for it.

(3) If trustees or managers to whom subsection (2)(a) applies fail to perform the obligation imposed by that provision, section 10 of the Pensions Act 1995 shall apply to any trustee or manager who has failed to take all reasonable steps to ensure that the obligation was performed.

(4) On the application of the trustees or managers of an occupational pension scheme who are subject to liability in respect of a pension credit, the Regulatory Authority may extend the implementation period for the credit for the purposes of this section if it is satisfied that the application is made in such circumstances as the Secretary of State may prescribe by regulations.

(5) In this section "the Regulatory Authority" means the Occupational Pensions Regulatory Authority.

34.—(1) For the purposes of this Chapter, the implementation period for a pension credit is the period of 4 months beginning with the later of—

(a) the day on which the relevant order or provision takes effect, and

(b) the first day on which the person responsible for the pension arrangement to which the relevant order or provision relates is in receipt of—

(i) the relevant matrimonial documents, and

(ii) such information relating to the transferor and transferee as the Secretary of State may prescribe by regulations.

(2) The reference in subsection (1)(b)(i) to the relevant matrimonial documents is to copies of—

(a) the relevant order or provision, and

(b) the order, decree or declarator responsible for the divorce or annulment to which it relates,

and, if the pension credit depends on provision falling within subsection (1)(f) of section 28, to documentary evidence that the agreement containing the provision is one to which subsection (3)(a) of that section applies.

(3) Subsection (1) is subject to any provision made by regulations under section 41(2)(a).

(4) The Secretary of State may by regulations—
    (a) make provision requiring a person subject to liability in respect of a pension credit to notify the transferor and transferee of the day on which the implementation period for the credit begins;
    (b) provide for this section to have effect with modifications where the pension arrangement to which the relevant order or provision relates is being wound up;
    (c) provide for this section to have effect with modifications where the pension credit depends on a pension sharing order and the order is the subject of an application for leave to appeal out of time.

(5) In this section—

"relevant order or provision", in relation to a pension credit, means the pension sharing order or provision on which the pension credit depends;

"transferor" means the person to whose rights the relevant order or provision relates;

"transferee" means the person for whose benefit the relevant order or provision is made.

35.—(1) Schedule 5 (which makes provision about how liability in respect of a pension credit may be discharged) shall have effect.

(2) Where the person entitled to a pension credit dies before liability in respect of the credit has been discharged—
    (a) Schedule 5 shall cease to have effect in relation to the discharge of liability in respect of the credit, and
    (b) liability in respect of the credit shall be discharged in accordance with regulations made by the Secretary of State.

Treatment of pension credit rights under schemes

36.—After section 68 of the Pension Schemes Act 1993 there shall be inserted—

"Part IIIA
Safeguarded rights

Safeguarded rights

68A.—(1) Subject to subsection (2), the safeguarded rights of a member of an occupational pension scheme or a personal pension scheme are such of his rights to future benefits under the scheme as are attributable (directly or indirectly) to a pension credit in respect of which the reference rights are, or include, contracted-out rights or safeguarded rights.

(2) If the rules of an occupational pension scheme or a personal pension scheme so provide, a member's safeguarded rights are such of his rights falling within subsection (1) as—

(a) in the case of rights directly attributable to a pension credit, represent the safeguarded percentage of the rights acquired by virtue of the credit, and

(b) in the case of rights directly attributable to a transfer payment, represent the safeguarded percentage of the rights acquired by virtue of the payment.

(3) For the purposes of subsection (2)(a), the safeguarded percentage is the percentage of the rights by reference to which the amount of the credit is determined which are contracted-out rights or safeguarded rights.

(4) For the purposes of subsection (2)(b), the safeguarded percentage is the percentage of the rights in respect of which the transfer payment is made which are contracted-out rights or safeguarded rights.

(5) In this section—

"contracted-out rights" means such rights under, or derived from—

(a) an occupational pension scheme contracted-out by virtue of section 9(2) or (3), or

(b) an appropriate personal pension scheme,

as may be prescribed;

"reference rights", in relation to a pension credit, means the rights by reference to which the amount of the credit is determined.

Requirements relating to safeguarded rights.

68B. Regulations may prescribe requirements to be met in relation to safeguarded rights by an occupational pension scheme or a personal pension scheme.

Reserve powers in relation to non-complying schemes

68C

(1) This section applies to—

    (a) any occupational pension scheme, other than a public service pension scheme, and

    (b) any personal pension scheme.

(2) If any scheme to which this section applies does not comply with a requirement prescribed under section 68B and there are any persons who—

    (a) have safeguarded rights under the scheme, or

    (b) are entitled to any benefit giving effect to such rights under the scheme,

the Inland Revenue may direct the trustees or managers of the scheme to take or refrain from taking such steps as they may specify in writing for the purpose of safeguarding the rights of persons falling within paragraph (a) or (b).

(3) A direction under subsection (2) shall be final and binding on the trustees or managers to whom the direction is given and any person claiming under them.

(4) An appeal on a point of law shall lie to the High Court or, in Scotland, the Court of Session from a direction under subsection (2) at the instance of the trustees or managers, or any person claiming under them.

(5) A direction under subsection (2) shall be enforceable—

    (a) in England and Wales, in a county court, as if it were an order of that court, and

    (b) in Scotland, by the sheriff, as if it were an order of the sheriff and whether or not the sheriff could himself have given such an order.

Power to control transfer or discharge of liability.

68D. Regulations may prohibit or restrict the transfer or discharge of any liability under an occupational pension scheme or a personal pension scheme in respect of safeguarded rights except in prescribed circumstances or on prescribed conditions."

37. After section 101 of the Pension Schemes Act 1993 there shall be inserted—

"PART IVA

REQUIREMENTS RELATING TO PENSION CREDIT BENEFIT

CHAPTER I

PENSION CREDIT BENEFIT UNDER OCCUPATIONAL SCHEMES

Scope of Chapter I.

101A.—(1) This Chapter applies to any occupational pension scheme whose resources are derived in whole or part from—

(a) payments to which subsection (2) applies made or to be made by one or more employers of earners to whom the scheme applies, or

(b) such other payments by the earner or his employer, or both, as may be prescribed for different categories of scheme.

(2) This subsection applies to payments—

(a) under an actual or contingent legal obligation, or

(b) in the exercise of a power conferred, or the discharge of a duty imposed, on a Minister of the Crown, government department or any other person, being a power or duty which extends to the disbursement or allocation of public money.

Interpretation

101B. In this Chapter—

"scheme" means an occupational pension scheme to which this Chapter applies;

"pension credit rights" means rights to future benefits under a scheme which are attributable (directly or indirectly) to a pension credit;

"pension credit benefit", in relation to a scheme, means the benefits payable under the scheme to or in respect of a person by virtue of rights under the scheme attributable (directly or indirectly) to a pension credit;

"normal benefit age", in relation to a scheme, means the earliest age at which a person who has pension credit rights under the scheme is entitled to receive a pension by virtue of those rights (disregarding any scheme rule making special provision as to early payment of pension on grounds of ill-health or otherwise).

Basic principle as to pension credit benefit.

101C.—(1) Normal benefit age under a scheme must be between 60 and 65.

(2) A scheme must not provide for payment of pension credit benefit in the form of a lump sum at any time before normal benefit age, except in such circumstances as may be prescribed.

Form of pension credit benefit and its alternatives.

101D.—(1) Subject to subsection (2) and section 101E, a person's pension credit benefit under a scheme must be—

(a) payable directly out of the resources of the scheme, or

(b) assured to him by such means as may be prescribed.

(2) Subject to subsections (3) and (4), a scheme may, instead of providing a person's pension credit benefit, provide—

(a) for his pension credit rights under the scheme to be transferred to another occupational pension scheme or a personal pension scheme with a view to acquiring rights for him under the rules of the scheme, or

(b) for such alternatives to pension credit benefit as may be prescribed.

(3) The option conferred by subsection (2)(a) is additional to any obligation imposed by Chapter II of this Part.

(4) The alternatives specified in subsection (2)(a) and (b) may only be by way of complete or partial substitute for pension credit benefit—

(a) if the person entitled to the benefit consents, or

(b) in such other cases as may be prescribed.

Discharge of liability where pension credit or alternative benefits secured by insurance policies or annuity contracts.

101E.—(1) A transaction to which section 19 applies discharges the trustees or managers of a scheme from their liability to provide pension credit benefit or any alternative to pension credit benefit for or in respect of a member of the scheme if and to the extent that—

(a) it results in pension credit benefit, or any alternative to pension credit benefit, for or in respect of the member being appropriately secured (within the meaning of that section),

    (b) the transaction is entered into with the consent of the member or, if the member has died, of the member's widow or widower, and

    (c) such requirements as may be prescribed are met.

(2) Regulations may provide that subsection (1)(b) shall not apply in prescribed circumstances.

CHAPTER II
TRANSFER VALUES

Power to give transfer notice.

101F.—(1) An eligible member of a qualifying scheme may by notice in writing require the trustees or managers of the scheme to use an amount equal to the cash equivalent of his pension credit benefit for such one or more of the authorised purposes as he may specify in the notice.

(2) In the case of a member of an occupational pension scheme, the authorised purposes are—

    (a) to acquire rights allowed under the rules of an occupational pension scheme, or personal pension scheme, which is an eligible scheme,

    (b) to purchase from one or more insurance companies such as are mentioned in section 19(4)(a), chosen by the member and willing to accept payment on account of the member from the trustees or managers, one or more annuities which satisfy the prescribed requirements, and

    (c) in such circumstances as may be prescribed, to subscribe to other pension arrangements which satisfy prescribed requirements.

(3) In the case of a member of a personal pension scheme, the authorised purposes are—

    (a) to acquire rights allowed under the rules of an occupational pension scheme, or personal pension scheme, which is an eligible scheme, and

    (b) in such circumstances as may be prescribed, to subscribe to other pension arrangements which satisfy prescribed requirements.

(4) The cash equivalent for the purposes of subsection (1) shall—

    (a) in the case of a salary related occupational pension scheme, be taken to be the amount shown in the relevant statement under section 101H, and

    (b) in any other case, be determined by reference to the date the notice under that subsection is given.

(5) The requirements which may be prescribed under subsection (2) or (3) include, in particular, requirements of the Inland Revenue.

(6) In subsections (2) and (3), references to an eligible scheme are to a scheme—

    (a) the trustees or managers of which are able and willing to accept payment in respect of the member's pension credit rights, and

    (b) which satisfies the prescribed requirements.

(7) In this Chapter, "transfer notice" means a notice under subsection (1).

Restrictions on power to give transfer notice

101G.—(1) In the case of a salary related occupational pension scheme, the power to give a transfer notice may only be exercised if—

    (a) the member has been provided with a statement under section 101H, and

    (b) not more than 3 months have passed since the date by reference to which the amount shown in the statement is determined.

(2) The power to give a transfer notice may not be exercised in the case of an occupational pension scheme if—

    (a) there is less than a year to go until the member reaches normal benefit age, or

    (b) the pension to which the member is entitled by virtue of his pension credit rights, or benefit in lieu of that pension, or any part of it has become payable.

(3) Where an eligible member of a qualifying scheme—

(a) is entitled to make an application under section 95 to the trustees or managers of the scheme, or

(b) would be entitled to do so, but for the fact that he has not received a statement under section 93A in respect of which the guarantee date is sufficiently recent,

he may not, if the scheme so provides, exercise the power to give them a transfer notice unless he also makes an application to them under section 95.

(4) The power to give a transfer notice may not be exercised if a previous transfer notice given by the member to the trustees or managers of the scheme is outstanding.

Salary related schemes: statements of entitlement.

101H.—(1) The trustees or managers of a qualifying scheme which is a salary related occupational pension scheme shall, on the application of an eligible member, provide him with a written statement of the amount of the cash equivalent of his pension credit benefit under the scheme.

(2) For the purposes of subsection (1), the amount of the cash equivalent shall be determined by reference to a date falling within—

(a) the prescribed period beginning with the date of the application, and

(b) the prescribed period ending with the date on which the statement under that subsection is provided to the applicant.

(3) Regulations may make provision in relation to applications under subsection (1) and may, in particular, restrict the making of successive applications.

(4) If trustees or managers to whom subsection (1) applies fail to perform an obligation under that subsection, section 10 of the Pensions Act 1995 (power of the Regulatory Authority to impose civil penalties) shall apply to any trustee or manager who has failed to take all such steps as are reasonable to secure that the obligation was performed.

Calculation of cash equivalents

101I. Cash equivalents for the purposes of this Chapter shall be calculated and verified in the prescribed manner.

101J. (1) Trustees or managers of a qualifying scheme who receive a transfer notice shall comply with the notice—

    (a) in the case of an occupational pension scheme, within 6 months of the valuation date or, if earlier, by the date on which the member to whom the notice relates reaches normal benefit age, and

    (b) in the case of a personal pension scheme, within 6 months of the date on which they receive the notice.

(2) The Regulatory Authority may, in prescribed circumstances, extend the period for complying with the notice.

(3) If the Regulatory Authority are satisfied—

    (a) that there has been a relevant change of circumstances since they granted an extension under subsection (2), or

    (b) that they granted an extension under that subsection in ignorance of a material fact or on the basis of a mistake as to a material fact,

they may revoke or reduce the extension.

(4) Where the trustees or managers of an occupational pension scheme have failed to comply with a transfer notice before the end of the period for compliance—

    (a) they shall, except in prescribed cases, notify the Regulatory Authority of that fact within the prescribed period, and

    (b) section 10 of the Pensions Act 1995 (power of the Regulatory Authority to impose civil penalties) shall apply to any trustee or manager who has failed to take all such steps as are reasonable to ensure that the notice was complied with before the end of the period for compliance.

(5) If trustees or managers to whom subsection (4)(a) applies fail to perform the obligation imposed by that provision, section 10 of the Pensions Act 1995 shall apply to any trustee or manager who has failed to take all such steps as are reasonable to ensure that the obligation was performed.

(6) Regulations may—
  (a) make provision in relation to applications under subsection (2), and
  (b) provide that subsection (4) shall not apply in prescribed circumstances.

(7) In this section, "valuation date", in relation to a transfer notice given to the trustees or managers of an occupational pension scheme, means—
  (a) in the case of a salary related scheme, the date by reference to which the amount shown in the relevant statement under section 101H is determined, and
  (b) in the case of any other scheme, the date the notice is given.

Withdrawal of transfer notice.

101K.—(1) Subject to subsections (2) and (3), a person who has given a transfer notice may withdraw it by giving the trustees or managers to whom it was given notice in writing that he no longer requires them to comply with it.

(2) A transfer notice may not be withdrawn if the trustees or managers have already entered into an agreement with a third party to use the whole or part of the amount they are required to use in accordance with the notice.

(3) If the giving of a transfer notice depended on the making of an application under section 95, the notice may only be withdrawn if the application is also withdrawn.

Variation of the amount required to be used

101L.—(1) Regulations may make provision for the amount required to be used under section 101F(1) to be increased or reduced in prescribed circumstances.

(2) Without prejudice to the generality of subsection (1), the circumstances which may be prescribed include—
  (a) failure by the trustees or managers of a qualifying scheme to comply with a notice under section 101F(1) within 6 months of the date by reference to which the amount of the cash equivalent falls to be determined, and
  (b) the state of funding of a qualifying scheme.

(3) Regulations under subsection (1) may have the effect of extinguishing an obligation under section 101F(1).

Effect of transfer on trustees' duties.

101M. Compliance with a transfer notice shall have effect to discharge the trustees or managers of a qualifying scheme from any obligation to provide the pension credit benefit of the eligible member who gave the notice.

Matters to be disregarded in calculations

101N. In making any calculation for the purposes of this Chapter—
    (a) any charge or lien on, and
    (b) any set-off against,
the whole or part of a pension shall be disregarded.

Service of notices

101O. A notice under section 101F(1) or 101K(1) shall be taken to have been given if it is delivered to the trustees or managers personally or sent by post in a registered letter or by recorded delivery service.

Interpretation of Chapter II.

101P.—(1) In this Chapter—
    "eligible member", in relation to a qualifying scheme, means a member who has pension credit rights under the scheme;

    "normal benefit age", in relation to an eligible member of a qualifying scheme, means the earliest age at which the member is entitled to receive a pension by virtue of his pension credit rights under the scheme (disregarding any scheme rule making special provision as to early payment of pension on grounds of ill-health or otherwise);

    "pension credit benefit", in relation to an eligible member of a qualifying scheme, means the benefits payable under the scheme to or in respect of the member by virtue of rights under the scheme attributable (directly or indirectly) to a pension credit;

    "pension credit rights", in relation to a qualifying scheme, means rights to future benefits under the scheme which are attributable (directly or indirectly) to a pension credit;

"qualifying scheme" means a funded occupational pension scheme and a personal pension scheme;

"transfer notice" has the meaning given by section 101F(7).

(2) For the purposes of this Chapter, an occupational pension scheme is salary related if—
(a) it is not a money purchase scheme, and
(b) it does not fall within a prescribed class.

(3) In this Chapter, references to the relevant statement under section 101H, in relation to a transfer notice given to the trustees or managers of a salary related occupational pension scheme, are to the statement under that section on which the giving of the notice depended.

(4) For the purposes of this section, an occupational pension scheme is funded if it meets its liabilities out of a fund accumulated for the purpose during the life of the scheme.

Power to modify Chapter II in relation to hybrid schemes.

101Q. Regulations may apply this Chapter with prescribed modifications to occupational pension schemes—
(a) which are not money purchase schemes, but
(b) where some of the benefits that may be provided are money purchase benefits."

38.—(1) In section 73 of the Pensions Act 1995 (treatment of rights on winding up of an occupational pension scheme to which section 56 of that Act (minimum funding requirement) applies), in subsection (3) (classification of liabilities), in paragraph (c) (accrued rights), at the end of sub-paragraph (i) there shall be inserted—
"(ia) future pensions, or other future benefits, attributable (directly or indirectly) to pension credits (but excluding increases to pensions),".

(2) In the case of an occupational pension scheme which is not a scheme to which section 56 of the Pensions Act 1995 applies, rights attributable (directly or indirectly) to a pension credit are to be accorded in a winding up the same treatment—
(a) if they have come into payment, as the rights of a pensioner member, and

(b) if they have not come into payment, as the rights of a deferred member.

(3)   Subsection (2) overrides the provisions of a scheme to the extent that it conflicts with them, and the scheme has effect with such modifications as may be required in consequence.

(4)   In subsection (2)—
   (a) "deferred member" and "pensioner member" have the same meanings as in Part I of the Pensions Act 1995,
   (b) "pension credit" includes a credit under Northern Ireland legislation corresponding to section 29(1)(b), and
   (c) references to rights attributable to a pension credit having come into payment are to the person to whom the rights belong having become entitled by virtue of the rights to the present payment of pension or other benefits.

Indexation

39.—(1)   The Pensions (Increase) Act 1971 shall be amended as follows.

(2)   In section 3 (qualifying conditions), after subsection (2) there shall be inserted—
   "(2A)   A pension attributable to the pensioner having become entitled to a pension credit shall not be increased unless the pensioner has attained the age of fifty-five years."

(3)   In section 8, in subsection (1) (definition of "pension"), in paragraph (a), the words from "(either" to "person)" shall be omitted.

(4)   In that section, in subsection (2) (when pension deemed for purposes of the Act to begin), after "pension", in the first place, there shall be inserted "which is not attributable to a pension credit", and after that subsection there shall be inserted—
   "(2A)   A pension which is attributable to a pension credit shall be deemed for purposes of this Act to begin on the day on which the order or provision on which the credit depends takes effect."

(5)   In section 17(1) (interpretation)—
   (a) for the definitions of "derivative pension" and "principal pension" there shall be substituted—
      ""derivative pension" means a pension which—

      (a) is not payable in respect of the pensioner's own
          services, and

      (b) is not attributable to the pensioner having
          become entitled to a pension credit;",

  (b) after the definition of "pension" there shall be
     inserted—

       ""pension credit" means a credit under section 29(1)(b)
    of the Welfare Reform and Pensions Act 1999 or under
    corresponding Northern Ireland legislation;

      "principal pension" means a pension which—

      (a) is payable in respect of the pensioner's own
          services, or

      (b) is attributable to the pensioner having become
          entitled to a pension credit;", and

  (c) for the definition of "widow's pension" there shall be
     substituted—

       ""widow's pension" means a pension payable—

      (a) in respect of the services of the pensioner's
          deceased husband, or

      (b) by virtue of the pensioner's deceased husband
          having become entitled to a pension credit."

40.—(1) The Secretary of State may by regulations make provision
for a pension to which subsection (2) applies to be increased, as a
minimum, by reference to increases in the retail prices index, so far as
not exceeding 5% per annum.

(2) This subsection applies to—

  (a) a pension provided to give effect to eligible pension credit
     rights of a member under a qualifying occupational pension
     scheme, and

  (b) a pension provided to give effect to safeguarded rights of a
     member under a personal pension scheme.

(3) In this section—

  "eligible", in relation to pension credit rights, means of a
    description prescribed by regulations made by the Secretary
    of State;

  "pension credit rights", in relation to an occupational pension
    scheme, means rights to future benefits under the scheme
    which are attributable (directly or indirectly) to a credit
    under section 29(1)(b) or under corresponding Northern
    Ireland legislation;

"qualifying occupational pension scheme" means an occupational pension scheme which is not a public service pension scheme;

"safeguarded rights" has the meaning given in section 68A of the Pension Schemes Act 1993.

Charges by pension arrangements

41.—(1) The Secretary of State may by regulations make provision for the purpose of enabling the person responsible for a pension arrangement involved in pension sharing to recover from the parties to pension sharing prescribed charges in respect of prescribed descriptions of pension sharing activity.

(2) Regulations under subsection (1) may include—
  (a) provision for the start of the implementation period for a pension credit to be postponed in prescribed circumstances;
  (b) provision, in relation to payments in respect of charges recoverable under the regulations, for reimbursement as between the parties to pension sharing;
  (c) provision, in relation to the recovery of charges by deduction from a pension credit, for the modification of Schedule 5;
  (d) provision for the recovery in prescribed circumstances of such additional amounts as may be determined in accordance with the regulations.

(3) For the purposes of regulations under subsection (1), the question of how much of a charge recoverable under the regulations is attributable to a party to pension sharing is to be determined as follows—
  (a) where the relevant order or provision includes provision about the apportionment of charges under this section, there is attributable to the party so much of the charge as is apportioned to him by that provision;
  (b) where the relevant order or provision does not include such provision, the charge is attributable to the transferor.

(4) For the purposes of subsection (1), a pension arrangement is involved in pension sharing if section 29 applies by virtue of an order or provision which relates to the arrangement.

(5) In that subsection, the reference to pension sharing activity is to activity attributable (directly or indirectly) to the involvement in pension sharing.

(6) In subsection (3)—
  (a) the reference to the relevant order or provision is to the order or provision which gives rise to the pension sharing, and
  (b) the reference to the transferor is to the person to whose rights that order or provision relates.

(7) In this section "prescribed" means prescribed in regulations under subsection (1).

Adaptation of statutory schemes

42.—(1) Power under an Act to establish a pension scheme shall include power to make provision for the provision, by reference to pension credits which derive from rights under—
  (a) the scheme, or
  (b) a scheme in relation to which the scheme is specified as an alternative for the purposes of paragraph 2 of Schedule 5,
of benefits to or in respect of those entitled to the credits.

(2) Subsection (1) is without prejudice to any other power.

(3) Subsection (1) shall apply in relation to Acts whenever passed.

(4) No obligation to consult shall apply in relation to the making, in exercise of a power under an Act to establish a pension scheme, of provision of a kind authorised by subsection (1).

(5) Any provision of, or under, an Act which makes benefits under a pension scheme established under an Act a charge on, or payable out of—
  (a) the Consolidated Fund,
  (b) the Scottish Consolidated Fund, or
  (c) the Consolidated Fund of Northern Ireland,
shall be treated as including any benefits under the scheme which are attributable (directly or indirectly) to a pension credit which derives from rights to benefits charged on, or payable out of, that fund.

(6) In this section—
  "pension credit" includes a credit under Northern Ireland legislation corresponding to section 29(1)(b);

  "pension scheme" means a scheme or arrangement providing benefits, in the form of pensions or otherwise, payable on termination of service, or on death or retirement, to or in respect of persons to whom the scheme or arrangement applies.

43.—(1) The appropriate minister may by regulations amend the Sheriffs' Pensions (Scotland) Act 1961, the Judicial Pensions Act 1981 or the Judicial Pensions and Retirement Act 1993 for the purpose of—

    (a) extending a pension scheme under the Act to include the provision, by reference to pension credits which derive from rights under—

        (i) the scheme, or

        (ii) a scheme in relation to which the scheme is specified as an alternative for the purposes of paragraph 2 of Schedule 5,

        of benefits to or in respect of those entitled to the credits, or

    (b) restricting the power of the appropriate minister to accept payments into a pension scheme under the Act, where the payments represent the cash equivalent of rights under another pension scheme which are attributable (directly or indirectly) to a pension credit.

(2) Regulations under subsection (1)—

    (a) may make benefits provided by virtue of paragraph (a) of that subsection a charge on, and payable out of, the Consolidated Fund;

    (b) may confer power to make subordinate legislation, including subordinate legislation which provides for calculation of the value of rights in accordance with guidance from time to time prepared by a person specified in the subordinate legislation.

(3) The appropriate minister for the purposes of subsection (1) is—

    (a) in relation to a pension scheme whose ordinary members are limited to those who hold judicial office whose jurisdiction is exercised exclusively in relation to Scotland, the Secretary of State, and

    (b) in relation to any other pension scheme, the Lord Chancellor.

(4) In this section—

"pension credit" includes a credit under Northern Ireland legislation corresponding to section 29(1)(b);

"pension scheme" means a scheme or arrangement providing benefits, in the form of pensions or otherwise, payable on termination of service, or on death or retirement, to or in respect of persons to whom the scheme or arrangement applies.

Supplementary

44.—(1) Nothing in any of the following provisions (restrictions on alienation of pension rights) applies in relation to any order or provision falling within section 28(1)—

(a) section 203(1) and (2) of the Army Act 1955, section 203(1) and (2) of the Air Force Act 1955, section 128G(1) and (2) of the Naval Discipline Act 1957 and section 159(4) and (4A) of the Pension Schemes Act 1993,

(b) section 91 of the Pensions Act 1995,

(c) any provision of any enactment (whether passed or made before or after this Act is passed) corresponding to any of the enactments mentioned in paragraphs (a) and (b), and

(d) any provision of a pension arrangement corresponding to any of those enactments.

(2) In this section, "enactment" includes an enactment comprised in subordinate legislation (within the meaning of the Interpretation Act 1978).

45.—(1) The Secretary of State may by regulations require the person responsible for a pension arrangement involved in pension sharing to supply to such persons as he may specify in the regulations such information relating to anything which follows from the application of section 29 as he may so specify.

(2) Section 168 of the Pension Schemes Act 1993 (breach of regulations) shall apply as if this section were contained in that Act (otherwise than in Chapter II of Part VII).

(3) For the purposes of this section, a pension arrangement is involved pension sharing if section 29 applies by virtue of an order or provision which relates to the arrangement.

46.—(1) In this Chapter—

"implementation period", in relation to a pension credit, has the meaning given by section 34;

"occupational pension scheme" has the meaning given by section 1 of the Pension Schemes Act 1993;

"pension arrangement" means—

(a) an occupational pension scheme,

(b) a personal pension scheme,

(c) a retirement annuity contract,

(d)   an annuity or insurance policy purchased, or transferred, for the purpose of giving effect to rights under an occupational pension scheme or a personal pension scheme, and

(e)   an annuity purchased, or entered into, for the purpose of discharging liability in respect of a credit under section 29(1)(b) or under corresponding Northern Ireland legislation;

"pension credit" means a credit under section 29(1)(b);

"pension debit" means a debit under section 29(1)(a);

"pensionable service", in relation to a member of an occupational pension scheme, means service in any description or category of employment to which the scheme relates which qualifies the member (on the assumption that it continues for the appropriate period) for pension or other benefits under the scheme;

"personal pension scheme" has the meaning given by section 1 of the Pension Schemes Act 1993;

"retirement annuity contract" means a contract or scheme approved under Chapter III of Part XIV of the Income and Corporation Taxes Act 1988;

"shareable rights" has the meaning given by section 27(2);

"trustees or managers", in relation to an occupational pension scheme or a personal pension scheme means—

(a)   in the case of a scheme established under a trust, the trustees of the scheme, and

(b)   in any other case, the managers of the scheme.

(2)   In this Chapter, references to the person responsible for a pension arrangement are—

(a)   in the case of an occupational pension scheme or a personal pension scheme, to the trustees or managers of the scheme,

(b)   in the case of a retirement annuity contract or an annuity falling within paragraph (d) or (e) of the definition of "pension arrangement" in subsection (1), to the provider of the annuity, and

(c)   in the case of an insurance policy falling within paragraph (d) of the definition of that expression, to the insurer.

(3) In determining what is "pensionable service" for the purposes of this Chapter—

(a) service notionally attributable for any purpose of the scheme is to be disregarded, and

(b) no account is to be taken of any rules of the scheme by which a period of service can be treated for any purpose as being longer or shorter than it actually is.

CHAPTER II
SHARING OF STATE SCHEME RIGHTS

47.—(1) Pension sharing is available under this Chapter in relation to a person's shareable state scheme rights.

(2) For the purposes of this Chapter, a person's shareable state scheme rights are—

(a) his entitlement, or prospective entitlement, to a Category A retirement pension by virtue of section 44(3)(b) of the Contributions and Benefits Act (earnings-related additional pension), and

(b) his entitlement, or prospective entitlement, to a pension under section 55A of that Act (shared additional pension).

48.—(1) Section 49 applies on the taking effect of any of the following relating to a person's shareable state scheme rights—

(a) a pension sharing order under the Matrimonial Causes Act 1973,

(b) provision which corresponds to the provision which may be made by such an order and which—

(i) is contained in a qualifying agreement between the parties to a marriage, and

(ii) takes effect on the dissolution of the marriage under the Family Law Act 1996,

(c) provision which corresponds to the provision which may be made by such an order and which—

(i) is contained in a qualifying agreement between the parties to a marriage or former marriage, and

(ii) takes effect after the dissolution of the marriage under the Family Law Act 1996,

(d) an order under Part III of the Matrimonial and Family Proceedings Act 1984 (financial relief in England and Wales in relation to overseas divorce etc) corresponding to such an order as is mentioned in paragraph (a),

(e) a pension sharing order under the Family Law (Scotland) Act 1985,

(f) provision which corresponds to the provision which may be made by such an order and which—

    (i) is contained in a qualifying agreement between the parties to a marriage,

    (ii) is in such form as the Secretary of State may prescribe by regulations, and

    (iii) takes effect on the grant, in relation to the marriage, of decree of divorce under the Divorce (Scotland) Act 1976 or of declarator of nullity,

(g) an order under Part IV of the Matrimonial and Family Proceedings Act 1984 (financial relief in Scotland in relation to overseas divorce etc) corresponding to such an order as is mentioned in paragraph (e),

(h) a pension sharing order under Northern Ireland legislation, and

(i) an order under Part IV of the Matrimonial and Family Proceedings (Northern Ireland) Order 1989 (financial relief in Northern Ireland in relation to overseas divorce etc) corresponding to such an order as is mentioned in paragraph (h).

(2) For the purposes of subsection (1)(b) and (c), a qualifying agreement is one which—

(a) has been entered into in such circumstances as the Lord Chancellor may prescribe by regulations, and

(b) satisfies such requirements as the Lord Chancellor may so prescribe.

(3) For the purposes of subsection (1)(f), a qualifying agreement is one which—

(a) has been entered into in such circumstances as the Secretary of State may prescribe by regulations, and

(b) is registered in the Books of Council and Session.

(4) Subsection (1)(b) does not apply if the provision relates to rights which are the subject of a pension sharing order under the Matrimonial Causes Act 1973 in relation to the marriage.

(5) Subsection (1)(c) does not apply if—

(a) the marriage was dissolved by an order under section 3 of the Family Law Act 1996 (divorce not preceded by separation) and the satisfaction of the requirements of section 9(2) of that Act (settlement of future financial arrangements) was a precondition to the making of the order,

   (b)   the provision relates to rights which are the subject of a pension sharing order under the Matrimonial Causes Act 1973 in relation to the marriage, or

   (c)   shareable state scheme rights have already been the subject of pension sharing between the parties.

(6)   For the purposes of this section, an order or provision falling within subsection (1)(e), (f) or (g) shall be deemed never to have taken effect if the Secretary of State does not receive before the end of the period of 2 months beginning with the relevant date—

   (a)   copies of the relevant matrimonial documents, and

   (b)   such information relating to the transferor and transferee as the Secretary of State may prescribe by regulations under section 34(1)(b)(ii).

(7)   The relevant date for the purposes of subsection (6) is—

   (a)   in the case of an order or provision falling within subsection (1)(e) or (f), the date of the extract of the decree or declarator responsible for the divorce or annulment to which the order or provision relates, and

   (b)   in the case of an order falling within subsection (1)(g), the date of disposal of the application under section 28 of the Matrimonial and Family Proceedings Act 1984.

(8)   The reference in subsection (6)(a) to the relevant matrimonial documents is—

   (a)   in the case of an order falling within subsection (1)(e) or (g), to copies of the order and the order, decree or declarator responsible for the divorce or annulment to which it relates, and

   (b)   in the case of provision falling within subsection (1)(f), to—

      (i)   copies of the provision and the order, decree or declarator responsible for the divorce or annulment to which it relates, and

      (ii)   documentary evidence that the agreement containing the provision is one to which subsection (3)(a) applies.

(9)   The sheriff may, on the application of any person having an interest, make an order—

   (a)   extending the period of 2 months referred to in subsection (6), and

   (b)   if that period has already expired, providing that, if the Secretary of State receives the documents and information concerned before the end of the period specified in the order, subsection (6) is to be treated as never having applied.

49.—(1) On the application of this section—
- (a)   the transferor becomes subject, for the purposes of Part II of the Contributions and Benefits Act (contributory benefits), to a debit of the appropriate amount, and
- (b)   the transferee becomes entitled, for those purposes, to a credit of that amount.

(2) Where the relevant order or provision specifies a percentage value to be transferred, the appropriate amount for the purposes of subsection (1) is the specified percentage of the cash equivalent on the transfer day of the transferor's shareable state scheme rights immediately before that day.

(3) Where the relevant order or provision specifies an amount to be transferred, the appropriate amount for the purposes of subsection (1) is the lesser of—
- (a)   the specified amount, and
- (b)   the cash equivalent on the transfer day of the transferor's relevant state scheme rights immediately before that day.

(4) Cash equivalents for the purposes of this section shall be calculated accordance with regulations made by the Secretary of State.

(5)   In determining prospective entitlement to a Category A retirement pension for the purposes of this section, only tax years before that in which the transfer day falls shall be taken into account.

(6) In this section—

"relevant order or provision" means the order or provision by virtue of which this section applies;

"transfer day" means the day on which the relevant order or provision takes effect;

"transferor" means the person to whose rights the relevant order or provision relates;

"transferee" means the person for whose benefit the relevant order or provision is made.

50.—(1) Schedule 6 (which amends the Contributions and Benefits Act for the purpose of giving effect to debits and credits under section 49(1)) shall have effect.

(2)   Section 55C of that Act (which is inserted by that Schedule) shall have effect, in relation to incremental periods (within the meaning of that section) beginning on or after 6th April 2010, with the following amendments—

    (a)   in subsection (3), for "period of enhancement" there is substituted "period of deferment",

    (b)   in subsection (4), for "1/7th per cent" there is substituted "1/5th per cent",

    (c)   in subsection (7), for "period of enhancement", in both places, there is substituted "period of deferment", and

    (d)   in subsection (9), the definition of "period of enhancement" (and the preceding "and") are omitted.

51.—In this Chapter—

"shareable state scheme rights" has the meaning given by section 47(2); and

"tax year" has the meaning given by section 122(1) of the Contributions and Benefits Act.

SCHEDULE 1
APPLICATION OF 1993 AND 1995 ACTS TO REGISTERED SCHEMES

1.—(1)   The provisions specified in sub–paragraph (2) shall apply as if any pension scheme established under a trust which—

    (a)   is not an occupational pension scheme, but

    (b)   is or has been registered under section 2,

were an occupational pension scheme.

(2)   The provisions are—

    (a)   subsections (4) to (9) of section 175 of the 1993 Act (levies towards certain expenditure); and

    (b)   the following provisions of Part I of the 1995 Act—

        (i)   sections 3 to 11, 13 and 15 (supervision by the Authority) except sections 8(1) and (2), 11(3)(c) and 15(1);

        (ii)   sections 27 to 31 (trustees: general);

        (iii)   sections 32 to 36 and 39 (functions of trustees) except the reference to sections 16(3)(b) and 25(2) in section 32(4), the reference to section 56 in section 35(2) and section 35(5)(b);

        (iv)   section 41 (functions of trustees or managers);

        (v)   sections 47 and 48 (advisers);

    (vi) section 49 (receipts, payment and records) except subsections (5) and (8) to (13);

    (vii)   section 50 (resolution of disputes);

    (viii)   section 68 (power of trustees to modify scheme by resolution) except subsection (3);

    (ix)   sections 81 to 86 (the compensation payments) except section 81(1)(b);

    (x)   sections 91, 92 and 94 (assignment and forfeiture etc) except section 91(5)(d);

    (xi)   section 96(2)(c) (review of decisions of the Authority);

    (xii)   section 108 (other permitted disclosures);

    (xiii)   section 110 (provision of information to Compensation Board);

    (xiv)   section 117 (overriding requirements); and

    (xv)   sections 124 and 125 (interpretation).

(3) Section 47(9) of the 1995 Act (as applied by sub-paragraph (1)) shall have effect as if the reference to any person who is or has been the employer were a reference to any person who, in pursuance of section 3(5), is or has been required—

    (a)   to deduct an employee's contributions to the scheme from his remuneration; and

    (b)   to pay them to the trustees or managers of the scheme or to a prescribed person.

(4) Section 68 of the 1995 Act (as so applied) shall have effect as if the purposes specified in subsection (2) included enabling the conditions set out in section 1 to be fulfilled in relation to the scheme.

(5) Section 124(1) of the 1995 Act (as so applied) shall have effect as if the definition of "member" were omitted.

2.—(1)   Sections 98 to 100 of the 1995 Act (gathering information: the Authority) shall apply as if any pension scheme which—

    (a)   is not an occupational pension scheme, but

    (b)   is or has been registered under section 2,

were an occupational pension scheme.

(2) Section 99 of the 1995 Act (as applied by sub-paragraph (1)) shall have effect as if the regulatory provisions, for the purposes of subsection (1) of that section, were—

    (a)   provisions made by or under the provisions specified in paragraph 1(2), other than section 110 of the 1995 Act;

    (b)   sections 111, 115 and 116 of that Act;

(c) any provisions in force in Northern Ireland corresponding to the provisions mentioned in paragraphs (a) and (b); and

(d) sections 1 and 2(4) to (6).

(3) Section 100 of the 1995 Act (as so applied) shall have effect as if the references in subsections (1)(c)(i) and (4)(b) to that Act included references to section 2(5).

(4) Any reference in this paragraph or paragraph 3 which is or includes a reference to, or to any subsection of, section 1 or 2 includes a reference to any provision in force in Northern Ireland corresponding to that section or (as the case may be) that subsection; and the reference in sub-paragraph (1) to any pension scheme includes a personal pension scheme (as well as an occupational scheme) within the meaning of the Pension Schemes (Northern Ireland) Act 1993.

3.—(1) Section 99 of the 1995 Act shall have effect in relation to any occupational pension scheme which is or has been registered under section 2 as if the regulatory provisions for the purposes of subsection (1) of section 99 included sections 1 and 2(4) to (6).

(2) Section 100 of the 1995 Act shall have effect in relation to any occupational pension scheme which is or has been registered under section 2 as if the references in subsections (1)(c)(i) and (4)(b) to that Act included references to section 2(5).

Appendix 2

STATUTORY INSTRUMENT

2000 No. 1403

PENSIONS

The Stakeholder Pension Schemes Regulations 2000

Made	*24th May 2000*
Laid before Parliament	*25th May 2000*
Coming into force	
Parts I to III and V	*1st October 2000*
Part IV	*8th October 2001*

ARRANGEMENT OF REGULATIONS

PART I

GENERAL

PART II

CONDITIONS APPLYING TO STAKEHOLDER PENSION SCHEMES

29. Amendment of the Protected Rights (Transfer Payment) Regulations 1996.
30. Amendment of the Occupational Pension Schemes (Member-nominated Trustees and Directors) Regulations 1996.
31. Amendment of the Occupational Pension Schemes (Investment) Regulations 1996.
32. Application of other Regulations to stakeholder pension schemes.

SCHEDULES

1.   Provisions conferring powers exercised in making these Regulations.

2.   Regulations applying to schemes which are or have been registered under section 2 of the Act.

The Secretary of State for Social Security, in exercise of the powers conferred upon him by the provisions set out in Schedule 1 and of all other powers enabling him in that behalf, after consultation with such persons as he considers appropriate, hereby makes the following Regulations:—

PART I

GENERAL

Citation, commencement and interpretation

1.—(1) These Regulations may be cited as the Stakeholder Pension Schemes Regulations 2000.

(2) Parts I to III and V of these Regulations shall come into force on 1st October 2000 and Part IV shall come into force on 8th October 2001.

(3) In these Regulations—

"the Act" means the Welfare Reform and Pensions Act 1999;

"the 1993 Act" means the Pension Schemes Act 1993;

"the 1995 Act" means the Pensions Act 1995;

"beneficiary", in relation to a stakeholder pension scheme, means any person who has rights under the scheme which have arisen as a result of the death of a member of the scheme;

"the Income and Corporation Taxes Act" means the Income and Corporation Taxes Act 1988;

"insurance company" means a company which is authorised under sections 3 or 4 of the Insurance Companies Act 1982;

"investment trust" means a company which is approved for the purposes of section 842 of the Income and Corporation Taxes Act;

"minimum contributions" means amounts paid by the Inland Revenue in accordance with section 43 of the 1993 Act (payment of minimum contributions to personal pension schemes);

"minimum payments" means payments made to an occupational pension scheme in respect of a person's employment by virtue of which (subject to there being in force a contracting-out certificate issued by the Inland Revenue in accordance with Chapter I of Part III of the 1993 Act) that employment is contracted-out employment by reference to the scheme under section 8(1) of the 1993 Act (meaning of "contracted-out employment" and "minimum payment");

"pension arrangement" means—
    (a) an annuity contract;
    (b) an insurance policy; or
    (c) a scheme or arrangement which is administered wholly or primarily outside the United Kingdom,
which has effect, or is capable of having effect, so as to provide benefits on termination of employment or on death or retirement, to or in respect of earners;

"property" includes land;

"qualifying scheme" shall, in respect of an employer, include any stakeholder pension scheme which has at any time been designated by the employer under section 3(2);

"reporting accountant" has the meaning given to it by regulation 11(3);

"securities" means investments falling within paragraphs 1 to 5 of Schedule 1 to the Financial Services Act 1986 (investments and investment business) but does not include shares in an investment trust;

"tax relief" means amounts which may be deducted from contributions, retained by members and recovered from the Inland Revenue by a scheme administrator under section 639 of the Income and Corporation Taxes Act;

"transfer payment" means a payment in respect of a person's accrued rights under a pension scheme or pension arrangement made with a view to acquiring rights under another pension scheme or pension arrangement for that person; and

"with-profits fund" means a fund, maintained by an insurance company in respect of a particular part of its long-term business for which—

(a) separate accounting records are maintained by the insurance company in respect of all income and expenditure relating to that part of its business; and

(b) the benefits payable in respect of policies allocated to that fund are determined partly by reference to a discretion exercisable by any person.

(4)   In these Regulations references to notice in writing include using electronic communications for sending a notice to an address notified by the member for that purpose.

(5) Sections 249 and 435 of the Insolvency Act 1986 (connected and associated persons) and section 74 of the Bankruptcy (Scotland) Act 1985 (associated persons), apply for the purposes of regulations 4(3) and 11(4) as they apply for the purposes of those Acts respectively.

(6) For the purposes of these Regulations and section 1(8) and (9) (which provide that stakeholder pension schemes must have tax-exemption or tax-approval and must not refuse to accept transfer payments except in so far as necessary to ensure that the scheme has such exemption or approval) "tax-exemption" and "tax-approval" mean tax-exemption and tax-approval under Chapter IV of Part XIV of the Income and Corporation Taxes Act.

(7) In these Regulations, unless the context otherwise requires, references to a section are to a section of the Act.

PART II

CONDITIONS APPLYING TO STAKEHOLDER PENSION SCHEMES

Manner of establishment

2.—(1) A stakeholder pension scheme may (where not established under a trust) be established by means of one or more instruments in writing which provide for one or more contracts to be entered into between the manager of the scheme and each member of the scheme, or a person acting on his behalf.

(2) The manager of the scheme must be a person who is mentioned in section 632(1) of the Income and Corporation Taxes Act (establishment of schemes approved as personal pension schemes under Chapter IV of Part XIV of that Act).

Requirements applying to all stakeholder pension schemes as regards instruments establishing such schemes

3.—(1) Subject to paragraph (2), the instruments establishing a stakeholder pension scheme (the "scheme instruments") must prohibit the acceptance of contributions, transfer payments and pension credits to the scheme before 6th April 2001.

(2) Paragraph (1) shall not apply to a scheme in respect of which an application for registration under section 2 (registration of stakeholder pension schemes) is first made on or after 6th April 2001.

(3) The scheme instruments must require that no member is required to make any choice as regards the investment under the scheme of any payment made to it by him or on his behalf, any amount credited to the member's account in respect of a credit within the meaning of section 29 (pension sharing: creation of pension debits and credits), or any income or capital gain arising from the investment of such a payment or credit.

(4) The scheme instruments must, except to the extent permitted under regulations 13 or 14, prohibit the use of —
- (a) any payment made to the scheme by or on behalf of a member;
- (b) any amount credited to a member's account in respect of a credit within the meaning of section 29 (pension sharing: creation of pension debits and credits);
- (c) any income or capital gain arising from the investment of such a payment or credit; or
- (d) the value of his rights under the scheme;

in any way which does not result in the provision of benefits for or in respect of the member.

(5) The scheme instruments must require that—

   (a) if the scheme ceases to be registered under section 2 the winding-up of the scheme be commenced on the date on which it is notified in writing by the Occupational Pensions Regulatory Authority that it is no longer so registered;

   (b) if the trustees or manager fix a time for winding-up a scheme for any reason other than because the scheme ceases to be registered under section 2, the winding-up of the scheme be commenced at the earliest time fixed by the trustees or manager as the time from which steps for the purposes of winding-up are to be taken;

   (c) within 2 weeks of the date of commencement of any winding-up, the trustees or manager notify in writing any employers whom they know to have designated the scheme for the purposes of section 3 (duty of employers to facilitate access to stakeholder pension schemes) of the fact of, and the reason for, the winding-up including, where the scheme has ceased to be registered under section 2, the reason for the cessation of registration;

   (d) any contributions made to a scheme after the date of commencement of any winding-up must be repaid —

      (i) to the member, to the extent of his contributions; and

      (ii) as to any remainder, to his employer;

   (e) subject to paragraphs (8) and (9) below, on any winding-up all rights under the scheme shall be discharged by the trustees or managers of the scheme within 12 months of the commencement of winding-up, or as soon thereafter as is practicable, by the making of transfer payments—

      (i) to other stakeholder pension schemes, or schemes registered under Article 4 of the Welfare Reform and Pensions (Northern Ireland) Order 1999; or

      (ii) in accordance with requests by one or more members or beneficiaries in respect of their rights, to the trustees or managers of pension schemes or pension arrangements which are not schemes mentioned in head (i) above,

in accordance with paragraphs (6) and (7) below and regulation 6 or, where regulation 7 applies, with regulation 7; and

   (f) if the scheme fails to complete winding-up within 12 months of commencing winding-up proceedings, the trustees or manager notify the Occupational Pensions Regulatory Authority of that fact within one month of so failing to complete the winding-up.

(6) A transfer payment referred to in paragraph (5)(e) must be of an amount not less than the cash equivalent of the member's rights under the scheme, as calculated and verified in a manner consistent with regulations made under section 97 of the 1993 Act (calculation of cash equivalents) on the date on which the payment is made.

(7) Where the member's rights include any protected rights within the meaning of section 10 of the 1993 Act (protected rights and money purchase benefits), the scheme must provide for any transfer payments to be made subject to the requirements of section 28 of that Act (ways of giving effect to protected rights).

(8) Paragraph (5)(e) does not apply to rights to which effect is given under the scheme by the payment of an annuity (not being a deferred annuity) or a lump sum either to the member or, on or after his death, to another person.

(9) For the purposes of paragraph (8), a deferred annuity is an annuity under the terms of which payment does not commence immediately but at a time in the future.

Additional requirements as regards instruments establishing a stakeholder pension scheme established under a trust

4.—(1) Subject to paragraph (2) and to regulation 17(1), except in so far as is necessary to ensure that the scheme has tax-exemption or tax-approval, the instruments establishing a stakeholder pension scheme established under a trust ("the trust instruments") must preclude any restriction on membership of the scheme by reference to financial status, the amount of contributions to be made to the scheme or the manner in which contributions may be made to the scheme.

(2) Paragraph (1) shall not preclude any restrictions on—
    (a) membership by reference to employment with a particular employer or in a particular trade or profession or by reference to membership of a particular organisation; or
    (b) the payment of contributions by means of cash or a credit card.

(3) The trust instruments must require that—
    (a) unless sub-paragraph (b) applies, at least one trustee and at least one-third of the total number of trustees is neither connected with nor an associate of any person providing services to or otherwise managing the scheme (other than as a trustee);

    (b)   where a company is trustee of the scheme and there is no trustee of the scheme who is not a company, at least one of the directors of the company and at least one-third of the total number of its directors is neither connected with nor an associate of any person providing services to or otherwise managing the scheme (other than as a trustee).

  (4) The trust instruments must not—
    (a)   enable any of the provisions required by regulation 3 or by this regulation to be modified or disapplied;
    (b)   have a condition that the trustees must obtain the consent of any person before making any decision about investments for the purposes of the scheme; or
    (c)   except in so far as otherwise required by or under any enactment, preclude the trustees from amending the trust instruments to provide for different investments to be held for the purposes of the scheme.

Additional requirements as regards instruments establishing a stakeholder pension scheme not established under a trust

5.—(1) Subject to paragraph (2) and to regulation 17(1), except in so far as is necessary to ensure that the scheme has tax-exemption or tax-approval, the instruments establishing a stakeholder pension scheme established otherwise than under a trust must preclude any restriction on membership of the scheme by reference to—
    (a)   employment with a particular employer, or in a particular trade or profession or by reference to membership of a particular organisation; or
    (b)   financial status, the amount of contributions to be made to the scheme or the manner in which contributions may be made to the scheme.

  (2) Paragraph (1) shall not preclude any restrictions on the payment of contributions by means of cash or a credit card.

Procedure for discharging rights on winding-up

6.—(1) The scheme instruments must require that, where the winding-up of a stakeholder pension scheme has commenced, the trustees or manager must, except in cases where regulation 7 applies, make transfer payments in respect of members' rights in accordance with the procedure set out in paragraphs (2) to (9) of this regulation.

  (2) The trustees or manager shall no later than 4 months after the commencement of winding-up give notice to each member stating—

(a) that they propose to make a transfer payment in respect of his rights under the scheme to their choice of a stakeholder pension scheme or a scheme registered under Article 4 of the Welfare Reform and Pensions (Northern Ireland) Order 1999, that scheme to be named in the notice, unless the member applies for the transfer payment to be made to a pension scheme or pension arrangement of his choice;

(b) the value of the member's rights at the date that the scheme commenced winding-up, being an amount not less than the cash equivalent of those rights on that date, as calculated and verified in a manner consistent with regulations made under section 97 of the 1993 Act (calculation of cash equivalents); and

(c) that, unless the member applies within 4 months of the date of the notice for a transfer payment to be made to a pension scheme or pension arrangement of his choice, a transfer payment may be made without his consent to the scheme named in the notice as the scheme of the trustees' or manager's choice.

(3) If any member makes an application for a transfer payment to be made to a pension scheme or pension arrangement of his choice (whether or not the application is made under section 95 of the 1993 Act (ways of taking right to cash equivalent)) the trustees or manager shall, unless paragraph (4) of this regulation applies, do what is needed to carry out what the member requires within one month of receiving the member's application.

(4) This paragraph applies where—
(a) it is not possible for the trustees or manager to do what is needed to carry out what the member requires within 12 months of the date of commencement of winding-up;

(b) it would contravene the terms of the scheme's tax-approval or tax-exemption, or any provision of the scheme required to be included as a condition of any such approval or exemption, for the trustees or manager to do what is needed to carry out what the member requires; or

(c) the member withdraws his application before the trustees have or the manager has done what is needed to carry out what he requires.

(5) Where paragraph (4)(a) or (b) applies in relation to the first such application made by the member as is mentioned in paragraph (3), the trustees or manager shall as soon as practicable give notice to the member stating—
(a) that they cannot carry out what he requires and the reasons why not;

(b) that if he does not make a further application such as is mentioned in paragraph (3) they propose to make a transfer payment in respect of his rights as set out in the notice given in accordance with paragraph (2); and

(c) that, unless he makes such further application within one month of the date of the notice given in accordance with this paragraph, such a transfer payment may be made without his consent.

(6) In any case where—

(a) the trustees do not or the manager does not receive any such application as is mentioned in paragraph (3) within 4 months of the date of the notice given in accordance with paragraph (2);

(b) the member withdraws his application and no further such application by him is received by the trustees or manager within one month of that date; or

(c) paragraph (4)(a) or (b) applied in respect of the first such application made by the member and—

(i) the trustees or manager, having given notice to the member in the terms set out in paragraph (5), do not receive any such further application as is mentioned in that paragraph within one month of the date of the notice, or

(ii) the trustees or manager, having given such notice, have received a further application such as is mentioned in paragraph (5) within one month of that date but paragraph (4) applies in respect of that further application,

the trustees or manager may make a transfer payment in respect of the member's rights to the pension scheme named in the notice mentioned in paragraph (2) as the scheme of their choice.

(7) The trustees or manager shall, within one month of making a transfer payment under paragraph (3) or (6), give notice to the member stating the amount of the payment, the name and address of the scheme to which it has been made and the date on which it was made.

(8) A notice given under this regulation shall be in writing and may be sent to the member's last known address.

(9) For the purposes of this regulation "member" includes "beneficiary".

Procedure for discharging on winding-up rights of members with whom the trustees or manager have lost contact

7.—(1) This regulation applies in respect of any member whose address for the time being is not known to the trustees or manager and in respect of whom—

(a) correspondence sent by them to the member at his last address known to them has been returned undelivered; and

(b) no contribution has been made to the scheme by him or on his behalf during the 2 years preceding the commencement of winding-up of the scheme.

(2) In cases where this regulation applies, the trustees or manager shall on the winding-up of the scheme make a transfer payment in respect of the member's rights to their choice of a stakeholder pension scheme, or to a scheme registered under Article 4 of the Welfare Reform and Pensions (Northern Ireland) Order 1999 and need give no notice of the transfer payment to the member either before or after it is made.

Requirement applying to all stakeholder pension schemes as regards investments

8.—(1) For the purposes of section 1(1)(b), it shall be a condition of a scheme being a stakeholder pension scheme that the requirements of this regulation are complied with.

(2) Except where monies are held temporarily on deposit in the course of dealing in assets for the purposes of the scheme, the trustees or manager must ensure that there is derived, from any part of the funds of the scheme that are held on deposit, a return accruing on a daily basis that is, net of any fees or charges, not less than the base rate minus 2 per cent. per annum.

(3) Where the base rate is increased, paragraph (2) shall apply as if the reference to the base rate in that paragraph were—

(a) within one calendar month of the date of the increase, a reference to the base rate immediately before the increase; and

(b) after that calendar month has elapsed, a reference to the base rate as increased.

(4) The trustees or manager shall not have scheme assets that are represented by units or shares in a collective investment scheme (within the meaning of section 75 of the Financial Services Act 1986 (interpretation: definition of 'collective investment scheme') unless it is a requirement of the collective investment scheme that the purchase and sale price of those units or shares shall, at any given time, not differ from each other.

(5) The trustees or manager shall not have scheme assets that are represented by rights under a contract of insurance which are expressed as units or shares in funds held by the insurance company unless it is a requirement of the contract of insurance that the purchase and sale price of those units or shares shall, at any given time, not differ from each other.

(6) In this regulation—

"base rate" means the rate for the time being quoted by the reference banks as applicable to sterling deposits or, where there is for the time being more than one such base rate, the rate which, when the base rate quoted by each bank is ranked in a descending sequence of seven, is fourth in the sequence;

"contract of insurance" means a pension fund management contract within Part VII of Schedule 1 to the Insurance Companies Act 1982 (classes of long term business) carried out by a person authorised to do so under that Act;

"deposit" has the meaning given to it in section 5 of the Banking Act 1987;

"reference banks" means the seven largest institutions for the time being which—

(a) are authorised by the Financial Services Authority under the Banking Act 1987;

(b) are incorporated in the United Kingdom and carrying on within it a deposit-taking business (as defined in section 6, but subject to any order under section 7, of that Act); and

(c) quote a base rate applicable to sterling deposits,

and for the purpose of this definition the size of an institution at any time is to be determined by reference to the gross assets denominated in sterling of that institution, together with any subsidiary (as defined in section 736 of the Companies Act 1985), as shown in the audited end of year accounts last published before that time.

Requirement for statement of investment principles for schemes not established under trust

9.—(1) Subject to paragraph (2), for the purposes of section 1(1)(b), it shall be a condition of a scheme being a stakeholder pension scheme that the requirements of this regulation are complied with.

(2) This regulation does not apply to a scheme established under a trust.

(3) The manager of the scheme must secure that there is prepared, maintained and from time to time revised a written statement of the principles governing decisions about investments for the purposes of the scheme.

(4) The statement must cover the manager's policy about the following matters—

    (a) the kinds of investments to be held;

    (b) the balance between different kinds of investments;

    (c) risk;

    (d) the expected return on investments;

    (e) the realisation of investments;

    (f) the extent (if at all) to which social, environmental or ethical considerations are taken into account in the selection, retention and realisation of investments; and

    (g) the exercise of the rights (including voting rights) attaching to investments.

(5) Subject to paragraph (6), where a copy of the latest statement mentioned in paragraph (3) is requested by a member, the statement shall, within 2 months of the request, be furnished to that member either—

    (a) free of charge; or

    (b) where a charge is made, at an amount that does not exceed the expense incurred in copying, posting and packing the statement.

(6) A copy of the statement mentioned in paragraph (3) need not be furnished to the same person within 12 months of the person last being given such a copy unless the statement has changed during that 12 month period.

(7) In this regulation "member" includes "beneficiary".

Requirement for manager of schemes not established under a trust to have regard to certain matters, and to take advice, relating to investment

    10.—(1) Subject to paragraph (2), for the purposes of section 1(1)(b), it shall be a condition of a scheme being a stakeholder pension scheme that the requirements of this regulation are complied with.

(2) This regulation does not apply to a scheme established under a trust.

(3) The manager of the scheme, and any person managing funds held for the purposes of the scheme, must, in investing such funds or in selecting investment options offered to members of the scheme, have regard to—

    (a) the need for diversification of investments, in so far as appropriate to the circumstances of the scheme; and

    (b) the suitability for the purposes of the scheme of any investment or investment option proposed.

(4) The manager of the scheme, and any person managing funds held for the purposes of the scheme, must, before making any investment or selecting any investment option for the purposes of the scheme, obtain and consider proper advice as to whether the investment is satisfactory having regard to the matters mentioned in paragraph (3) and the principles contained in the statement under regulation 9.

(5) For the purposes of paragraph (4), "proper advice" means—

    (a) where giving the advice constitutes carrying on investment business in the United Kingdom within the meaning of the Financial Services Act 1986, advice—

        (i) given by a person authorised under Chapter III of Part I of that Act,

        (ii) given by a person exempted under Chapter IV of that Part who, in giving the advice, is acting in the course of the business in respect of which he is exempt,

        (iii) given by a person where, by virtue of paragraph 27 of Schedule 1 to that Act, paragraph 15 of that Schedule does not apply to the giving of the advice, or

        (iv) given by a person who, by virtue of regulation 5 of the Banking Coordination (Second Council Directive) Regulations 1992, may give the advice though not authorised as mentioned in head (i) above;

    (b) in any other case, the advice of a person whom the manager or person managing funds held for the purposes of the scheme reasonably believes to be qualified by his ability in and practical experience of financial matters and to have the appropriate knowledge and experience of the management of the investments of pension schemes.

(6) Paragraph (4) does not apply to the extent that the manager or the person managing the scheme's funds is a person who may themselves give proper advice.

(7) To the extent that paragraph (4) is disapplied by virtue of paragraph (6), the manager or person managing the scheme's funds,

being persons who may themselves give proper advice, must, before making any investment or selecting any investment option for the purposes of the scheme, consider whether the investment is satisfactory having regard to the matters mentioned in paragraph (3) and the principles contained in the statement under regulation 9, and must record in writing the reasons why they consider that any investment made or investment option chosen is satisfactory having regard to those matters.

(8) No person shall be regarded as having complied with paragraph (4) unless the advice mentioned in that paragraph is given or confirmed in writing.

Requirement for manager of schemes not established under trust to appoint a reporting accountant

11.—(1) Subject to paragraph (2), for the purposes of section 1(1)(b), it shall be a condition of a scheme being a stakeholder pension scheme that the requirements of this regulation are complied with.

(2) This regulation does not apply to a scheme established under a trust.

(3) There shall be a person appointed by the manager of the scheme as reporting accountant for the scheme ("the reporting accountant").

(4) A person shall not be appointed as the reporting accountant where—
    (a) he is a member of the scheme; or
    (b) he is connected with or an associate of the manager of the scheme.

(5) The reporting accountant shall be appointed in writing and the notice of appointment shall specify—
    (a) the date on which the appointment is due to take effect;
    (b) to whom the reporting accountant is to report; and
    (c) from whom the reporting accountant is to take instructions.

(6) The manager shall procure from the reporting accountant within one month of his receiving his notice of appointment a statement—
    (a) acknowledging in writing his receipt of his notice of appointment; and
    (b) confirming in writing that he will notify the manager of any conflict of interest to which he is subject in relation to the scheme immediately he becomes aware of its existence.

(7)   It shall be a condition of the appointment of the reporting accountant that he agrees, in the event of his resignation, to serve on the manager a written notice of resignation containing—

    (a)   a statement specifying any circumstances connected with the resignation which in his opinion significantly affect the interests of the members or prospective members of, or of beneficiaries under, the scheme; or

    (b)   a declaration that he knows of no such circumstances.

(8)   Where the reporting accountant is removed by the manager or resigns or dies, the manager shall appoint another reporting accountant within 3 months from the date of the removal, resignation or death.

Requirement for annual declaration

12.—(1)   For the purposes of section 1(1)(b), it shall be a condition of a scheme being a stakeholder pension scheme that the requirements of this regulation are complied with.

(2)   The trustees or manager of the scheme shall, at least once a year, make a declaration in writing signed by the trustees or manager containing the following statements in relation to the period of 12 months ending on a date not earlier than 3 months prior to the date of the declaration—

    (a)   that regulations 13 and 14 of these Regulations have been complied with in relation to the scheme;

    (b)   that the scheme's systems and controls are designed and used in a way that ensures that transactions in securities, property or other assets occur at a fair market value;

    (c)   that the scheme's system of determining the value of members' rights is designed and used in a way that ensures that the value of members' rights has been determined in accordance with the provisions in the instruments establishing the scheme; and

    (d)   that adequate accounts and records have been maintained for the purposes of providing to members the statement required by regulation 18(2) of these Regulations.

(3)   The declaration mentioned in paragraph (2) shall also contain a statement which—

    (a)   explains that regulations 13 and 14 of these Regulations impose limits on the amount of charges which may be made by a stakeholder pension scheme and on the manner in which charges may be made by such a scheme;

(b) explains that regulation 18(2) of these Regulations requires a stakeholder pension scheme to provide an annual benefit statement to each member.

(4) In the case of a scheme established under a trust, the trustees shall, within 3 months of the date of the declaration, obtain from the scheme auditor appointed by virtue of section 47(1) of the 1995 Act (professional advisers) or from the reporting accountant—

(a) a statement whether, in the auditor's or reporting accountant's opinion, it was or was not unreasonable for the trustees to make the statements contained in the declaration, or

(b) to the extent that the auditor or reporting accountant is unable to express such an opinion, an explanation of why he is unable to do so.

(5) In the case of a scheme not established under a trust, the manager shall, within 3 months of the date of the declaration, obtain from the reporting accountant appointed by virtue of regulation 11—

(a) a statement whether, in the opinion of the reporting accountant, it was or was not unreasonable for the manager to make the statements contained in the declaration, or

(b) to the extent that the reporting accountant is unable to express such an opinion, an explanation of why he is unable to do so.

(6) The trustees or manager shall annex to the declaration mentioned in paragraph (2) the statement obtained in accordance with paragraph (4) or (5).

(7) The trustees or manager shall make available to members and beneficiaries of the scheme on request the declaration mentioned in paragraph (2) annexing the statement obtained in accordance with paragraph (4) or (5).

Expenses, commission etc. – principles

13.—(1) Except to the extent permitted by regulation 14—

(a) no payment made to a stakeholder pension scheme by or on behalf of any member;

(b) no income or capital gain arising from the investment of such a payment;

(c) no amount credited to a member's account in respect of a credit within the meaning of section 29 (pension sharing: creation of pension debits and credits); and

(d)   no amount representing the value of any rights of a member under the scheme,

shall be used in any way which does not result in the provision of benefits for or in respect of members.

(2)   Paragraph (1) does not apply—

(a)   to the extent that section 31 (pension sharing: pension debits), or any enactment in force in Northern Ireland corresponding to that section, applies to reduce the benefits or future benefits to which a member may be entitled under the scheme; or

(b)   to prevent the trustees or manager of a scheme from complying with their obligations under an order made by a court—

(i)   under section 23 of the Matrimonial Causes Act 1973 (financial provision in connection with divorce proceedings, etc.) by virtue of section 25B or 25C of that Act (powers to include provision about pensions),

(ii)   under Article 25 of the Matrimonial Causes (Northern Ireland) Order 1978 by virtue of Article 27B or 27C of that Order (Northern Ireland powers corresponding to section 25B and 25C of the Matrimonial Causes Act 1973), or

(iii)   under section 12A(2) or (3) of the Family Law (Scotland) Act 1985 (powers in relation to pensions lump sums when making a capital sum order).

(3)   In this regulation and in regulation 14 below "member" includes "beneficiary".

Charges etc. — *permitted reductions in members' rights*

14.—(1) The value of a member's rights under the scheme may be reduced in the circumstances, and to the extent, set out in paragraphs (2) to (5) of this regulation.

(2)   To the extent that a member's rights are represented by a fund allocated to him to the exclusion of other members, the value of those rights may be reduced by the making of deductions from that fund no greater than 1/365 per cent. of its value for each day on which it is held for the purposes of the scheme.

(3)   To the extent that a member's rights are represented by a share of funds held for the purposes of the scheme, the amount of that share not being determined by reference to a discretion exercisable by any person, the value of those rights may be reduced by the making of deductions from that share no greater than 1/365 per cent. of its value for each day on which it is so held.

(4) To the extent that a member's rights are represented by rights in a with-profits fund, the value of those rights may be reduced by the making of deductions from the with-profits fund no greater than 1/365 per cent. of the value of the member's rights in the fund for each day on which it is held for the purposes of the scheme.

(5) The value of a member's rights under the scheme may be reduced—

(a) where administrative expenses are incurred by the trustees or manager in—

(i) the purchase or provision of an annuity for the member in accordance with the scheme, or

(ii) the making of payments of income (otherwise than by way of an annuity) to a member under arrangements made in accordance with the scheme,

by the amount of those expenses;

(b) by such amount, and in such manner, as is permitted by regulations under section 24 or 41 (charges in respect of pension sharing costs);

(c) where any stamp duty or other charges are incurred directly in the sale or purchase of securities or property held for the purposes of the scheme, by the amount of such of those charges as are attributable to the member's rights;

(d) where the member is the transferor for the purposes of section 29 (pension sharing: creation of pension debits and credits), by the amount of any payment made to discharge the liability of the trustees or manager in respect of a credit within the meaning of that section;

(e) by the amount of any payment made for the purpose of returning excessive contributions made in relation to the member, in accordance with the arrangements that the scheme must have in order to be approved under Chapter IV of Part XIV of the Income and Corporation Taxes Act 1988 (pension schemes, social security benefits, life annuities etc.);

(f) by the amount required to discharge any monetary obligation due from the member to the scheme which—

(i) arises out of a criminal, negligent or fraudulent act or omission by him; or

(ii) in the case of a trust scheme of which the person in question is a trustee, arises out of breach of trust by him,

and which is either not in dispute or, if there is a dispute, where the obligation in question has become enforceable under an order of a competent court or in consequence of an award of an arbitrator or, in Scotland, an arbiter appointed (failing agreement between the parties) by the sheriff.

(6) When calculating the value of a member's rights for the purposes of paragraphs (2) to (4) above, where the trustees or manager have specified under paragraph (7) below that such rights are to be valued weekly or monthly—

(a) where the rights are to be valued weekly, they are to be valued on such day of the week ("the specified day") as has been so specified by the trustees or manager (except that, where that day is not a working day, the rights are to be valued on the next working day), and the value of the rights on each subsequent day prior to the next specified day is to be taken to be the value of the rights on the previous specified day; and

(b) where the rights are to be valued monthly, they are to be valued on such date in each month ("the specified date") as has been so specified by the trustees or manager (except that, where that date is not a working day, the rights are to be valued on the next working day), and the value of the rights on each subsequent day prior to the next specified date is to be taken to be the value of the rights on the previous specified date.

(7) For the purposes of paragraph (6) above—

(a) the frequency, which must be daily, weekly or monthly, with which rights are to be valued; and

(b) where valuation is to take place weekly or monthly, the day of the week or, as the case may be, the date in the month on which it is to take place,

must be specified in writing by the trustees or manager of the scheme; and the specification may not be amended during the period of 12 months after the date on which it is made.

(8) Where the value of any member's rights is reduced by reference to an amount of costs or charges referred to in paragraph (5)(c) above, then, for the purposes of calculating any reduction under paragraph (2), (3) or (4) above, the funds held by the scheme are to be calculated after the deduction of any such amount.

Requirement for trustees or manager to satisfy certain conditions in relation to with-profit funds
15.—(1) Where all or any of a stakeholder pension scheme's assets are invested in a with-profits fund it shall, for the purposes of section 1(1)(b), be a condition of the scheme being a stakeholder pension scheme that the requirements of this regulation are complied with.

(2) A stakeholder pension scheme shall not invest any assets in a with-profits fund that includes non-stakeholder pension scheme assets.

(3) Prior to entering into any agreement whereby any assets of the scheme will be invested in a with-profits fund, the trustees or manager of that scheme shall take such steps as are necessary to ensure that they obtain a written contract from the insurance company maintaining the with-profits fund which provides that the insurance company will, in respect of any period that the stakeholder pension scheme has assets invested in the with-profits fund—

  (a) provide such information to the trustees or manager of the stakeholder pension scheme as is necessary to allow the trustees or manager to operate in compliance with the requirements of regulations 13 or 14;

  (b) ensure that members of the stakeholder pension scheme will not be treated less favourably than any other members of stakeholder pension schemes who may have assets invested in the with-profits fund;

  (c) provide to the trustees or manager of the stakeholder pension scheme any certificates from the auditor and actuary to the company that are necessary to allow the stakeholder pension scheme's auditor or reporting accountant to certify that the requirements of regulations 13 and 14 have been complied with

  (d) ensure that no investments are made in the fund other than the investment of stakeholder pension scheme assets; and

  (e) take such steps as are necessary to comply with paragraph (4).

(4) The insurance company must, at least annually, provide the trustees or manager of the stakeholder pension scheme with a certificate from the auditor to the insurance company or the appointed actuary to the insurance company certifying that the insurance company has systems and controls that are designed and used so that—

  (a) proper accounting records are maintained in respect of all income and expenditure relevant to regulations 13 and 14 and the terms of the contract referred to in paragraph (3);

  (b) the records referred to in sub-paragraph (a) are provided at least annually to the auditor or reporting accountant, as the case may be, of the scheme;

  (c) no expenditure is charged to the with-profits fund where that expenditure would be contrary to the requirements of regulation 13 or 14; and

(d)   the terms of the contract referred to in paragraph (3) have been complied with.

(5)   Where the insurance company does not comply with the agreement referred to in paragraph (3), the trustees or managers must take such steps as are necessary to ensure that the insurance company does so comply.

(6)   In this regulation "appointed actuary" means a person appointed as actuary to the person responsible for managing the with-profits fund in which assets of the stakeholder pension scheme are invested.

Requirements as regards the provision of other services
16.   For the purposes of section 1(1)(b), it shall be a condition of a scheme being a stakeholder pension scheme that —
  (a)   the scheme does not provide any service other than the management of the scheme and its funds unless -
      (i)   any such service is provided under a contract separate from any contract of membership of the scheme, is provided free of charge or is consistent with regulations 13 and 14, and
      (ii)   any contract for such service is in writing and sets out the amount of any charge for the service and the terms on which it is to be paid; and
  (b)   it is not a condition of membership of the scheme that any person enter into any contract, whether with the trustees or manager of the scheme or any other person, other than the contract of membership of the scheme.

Restrictions on contributions
17.—(1)   Subject to paragraph (2), the rules of a stakeholder pension scheme may permit the trustees or manager to refuse to accept a payment to the scheme of less than £20.

(2)   Paragraph (1) does not permit the trustees or manager to refuse to accept any payment made to the scheme by the Inland Revenue by way of tax relief, minimum contributions, minimum payments or any payment under section 42A(3) of the 1993 Act (reduced rate of Class 1 contributions, and rebates).

(3)   For the purposes of paragraph (1), amounts in respect of income tax deducted and retained by a member as permitted by section 639 of the Income and Corporation Taxes Act (tax reliefs: member's contributions) shall not be treated as payments to the scheme.

(4) The trustees or manager of a stakeholder pension scheme may refuse to accept any contribution if its acceptance would contravene the terms of the scheme's tax-exemption or tax-approval under Chapter IV of Part XIV of the Income and Corporation Taxes Act.

Disclosure of information to members

18.—(1) For the purposes of section 1(1)(b), it shall be a condition of a scheme being a stakeholder pension scheme that the trustees or manager of the scheme comply with the requirements set out in this regulation in addition to such requirements of regulations under section 113 of the 1993 Act (disclosure of information about schemes to members) as are applicable to the scheme.

(2) Where a person is a member for all or part of a statement year, there shall be provided to the person within 3 months of the end of the statement year to which it relates, a statement which contains the information mentioned in paragraph (5), in so far as the information relates to that statement year.

(3) For the purposes of this regulation "statement year" means the period of 12 months beginning on a date chosen by the trustees or manager which falls on or before the day that the scheme is registered under section 2 (such date to be chosen on or before the scheme is so registered) and, subject to paragraph (4), each subsequent period ending on the anniversary of the ending of the first statement year.

(4) For the purposes of paragraph (3) the trustees or manager may choose a new date for the ending of the statement year if—
  (a) the date chosen—
      (i) is specified in writing; and
      (ii) falls before the end of the statement year during which the trustees or managers specify the new date; and
  (b) no other date has been chosen by the trustees or managers under this paragraph during the previous period of 12 months;
and, if a new date is chosen under this paragraph, "statement year" shall mean the period of 12 months ending on the date chosen and each subsequent period ending on the anniversary of that date.

(5) The information to be provided under paragraph (2) is—

  (a) the value of the member's rights under the scheme on the day before the first day of the statement year, being an amount which is not less than the cash equivalent of those rights on that date, as calculated and verified in a manner consistent with regulations made under section 97 of the 1993 Act (calculation of cash equivalents);

(b) the value of the member's rights on the last day of the statement year, being an amount which is not less than the cash equivalent of those rights on that date, as calculated and verified in a manner consistent with regulations made under section 97 of the 1993 Act (calculation of cash equivalents);

(c) the amount of the value mentioned in sub-paragraph (b) that is attributable to investment gains or losses made or sustained by the scheme during that statement year;

(d) the amount of each contribution made by the member and the date on which it was received;

(e) the amount of each contribution made by any employer on behalf of the member and the date on which it was received;

(f) except where contributions referred to in sub-paragraphs (d) and (e) are increased by the trustees or manager in anticipation of a payment to the scheme by the Inland Revenue by way of tax relief in respect of the member, the amount of each such payment by the Inland Revenue and the date on which it was received;

(g) the amount of each payment to the scheme by way of minimum contributions in respect of the member and the date on which it was received;

(h) the amount of each payment made to the scheme by way of minimum payments in respect of the member and the date on which it was received;

(i) the amount of each payment made to the scheme under section 42A(3) of the 1993 Act (reduced rates of Class 1 contributions, and rebates) in respect of the member and the date on which it was received;

(j) the amount of any transfer payment made to the scheme in respect of the member, the name of the scheme or arrangement from which the payment was made and the date on which it was made;

(k) any amount credited to the member's account in respect of a credit within the meaning of section 29 (pension sharing: creation of pension debits and credits);

(l) any reduction under section 31 (pension sharing: reduction of benefit), or any enactment in force in Northern Ireland corresponding to that section, in the benefits or future benefits to which the member is entitled under the scheme;

(m) any contributions refunded under the provisions of Chapter IV of Part XIV of the Income and Corporation Taxes Act (pension schemes, social security benefits, life annuities etc);

(n) any amount paid to the member in accordance with section 634A of the Income and Corporation Taxes Act (income withdrawals by member) or section 636A of that Act (income withdrawal after death of member);

(o) any other amount deducted from the member's account, the nature of the deduction and the date on which it was made;

(p) the total amount of any part of any of the contributions and payments mentioned in sub-paragraphs (d) to (k) which has not been credited to the member's account and the manner in which that amount has been used;

(q) the member's date of birth used in determining the appropriate age-related percentage for the purposes of section 42A of the 1993 Act and the name and address of whom to contact should that date be incorrect; and

(r) where the whole or any part of the member's rights under the scheme is represented by rights in a with-profits fund –

    (i) the principles adopted in allocating rights under that fund, including the extent of any smoothing of investment returns and the levels of any guarantees, and

    (ii) the principles which will be adopted in allocating such rights if the member's rights under the scheme cease to be represented by rights in that fund.

(6) Each member must be provided with a statement setting out any change in the scheme's rules or practice as regards the extent to which or the circumstances in which—

(a) any payment made to the scheme by or on behalf of a member,

(b) any amount credited to the member's account in respect of a credit within the meaning of section 29 (pension sharing: creation of pension debits and credits),

(c) any income or capital gain arising from the investment of such a payment, or

(d) the value of any rights under the scheme,

may, in accordance with regulations 13 and 14, be used otherwise than to provide benefits for or in respect of that member.

(7) The statement mentioned in paragraph (6) must be provided within one month of the change.

(8)   The statements mentioned in paragraphs (2) and (6) may be provided by sending them by post to the member at his last address known to the trustees or manager.

(9)   For the purposes of this regulation "member" shall not include any member whose present address is not known to the trustees or manager and in respect of whom—

    (a)   correspondence sent by them to the member at his last address known to them has been returned undelivered; and

    (b)   no contribution has been made to the scheme by him or on his behalf during the 2 years preceding the most recent date on which they would, apart from this paragraph, be required to provide him with a statement under this regulation.

(10)   For the purposes of this regulation "member" shall include a beneficiary making income withdrawals from the scheme in accordance with section 636A of the Income and Corporation Taxes Act 1988 (income withdrawals after death of member).

Requirement for trustees of a stakeholder pension scheme established under a trust

19.   For the purposes of section 1(1)(b), it shall be a condition of a scheme which is established under a trust being a stakeholder pension scheme that the scheme comply with sections 35 and 36 (functions of trustees) of the 1995 Act except the reference to section 56 in section 35(2) and 35(5)(b) of that Act.

PART III

REGISTRATION OF STAKEHOLDER PENSION SCHEMES

Persons who may apply for registration of stakeholder pension schemes not established under trust

20.   For the purposes of subsections (2) and (4) of section 2 (prescribed persons may apply for registration of stakeholder pension schemes and will be liable to penalties in certain circumstances connected with such application) the prescribed person in relation to a scheme not established under a trust is the manager of the scheme.

Access to the register

21.—(1) The Occupational Pensions Regulatory Authority shall supply the most recent copy of the register to any person on request either—

(a) free of charge; or
(b) where a charge is made, at an amount that does not exceed the expense incurred in copying, posting and packing the statement.

(2) The Authority may publish the register in any way.

PART IV

EMPLOYER REQUIREMENTS

Exemptions from employer access and consultation requirements
22.—(1) An employer need not comply with the requirements set out in section 3 (duty of employers to facilitate access to stakeholder pension schemes) and this Part of these Regulations if he has fewer than 5 employees.

(2) An employer need not comply with the requirements set out in section 3 and this Part of these Regulations if—
(a) it is a term of the contract of every relevant employee (other than any employee who has not attained the age of 18) that—
(i) the employer will make contributions to a personal pension scheme in respect of the employee, in accordance with paragraph (3) and subject to paragraph (4), for any period for which that employee, while in his employment, is a member of that scheme; and
(ii) the employer will, if he is requested to do so by the employee, deduct the employee's contributions to that scheme from his remuneration and pay them to the trustees or manager of the scheme; and
(b) subject to paragraph (7), no charge or penalty is imposed by the personal pension scheme in question on any member in respect of whom the employer has made any contributions to the scheme for transferring all or any of his funds out of that scheme or for ceasing to contribute to the scheme.

(3) Contributions are made in accordance with this paragraph if they are made on each occasion on which the employee is paid remuneration by the employer (or, if the employer and employee agree longer intervals, at such longer intervals as are agreed) and at a rate of at least 3% of the amount of remuneration paid.

(4) Contributions made by the employer in accordance with paragraph (3) may be conditional on the employee making contributions

to the same scheme at a specified rate on each occasion on which he is paid (or, if the employer and employee agree longer intervals, at such longer intervals as are agreed) while—

    (a)   if the arrangement is in place as at 8th October 2001, the employer is making contributions equal to or exceeding that of the employee; and

    (b)   if the condition is first imposed on or after 8th October 2001 or if sub-paragraph (a) ceases to apply after that date, the employee is not required to make contributions exceeding 3% of the amount of remuneration paid to him on any such occasion or for each such interval.

(5) For the purposes of paragraphs (3) and (4) only payments made in respect of basic pay shall be taken into account and payments in respect of bonuses, commission, overtime or similar payments shall be disregarded.

(6) In calculating the amount paid to an employee for the purposes of paragraphs (3) and (4) no account shall be taken of any deductions from the employee's remuneration which are made in respect of tax, national insurance contributions or pension contributions.

(7) For the purposes of paragraph (2)(b) deductions in the member's accrued rights to take account of —

    (a)   costs or charges that have not previously been taken into account and which would otherwise have been deductible under the terms and conditions of the scheme by the trustees or manager of the scheme in question, had contributions continued or a transfer not occurred, in respect of the member's rights under the scheme on or before the day the cessation takes effect or the day that member's rights are transferred from that scheme; or

    (b)   market value adjustments which occur in relation to a with-profit fund,

shall not be taken to be charges or penalties for transferring those funds or for ceasing to contribute to that scheme.

(8) An employer need not comply with the requirements set out in section 3 and this Part of these Regulations if the employer can provide written evidence to show that contributions are being made, and have continuously been made from a date prior to 8th October 2001, as if each relevant employee had a term in his contract that would satisfy the requirements set out in paragraph (2)(a) above.

(9) An employer need not comply with the requirements set out in section 3 and this Part of these Regulations to the extent that it is not practicable for him to do so because—

(a) on section 3 first applying to him (unless, subject to sub-paragraph (b), that section first applied to him on 8th October 2001), he has not had sufficient time to select a scheme which he wishes to designate for the purposes of that section and to complete the designation process, provided that the exemption under this sub-paragraph shall not apply for more than 3 months from the date on which that section first applies;

(b) on employing a fifth employee in the period from 8th July 2001 to 8th October 2001 after a period when he had fewer than 5 employees, he has not had sufficient time to select a scheme which he wishes to designate and to complete the designation process, provided that the exemption under this sub-paragraph shall not apply for more than 3 months from the date on which he employed that fifth employee;

(c) on section 3 applying to him after a period when it did not so apply, he has not had sufficient time to select a scheme which he wishes to designate and to complete the designation process, provided that the exemption under this sub-paragraph shall not apply for more than 3 months from the date on which that section begins to apply after such a period; or

(d) on having withdrawn his designation of a scheme due to reasons beyond his control he has not had sufficient time to select another scheme which he wishes to designate and to complete the designation process, provided that the exemption under this sub-paragraph shall not apply for more than 4 months from the withdrawal of designation.

(10) Where a stakeholder pension scheme commences winding-up, the employer need not comply with the consultation requirements in section 3(2) if, within 4 months of the scheme commencing to wind up, he designates for the purposes of that section the stakeholder pension scheme named in the notice mentioned in regulation 6(2) as the scheme of the trustees' or manager's choice

Definition of relevant employees

23.—(1) The following persons shall not be an employer's relevant employees for the purposes of section 3 —

(a) any employee whose employment would qualify him for membership of an occupational pension scheme of the employer had he been employed by that employer for more than 12 months;

(b) any employee whose employment would qualify him for membership of an occupational pension scheme of the employer if he were over the age of 18, or was more than 5 years younger than the age which would be his normal pension age were he a member of the scheme;

(c) any employee who—

(i) had he wished to join an occupational pension scheme of the employer at some time in the past, would have qualified for membership of the scheme; and

(ii) is now excluded from membership of that scheme because he did not join the scheme at an earlier time;

(d) any employee who has been employed by the employer for a continuous period of less than three months;

(e) any employee whose earnings have fallen below the lower earnings limit for one or more weeks within the last 3 months; and

(f) any employee who is ineligible, by virtue of any enactment relating to tax or any restriction imposed by the Inland Revenue, to make contributions to a stakeholder pension scheme.

(2) For the purposes of paragraph (1)(b) "normal pension age" means the earliest age at which the employee in question would, if he were a member of the scheme in question, be entitled to receive benefits (other than a guaranteed minimum pension) on retirement from employment to which the scheme applies, disregarding any rule of the scheme which makes special provision as to early retirement on grounds of ill-health or otherwise.

Payroll deduction of contributions

24.—(1) Subject to paragraph (2), where an employee requests an employer to make or vary (but not cease) deductions of the employee's contributions to a qualifying scheme from his remuneration ("the request"), the employer must comply with the request as soon as possible, but no later than the end of the pay period following that in which the request is made.

(2) Where an employee makes the request within 6 months of requesting the same employer to make, vary or cease deductions of the employee's contributions to a qualifying scheme from the employee's remuneration, the employer need not comply with the request but, where he does not do so, he must give notice to the employee in writing—

(a) that he is not complying with the request;

(b)   informing him of the date (which must be no later than 6 months after the date of the employee's previous request to make, vary or cease such deductions) that the employee can make a new request to make or vary deductions of the employee's contributions; and

(c)   informing him that—

(i)   he may require the employer to cease such deductions immediately (if deductions are being made at the time of the request) but, if the employee makes such a request, the employer is not required to comply with any further request to make such deductions if that further request is made within 6 months of the employee requesting that the deductions cease; and

(ii)   the employee may make payments, at a rate of his choosing, directly to the qualifying scheme.

(3)   Where an employee requests an employer to cease to make deductions from the employee's remuneration on account of contributions to a qualifying scheme, the employer must cease such deductions as soon as possible, but no later than the end of the pay period following that in which the request is made, and must give notice to the employee in writing—

(a)   that the employer is not obliged to make any further such deductions if a request to make those deductions is made by the employee within 6 months of the employee requesting that deductions cease; and

(b)   that the employee may make payments, at a rate of his choosing, directly to the qualifying scheme.

(4)   If an employer ceases on an employee's request to make deductions from the employee's remuneration of contributions to a qualifying scheme, the employer need not comply with any further request to make such deductions if that request is made within 6 months from the date when the employee requested the employer to cease deductions.

(5)   Where an employer is notified that a stakeholder pension scheme that has been designated by him for the purposes of section 3(2) of the Act has commenced winding–up, the employer must immediately cease making deductions from the employee's remuneration on account of contributions to that scheme and notify the employee in writing as soon as is practicable that those deductions have ceased.

Disclosure of information to relevant employees

25.—(1) Where an employee for the first time requests an employer to make or vary (but not cease) deductions of the employee's contributions to a qualifying scheme from his remuneration, the employer must, within 2 weeks of receiving that request, give notice in writing to the employee containing the information referred to in paragraph .

(2) The information to be provided under paragraph (1) is—

(a) the manner in which the employer will accept requests to make, vary or cease such deductions;

(b) advice that, where an employee requests an employer to make or vary deductions of the employee's contributions to a qualifying scheme from the employee's remuneration, the employer need not comply with that request—

(i) within 6 months of the date of any previous request to make, vary or cease such deductions; or

(ii) where the employer is agreeable to complying with the request within a lesser period than 6 months of a previous request, that lesser period;

(c) advice that the employee may, at any time, require the employer to cease such deductions immediately; and

(d) advice that, where the employer is required to comply with a request to make, vary or cease such deductions, the request will be complied with as soon as possible but no later than the end of the pay period following that in which the request is made.

PART V

AMENDMENT OF REGULATIONS UNDER THE PENSION SCHEMES ACT 1993 AND THE PENSIONS ACT 1995

Amendment of the Personal Pension Schemes (Disclosure of Information) Regulations 1987

26.—(1) The Personal Pension Schemes (Disclosure of Information) Regulations 1987 shall be amended as set out in this regulation.

(2) After regulation 2 there shall be inserted:

" *Limited exemption for stakeholder pension schemes* **2A.** In the case of a scheme which is a stakeholder pension scheme within the meaning of section 1 of the Welfare Reform and Pensions Act 1999, regulation 5 shall have effect as if paragraph (2) were omitted."

(3) In regulation 5—

(a) in paragraph (1) for the words "regulation 2" there shall be substituted "regulations 2 and 2A"; and

(b) the following paragraph shall be inserted after paragraph (7)—

" (7A) Where a stakeholder pension scheme within the meaning of section 1 of the Welfare Reform and Pensions Act 1999 (meaning of "stakeholder pension scheme") is removed from the register of such schemes kept under section 2 of that Act (registration of stakeholder pension schemes) the trustees shall—

(a) within 2 weeks of being notified of the removal from the register inform each member of the scheme except an excluded person that the scheme has been removed from the register of stakeholder pension schemes and is no longer a stakeholder pension scheme and that it is required to commence winding-up under the scheme rules;

(b) as soon as practicable and in any event not more than 4 months after such removal provide each member of the scheme except an excluded person with the information mentioned in paragraphs 1, 2 and 7 of Schedule 2; and

(c) where the scheme is unable to meet in full its liabilities to its members, as soon as is practicable and in any event not more than 4 months after such removal provide each member except an excluded person with the information mentioned in paragraph 8 of Schedule 2.".

Amendment of the Occupational Pension Schemes (Preservation of Benefit) Regulations 1991

27. In regulation 12 of the Occupational Pension Schemes (Preservation of Benefit) Regulations 1991—

(a) after paragraph (1) there shall be added—

"(1A) For the purposes of section 73(4) of the Act, a scheme may provide for a transfer payment to be made to another occupational or personal pension scheme (as described in section 73(2)(a)(i) of the Act) without the member's consent where the conditions set out in paragraph (6) of this regulation are satisfied."; and

(b) after paragraph (5) there shall be added—

"(6) The conditions set out in this paragraph are that—

(a) the transferring scheme is or has been a stakeholder pension scheme, within the meaning of section 1 of the Welfare Reform and Pensions Act 1999 or Article 3 of the Welfare Reform and Pensions (Northern Ireland) Order 1999, and the receiving scheme is such a scheme;

   (b)   the transferring scheme has commenced winding-up; and

   (c)   the transfer payment is of an amount at least equal to the cash equivalent of the member's rights under the scheme, as calculated and verified in a manner consistent with regulations made under section 97 of the 1993 Act (calculation of cash equivalents).".

Amendment of the Occupational Pension Schemes (Disclosure of Information) Regulations 1996

28.—(1) The Occupational Pension Schemes (Disclosure of Information) Regulations 1996 shall be amended as set out in this regulation.

   (2) In regulation 1—

   (a)   in the definition of "prospective member" for "and the scheme rules" there shall be substituted "or the scheme rules or both"; and

   (b)   the following paragraph shall be added at the end of the definition of "tax-approved scheme"—

      " (c) approved by the Commissioners of the Inland Revenue under Chapter IV of Part XIV of that Act;".

   (3) In regulation 2—

   (a)   in paragraph (1) for the words "paragraphs (2) and (3)" there shall be substituted "paragraphs (2), (3) and (3A)";

   (b)   after paragraph (3) there shall be inserted—

      "(3A) In the case of a scheme which is a stakeholder pension scheme within the meaning of section 1 of the Welfare Reform and Pensions Act 1999, regulation 5 shall have effect as if paragraph (5) were omitted."

   (4) In regulation 5—

   (a)   at the beginning of paragraph (5) for "In" there shall be substituted "Subject to paragraph (3A) of regulation 2, in"; and

   (b)   the following paragraph shall be inserted after paragraph (10)—

      "(11) Where a stakeholder pension scheme within the meaning of section 1 of the Welfare Reform and Pensions Act 1999 is removed from the register of such schemes kept under section 2 of that Act the trustees shall within 2 weeks of being notified of that removal inform each member of the scheme except an excluded person that the scheme has been removed from the register of stakeholder pension schemes and is no longer a stakeholder pension scheme, and that it is required to commence winding-up under the scheme rules."

Amendment of the Protected Rights (Transfer Payment) Regulations 1996

29.—(1) The Protected Rights (Transfer Payment) Regulations 1996 shall be amended as set out in this regulation.

(2) In regulation 3(a) after "consents in writing" there shall be inserted "or regulation 3A applies".

(3) After regulation 3 there shall be inserted—

> *"Transfer payments from stakeholder pension schemes without the member's consent*
>
> **3A.** This regulation applies where—
>> (a) a transfer payment is made to a scheme, which is registered as a stakeholder pension scheme under section 2 of the Welfare Reform and Pensions Act 1999 or under Article 4 of the Welfare Reform and Pensions (Northern Ireland) Order 1999, from a scheme which is or was so registered and which has commenced winding-up; and
>> (b) regulation 6 of the Stakeholder Pension Schemes Regulations 2000 is complied with."

Amendment of the Occupational Pension Schemes (Member-nominated

30.—(1) The Occupational Pension Schemes (Member-nominated Trustees and Directors) Regulations 1996 shall be amended as set out in this regulation.

(2) In regulation 4(1)—
> (a) "or" at the end of sub-paragraph (l) shall be deleted; and
> (b) after sub-paragraph (m) there shall be added—
>> "or
>> (n) which is a stakeholder pension scheme within the meaning of section 1 of the Welfare Reform and Pensions Act 1999."

(3) In regulation 6(1)—
> (a) "or" at the end of sub-paragraph (m) shall be deleted; and
> (b) after sub-paragraph (m) there shall be added—
>> " or
>> (o) which is a stakeholder pension scheme within the meaning of section 1 of the Welfare Reform and Pensions Act 1999".

Amendment of the Occupational Pension Schemes (Investment) Regulations 1996

31.—(1) The Occupational Pension Schemes (Investment) Regulations 1996 shall be amended as set out in this regulation.

(2) In regulation 10(3)(a) after "Chapter I" there shall be inserted "or Chapter IV".

(3) In regulation 10(3)(e) there shall be inserted after "wholly insured scheme" ", other than a stakeholder pension scheme within the meaning of section 1 of the Welfare Reform and Pensions Act 1999,".

Application of other Regulations to stakeholder pension schemes

32. The regulations listed in Schedule 2 shall apply to a pension scheme established under a trust which—
    (a) is not an occupational pension scheme; but
    (b) is or has been registered under section 2
as if it were an occupational pension scheme.

Signed by authority of the Secretary of State for Social Security.

Jeff Rooker
Minister of State, Department of Social Security

24th May 2000

SCHEDULE 1

PROVISIONS CONFERRING POWERS EXERCISED IN MAKING THESE REGULATIONS

Title of Act	*Powers*
Pension Schemes Act 1993[38]	section 28(2)(b) section 73(4) section 113 section 181(1)
Pensions Act 1995[39]	section 3(2) section 10(1) and (2)(b) section 17(4)(b) section 19(4)

	section 27(3) and (5) section 32(2)(b) and (3) section 35(7) section 41(1)(a) and (b) and (6) section 47(5)(a) and (b), (6) and (9)(b) section 49(1),(2) and (4) section 50(1),(2)(a),(3) and (7) section 81(1)(c) and (2) section 83(2) and (3)(a) section 84(1)(b), (2) and (3) section 86 section 91(5)(c) and (e) section 92(3) and (6) section 94(1) section 124(1) section 174(2) and (3)
Welfare Reform and Pensions Act 1999[40]	section 1(1)(b), (2), (3), (4), (5) and (7) section 2(2), (4) and (7) section 3(1), (3)(b), (5) and (9) section 8(1) and (2) section 83(4), (5) and (6)(a) and (b)

SCHEDULE 2

Regulation 32

REGULATIONS APPLYING TO SCHEMES WHICH ARE OR HAVE BEEN REGISTERED UNDER SECTION 2

Statutory Instrument	*Regulations applying*
The Occupational Pension Schemes (Assignment, Forfeiture, Bankruptcy etc.) Regulations 1997	The whole of the Regulations except regulations 3, and 8(1) and (1A).
The Occupational Pension Schemes (Disclosure of Information) Regulations 1996	Regulations 1, 2, 6 and 7 and Schedule 3 (except paragraph 16 of that Schedule)

The Occupational Pension Schemes (Internal Dispute Resolution Procedures) Regulations 1996	The whole of the Regulations
The Occupational Pension Schemes (Investment) Regulations 1996	Regulations 1 and 10
The Occupational and Personal Pension Schemes (Levy) Regulations 1997	Regulations 5 to 8 and regulation 1 so far as relevant to those regulations.
The Occupational Pension Schemes (Pensions Compensation Provisions) Regulations 1997	The whole of the Regulations except regulation 8
The Occupational Pension Schemes (Prohibition of Trustees) regulations 1997	The whole of the Regulations
The Occupational Pension Schemes (Requirement to obtain Audited Accounts or a Statement from the Auditor) Regulations 1996	The whole of the Regulations except paragraph 5 of the Schedule to the Regulations
The Occupational Pension Scheme(Scheme Administration) Regulations 1996	Regulations 1, 3(2)(a), (3) and (5) to (7), 4(1) and (2)(a) and (b), 5(1) to (10), 6(3), 7 to 11, 12(1) except sub-paragraph (b)(ix), 13(1) and 14

Appendix 3

Legislation and Guidance awaited for stakeholder pensions at June 2000

FSA

○ Details of the authorisation process for stakeholder managers
○ Details of documentation for contract based stakeholder schemes
○ Consultation paper on the conduct of stakeholder pension business (to include 'decision trees').

Inland Revenue

○ Tax regulations for the new DC tax regime (these are in draft in the Finance Bill, which is expected to be enacted in July/August 2000).
○ Regulations for employer payments to personal pensions (these were issued in draft in March 2000).
○ Model rules for stakeholder pension schemes.
○ Regulations concerning who can establish a stakeholder scheme (to bring in affinity groups).
○ Regulations to define scheme overfunding.
○ Regulations on documents and information to submit to establish a stakeholder scheme.
○ Regulations on the information requirements for higher level contributions.
○ Tax changes to cover the introduction of Pooled Pension Investments and the *Financial Services and Markets Act 2000*.

Relevant legislation currently before Parliament

○ The Child Support, Pensions and Social Security Bill (due to be enacted later this year) has details of the S2P rebates for contracted out stakeholder schemes and their members.

Index